D1496743

URBAN TRANSPORT PLANNING

URBAN TRANSPORT PLANNING

A developmental approach

Harry T. Dimitriou

London and New York

First published 1992
by Routledge
11 New Fetter Lane, London EC4P 4EE

Simultaneously published in the USA and Canada
by Routledge
a division of Routledge, Chapman and Hall, Inc.
29 West 35th Street, New York, NY 10001

Typeset in Garamond by Michael Mepham, Frome, Somerset
Printed and bound in Great Britain by
Mackays of Chatham plc, Chatham, Kent

British Library Cataloguing in Publication Data
Dimitriou, Harry T.
Urban transport planning: a
developmental approach
I. Title
338.4091724
ISBN 0-415-03857-X

Library of Congress Cataloging in Publication Data
Dimitriou, Harry T.
Urban transport planning: a developmental
approach / Harry T. Dimitriou.
p. cm.
Includes bibliographical references and index.
ISBN 0-415-03857-X
1. Urban transportation—Developing
countries—Planning. 2. Urban
transportation policy—Developing
countries. 3. Urban transportation—Planning.
4. Urban transportation policy.
I. Title

HE311.D44D56 1992
388.4'068—dc20 91-21438
CIP

CONTENTS

Part II A developmental approach to UTP for Third World cities

LIST OF FIGURES

LIST OF TABLES

PREFACE

This book represents the culmination of some ten years' research presented here in two parts.

The first of these is an examination of the evolution of the Urban Transport Planning (UTP) Process and its derivatives in the USA. This involved interviewing some forty persons, most of whom are internationally renowned as pioneers of the UTP process or some aspects of its application. Although the comments recorded are some twelve years old, their significance is as relevant as ever. Indeed, it might be argued that their inclusion in this text in the 1990s – at a time when there is a renewed concern for environmental, land use and broader development issues of urban transport planning – could well attract a more sympathetic reception than at the time they were first made. The research conducted for this part of the publication was financed by Sheffield University and undertaken when the author was a Faculty member of the Department of Town and Regional Planning. This provided much of the stimulus and analytical framework for the following parts of the book.

The second part concerning the technology transfer of this same process and its derivatives to Third World countries, and the subsequent formulation of the theoretical basis of a 'developmental approach' to urban transport planning, was expanded upon while teaching at the Development Planning Unit, University College London. As in the earlier part of the book, the conceptual spadework undertaken here also drew from material collected in interviews. Some thirty academics and international development agency representatives concerned with Third World development were interviewed.

The examination and assessment of the application of a 'developmental approach' to urban transport planning was refined while in professional practice as a consultant to Training and Development Consultants, (TDC S.A.) of Lausanne, Switzerland, in a study conducted for the Ministry of Public Works of the Government of Indonesia. This focused on the development of national urban transport planning guidelines for integrated urban infrastructure development and was financed by the United Nations Centre for Human Settlements (UNCHS), Nairobi and the United Nations Development Programme (UNDP), New York. The writing up of this last part of the research was completed during my tenure as a faculty member at the University of Hong Kong.

The importance placed on the need to address the principal areas of study covered by the book, and to arrive at the conclusions presented, has its origin in my concern with a number of academic and professional issues in urban transport. Foremast of these, from an academic perspective, is a concern for the current 'conceptual disarray' in city-wide transport planning. This is reported on in the book and unless appropriately addressed, will encourage further undesirable *ad hoc* developments in cities, as well as the continued demise of the planning ethic in the urban transport field. From a professional practice point of view, my concerns have to do with the rapidly rising international investments being made in urban transport without the use of adequate developmentally-sensitive guidelines. Both sets of concern are today as prevalent in cities of the industrialised world as they are in those of the Third World, even though the emphasis of the book is on the latter. This makes the need for more appropriate guidelines to plan transport systems and better assess their impacts more urgent than ever. One can only hope that this book may make some modest contribution to the formulation of such guidelines.

Harry T. Dimitriou
Hong Kong

FOREWORD

This is a global modern history of urban transportation planning. It is what we need as a source book to organise reformulations of the field for contemporary use. We should be grateful to Harry Dimitriou for providing it.

It was a large task, but not so difficult as its span might imply because this is a remarkably compact field. It was created in the United States during the dramatic enlargement of its natural highway system after the Second World War, then exported to the United Kingdom and Europe, afterwards to the rest of the world.

Most of the original participants in this technical movement are still alive and working. Its US contingent has been convened throughout by the Transportation Research Board of the National Academy of Sciences. The number of papers we have generated is prodigious, but the number of books (other than textbooks) has been very few. It is a field in which the principal contributors have focused on the details of technique. Books in the field have been mostly compilations of technique. There has been little overview. Yet overview is important because of the very comprehensiveness of the transportation planning effort to which the field applies. That is especially true now.

This is a timely book, even though a good bit of the data it draws upon was collected years ago. The US land use transportation planning effort of the 1950s and 1960s fell upon bad times in the 1970s and 1980s because of more pressing social commitments in the cities during the poverty-fighting years than stalemates between highway-building and environmental interests along with general budget stringencies. During much of this period there was more land use/transportation planning done in the poor countries than in the north. Planning programmes resorted to a futile faith in traffic management as the means to provide more capacity and alleviate congestion. But congestion continued to grow. Meanwhile, efforts in the developing world, led by the international agencies – especially the World Bank – shifted to a thrifty and socially committed approach to urban transportation by focusing narrowly on problems of the poorest parts of urban populations with low-cost, replicable solutions that ignored comprehensive thinking about the transportation system as a luxury.

But the more recent years of change and reformulation are those that provide the platform for this global history Dimitriou has provided. The USA has woken up after twenty years of virtually no metropolitan highway building to a nightmare of urban and suburban congestion. The first reaction is to intensify an effort at system management that leaves land development alone, but by now most of us are fully convinced that this will not solve the problem. Indeed, most of us always were convinced. It is just that now the seriousness of the rising problem forces us to admit it. So as a last resort we return to that hard chestnut, the land use/transportation interaction. It worked reasonably well when we were only documenting expected urban growth to justify new roads, but it was analytically unsatisfying at best and unmanageable as a tool for anything but building roads to meet the rising demand. Nonetheless, now that all else has failed we turn back to it, this time with a determination to plan the land use part as well as the transportation part.

Current hope is pinned to the recent activation of states' authority in the control of land use and trip production: growth management. This motivates a new look at land use/transportation planning, but the angle of view is different. Our poor analytical capability at following the land/transport relationship will be shored up by unaccustomed direct control of the land use side. What does this mean toward redevelopment of the survey and analysis? In contemplating the answer to this question we must consider the strength of the growth management movement, the agility of new computer software, and we should turn the pages of this book.

Meanwhile, in the developing world a different but intersecting series of events has taken place. Isolating the trip needs of the poor has been de-emphasised on the grounds that when we do not account for system-wide considerations our targeted efforts are swamped by overall system ineffectiveness. Further, the international agencies have lately rediscovered the city after decades of inattention in favour of other development perspectives. Most of the major multilateral and bilateral agencies have published new urban sector policy papers in the last year or two. They have rediscovered that a large part of GNP comes from the urban areas, so the way to enhance it is to make cities more effective as economies. That means reducing their congestion. Poverty remains a concern and environment too, but their context is now productivity. Another motivation for turning the pages of this work.

For developing countries' interpretations we must answer a variety of questions with attention to the experience of this field. How do you deal with a city growing at 4 per cent a year? How do you deal with sixteen modes of urban transportation simultaneously, as in the cities of India? What do you do when the important modal split is between bus and walking but the cars are causing most of the congestion? What study models do you use when uncertainties make future estimates extremely unreliable but answering questions about the outcomes of generically different policies might be feasible? Above all, catching Dimitriou's subtitle, we now have a mandate that for the first time expects transportation planning to be 'developmental' rather than just accommodative.

These queries should guide our attention to this book. The search could be rewarding.

Ralph Gakenheimer,
Professor of Urban Planning and
Urban Studies and Civil Engineering,
Massachusetts Institute of Technology

ACKNOWLEDGEMENTS

In addition to those persons listed in Appendixes 1 and 3 who were interviewed in support of this research (of whom many have been quoted in the text), I am indebted to numerous other people for the development of my initial interest in urban transport and their encouragement for me to complete the research outlined here.

Chronologically, it would be fitting first to acknowledge Barry Hutton (sometime Head of the Planning School at Bristol Polytechnic and lecturer at the University of Wales Institute of Science and Technology – now the University of Wales College at Cardiff), who as my one-time lecturer in transport (when I was an undergraduate at Leeds School of Town Planning) was the first to nurture my interest in urban transport policy and planning.

I am also particularly indebted to two of my ex-colleagues at the Development Planning Unit, University College, London – Otto Koenigsberger and Michael Safier – for their consistent interest in and support of my research, and their valuable comments on the Third World urban development aspects of my study.

Special gratitude is due to Emiel Wegelin of the Netherlands Economic Institute (sometime, UNDP/UNCHS Technical Advisor to the Directorate of Human Settlements and Housing of the Government of Indonesia), and to the late Wiyoto Wiyono, (sometime Secretary of the Directorate of Urban Highways of the Ministry of Public Works, also of the Government of Indonesia). They both provided me with the opportunity to apply and further develop my thoughts regarding the 'developmental approach' to urban transport planning and its application to Indonesia. Acknowledgements are also due to Ralph Gakenheimer of the Massachusetts Institute of Technology, who commented on the manuscripts for Chapters

3, 4 and 7, and whose writing and consultancy work in the field of urban transport has long been a considerable inspiration to my academic and professional work throughout the years I have known him.

I am very grateful to Michael Batty of the University of Wales at Cardiff, now at the State University of New York at Buffalo, who has shown consistent enthusiasm for the research I have reported on here, and who convinced me to write the findings up as a book. No acknowledgement would be complete without expressing my immeasurable gratitude to my wife, Vicky Dimitriou, for transcribing all interviews used as a source for this research and typing the manuscript for this book; Diana Martin who copy edited the manuscript, and both Norita Lau and Lau Kwan Wai who were responsible for the graphics; and last but not least, to my children who showed immense patience during the preparation of the book.

As with my first (edited) book, I am once again indebted financially to Training and Development Consultants (TDC S.A.), Lausanne – a Swiss consultancy firm specialising in planning and training aspects of Third World urban transport which met most of my costs associated with the writing of this book.

Finally, I am grateful to the authors and publishers for the permission to reproduce in a revised or redrawn form the following copyright materials:

Figure from Proudlove, J. A. (1968) *Some Comments on the West Midlands Transport Study, Traffic Engineering and Control* (reproduced here as Figure 2.1).

Figure 11.1 from 'Institution of Highways and Transportation, and Department of Transport' (1987) *Roads and Traffic in Urban Areas*, HMSO, London (reproduced here as Figure 2.3).

Figure 1.1 from Hutchinson, B. G. (1974) *Principles of Urban Transport Systems Planning*, McGraw-Hill and Hemisphere Publishing Corporation, New York (reproduced here as Figure 2.4).

Figure 4.3 from World Bank (1984) *World Development Report*, Oxford University Press, Oxford (reproduced here as Figure 5.2).

Figures 4 and 6 from World Bank (1986) *Urban Transport: A World Bank Policy Paper*, Washington DC (reproduced here as Figures 6.2 and 6.3 respectively).

Figure 4 from Banjo, G. A. and Dimitriou, H. T. (1983) *Urban Transport Problems of Third World Cities –The Third Generation*,

Habitat International, Vol. 7, No. 3/4 (reproduced here as Figure 6.6).

Figures 4.2, 5.1 and 3.7 from TDC S.A. (1988) *IUIDP Policy, Planning and Design Guidelines for Urban Road Transport*, Report to Ministry of Public Works, Government of Indonesia and UNDP/UNCHS (reproduced here as Figure 8.3, 8.6, 8.7 and 8.8).

Figure 3 from Dimitriou, H. T. (1988) *Urban Transport and Manpower Development and Training Needs of Four Asian Cities*, Habitat International, Vol. 12, No. 3 (reproduced here as Figure 8.4).

Figure from Transport Gaps from Bouladon, G. (1967b) 'The Transport Gaps', *Science Journal*, April (reproduced here as Figure 8.5).

Table A.1 from World Bank (1986) *Urban Transport, A World Bank Policy Study*, Washington DC (reproduced here as Table 6.1).

Table 11.2 from Armstrong-Wright (1986) *Urban Transit Systems: Guidelines for Examining Options*, World Bank, Washington DC (reproduced here as Table 6.2).

Table A.7 from World Bank (1986) *Urban Transport, A World Bank Policy Study*, Washington DC (reproduced here as Table 6.3).

Tables 1, 26 and 31 from World Bank (1990) *World Development Report*, Oxford University Press, Oxford (reproduced here as Appendix 6: Table A6.1, Table A6.2 and Table A6.3).

Appendix B from Weiner, E. (1986) *Urban Transportation in the United States: A Historical Overview*, US Department of Transportation, Washington DC (reproduced as Appendix 5).

1

INTRODUCTION

BACKGROUND

The purpose of this book is twofold. First, it is to examine the contribution of applying to Third World countries a particular planning approach (the UTP process) and its derivatives to urban transport infrastructure and facility provision. Secondly, to respond to the identified weaknesses and strengths of this approach and help arrive at conceptually more appropriate transport policy and planning guidelines for cities in such countries.

Both the UTP process investigated and many of its derivatives were conceived in the USA. The process evolved especially rapidly during the two decades immediately following the Second World War. By the late 1960s it had developed into a standard framework with sub-components and sub-models, by which time it was beginning to be applied world-wide. The process initially incorporated a heavy emphasis on road-building solutions and the needs of the motorcar. By the 1970s, however, it was adapted to include public transport and environmental considerations, and spawned various derivatives. By the 1980s both the UTP process and its derivatives focused more on traffic management, travel behaviour issues and cost recovery measures.

The disenchantment with these city-wide, long-range efforts at transport planning which emerged in the industrialised countries during the 1970s, and subsequently in some parts of the Third World in the early 1980s, has now become so widespread that there is an urgent need for a re-assessment of the contribution of the process and its derivatives to the planning of urban transport in Third World countries. An assessment of this kind is especially warranted if this disenchantment is to be prevented from overshadowing the progress that has been made to date in the field.

It is very apparent that many Third World cities are currently in critical need of planning guidelines to help tackle their rapidly growing and complex transport problems. Without guidelines such settlements are in danger of being confronted with one of two seemingly undesirable courses of action. They can either continue to employ the UTP process (or components and derivatives of it) irrespective of associated limitations, or they can resort to conventional traffic engineering and public transport optimisation schemes outside any wider planning context.

The book has been written in two parts. The first (Chapters 1–4) provides an outline and critique of the Urban Transport Planning (UTP) process and its derivatives, tracing its evolution in the USA and its application to other industrialised nations. The critique of this methodology and set of techniques is based on an extensive literature review and set of interviews conducted by the author with theorists and practising professionals in the USA, most of whom have been/are at the forefront of the field or who have been pioneers of the approach. The second part of the book (Chapters 5–9) concerns the technology-transfer of this same process to the Third World and the formulation of a more appropriate approach to urban transport planning for related development contexts. The discussion draws from a review of literature in the field and interviews conducted by the author among those concerned with Third World urban transport. This latter part of the book commences by outlining the general features of Third World urban development as a basis for assessing the suitability of urban transport planning studies employing the UTP process and its derivatives. Particular attention is paid to the agents of technology-transfer in this field, the role of technical assistance, and the function of consultants. The need to incorporate some consideration of settlement and transport hierarchies in the planning response to urban movement problems is also discussed. The observations of the preceding chapters provide the basis for the proposed 'developmental approach' to Third World city transport planning outlined in Chapter 8, which among other things, advocates the assessment of transport plans – first, on the basis of their contribution to development goals ('developmental effectiveness') and second, in terms of transport systems efficiency ('operations efficiency'). The concluding chapter (Chapter 9) seeks to draw together the principal observations and findings of the study both from a theoretical and professional practice perspective which can provide transport policy and planning guidance that are conceptually more appropriate to the development circumstances of Third World cities.

The study is based upon a number of premises, namely that the UTP process is essentially a standardised process which (either in part or in derivative form) is still applied throughout the world with essentially only marginal modifications made to its fundamental concepts since its inception in the mid 1950s (see Chapters 2 and 3). Another premise is that the process and its derivatives are ostensibly a product of the socio-economic and political environment in which they evolved, and consequently, many of the underlying assumptions and concepts they employ reflect the values, perceptions and technologies of the USA and (to a lesser extent) European societies at the time of their major development (see Chapters 3 and 4). Finally, there is the premise that there are certain inherent conceptual limitations to the UTP process and its derivatives which are transferred to Third World countries through studies conducted by international planning consultants and development agencies, as well as leading universities and professional institutions of the industrialised countries through many of their teaching, training and research programmes (see Chapters 6, 7 and 9).

The investigation outlined in this publication rests upon a number of assumptions, the most important of which are that:

1 Developments of urban transport planning in the USA and Europe (the industrialised countries), represent the main acknowledged international advances in the field of urban transport planning.
2 Different development circumstances warrant different urban transport planning approaches.
3 The political, social, economic and physical environments of development in which the UTP process and its derivatives have principally evolved are markedly different from those of the Third World.
4 The developmental conditions of most Third World countries are more akin to each other than to those of the industrialised countries (especially the USA), and although variations in the

Figure 1.1 Inter-relationship of areas of study

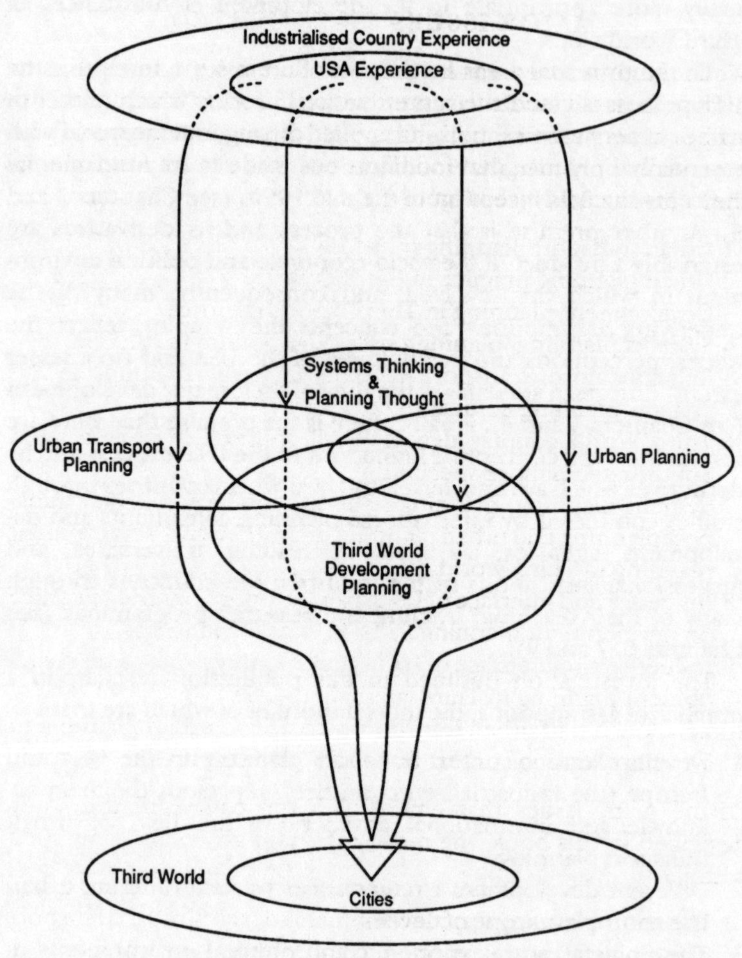

Source: Adapted from Figure 1.1, Dimitriou, 1989

circumstances of the Third World are considerable, the term 'Third World country' is a meaningful classification.

MAJOR ISSUES INVESTIGATED

While the principal areas investigated here are too numerous to discuss in detail, and their interrelationships too complex to describe at this juncture, both have their origins in conceptual and professional practice developments over the last four decades in the following fields (see Figure 1.1):

1. Urban transport planning in the USA.
2. Urban planning practice in the USA.
3. Development planning in Third World countries.
4. Systems planning, planning styles and politics in the USA.
5. Relationship of transport planning to urban planning in the systems planning context of the USA.
6. Third World country development contexts in general, and Southeast Asia more specifically.
7. Systems planning, planning styles and politics in urban transport planning and urban planning in the USA, and development planning in Third World countries.
8. Influence and interface of US urban transport planning practice on development planning in Third World countries.
9. Influence and interface of US urban planning practice on development planning in Third World countries.
10. Relationship of urban transport planning to urban planning in systems planning context in Third World countries.

Of the many issues that emerged in the course of the study described in this book, the most important are those concerned with:

1. The nature and scope of development to which urban transport planning efforts are expected to contribute.
2. The dominant transport technologies to be encouraged in Third World countries, and the criteria for their selection.
3. The relevance of the industrialised country (particularly the USA) experience of urban transport planning which has primarily focused upon metropolitan areas, for transport planning in Third World cities (particularly those with a population greater than 150,000).

4 The extent of the 'mismatch' between the development context in which much of urban transport planning practice has evolved in the industrialised countries, and the development context of Third World cities.
5 The nature of the 'mismatch' between transport characteristics of metropolitan areas and those of small and medium-sized settlements, and the impact of this on the generalised principles of urban transport planning practice.

The principal sources of data and research material employed to investigate the above are as follows. Interviews in the USA with academics, consultants and government officials responsible for selected urban transport planning studies (see Appendixes 1 and 2). Discussions with academics, consultants and representatives of international development agencies and government officials from Third World countries concerned with the urban transport sector (see Appendixes 3 and 4). Desk study reviews of selected urban transport planning studies made available by consultants, international development agencies and governments, and desk study literature reviews of books, articles and conference papers.

Part I

DEVELOPMENTS OF THE UTP PROCESS AND ITS DERIVATIVES

2

THE UTP PROCESS AND ITS DERIVATIVES

THE PROCESS

Purpose and functions

The conventional wisdom of transport planning practice in urban areas is closely identified with the application of the 'urban transport planning (UTP) process' and its derivatives.[1] This process is a formalised planning methodology designed to provide guidelines and priorities for future investment and construction of urban transport infrastructure and facilities. In some countries such as Brazil, the UK and the USA, the methodology has in the past been institutionalised by government and supported by legislation, obliging planning agencies to adopt particular procedures of the process in order to qualify for central government funding.

In character, the UTP process represents a 'scientific effort' at planning urban transport demand, particularly motorised road traffic, by:

1 observing current travel behaviour;
2 advancing certain hypotheses concerning the relationship between urban land use and movement;
3 testing these hypotheses as a basis for making estimates of future travel demand; and
4 ultimately recommending additional transport capacity.

Different versions and derivatives of this process have been widely adopted over time by policy-makers and technocrats throughout the world – usually when confronted with major traffic congestion problems thought to require a city-wide planning response.

An indication of the extent of international application of the process is illustrated by the fact that in 1975 the World Bank issued

Figure 2.1 The urban transport planning process

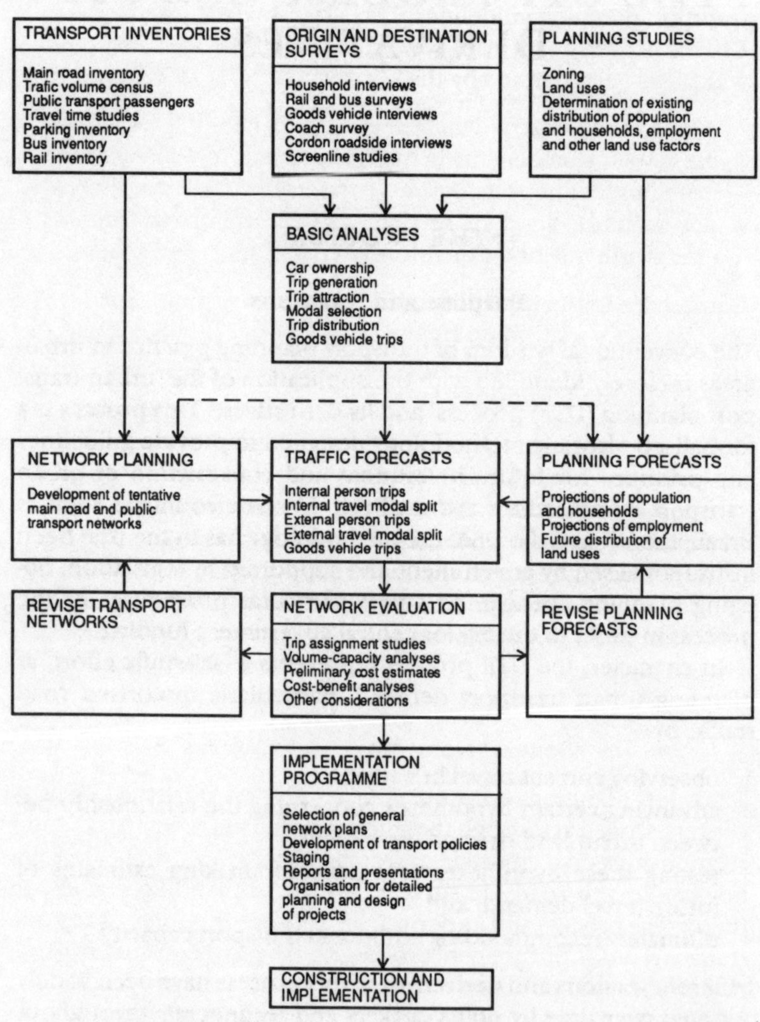

Source: Proudlove J.A., 1968. 'Some comments on the West Midlands Transport Study' *Traffic Engineering and Control*, November

guidelines to its staff based upon the UTP process for standard formatting of its urban transport studies.[2] The US Department of Transport (US DOT) in the late 1970s similarly made available to some thirty countries (many of them in the Third World) its urban transport planning guidelines. The latter, initially intended for US Federal Government use, were also based on the UTP process which has been defined by the agency (US DOT, 1973) as:

> a long range system, wherein the alternatives to be analysed are few in number but in sufficient detail to estimate land development impacts, system costs, major facility and corridor volumes, level of service, and some impacts such as energy use, major air quality effects, accidents and others.

Confidence in the versatility of the process was proclaimed by US DOT agency's staff, when Heanue and Ettinger (1978) argued that the methodology was also applicable to public transport planning with minor modifications:

> The Process is not a 'strait-jacket' – it can be made to do whatever we (the US DOT) want it to do. In fact, we are still using it at present.... Most of the (public) transit planning methodology has grown from highway planning. It is the same body of research that was attempting all along to do a good job of a multi-modal transport study. The researchers do not make any distinction as to whether they are dealing with highways or transit – it is still transportation planning.

General framework and features

Transport planning recommendations derived from the UTP process are arrived at through the simulation of land use and transport relationships on a city-wide and zonal basis, employing data from household and roadside surveys, as well as planning studies. In theory, the process and its derivatives are not supportive of any one transport mode but are concerned with the provision and distribution of *all* types of urban transport facilities – a claim challenged by many, including professionals and community groups.

The general framework of the process (see Figure 2.1) is traditionally believed to have its origin in the urban transport studies of Detroit (Detroit City, 1953–5) and Chicago (Chicago City, 1955–61), as well as the seminal research conducted by Mitchell and

Table 2.1 Some major transport planning studies in Third World cities, 1955–84

Place	*Date*	*Title*	*Consultants*	*Nationality*
Bombay	1955	Bombay Traffic & Transportation Study	Wilbur Smith & Associates	American
San Jose City Puerto Rico	1959	San Jose Urban Transportation Study	Wilbur Smith & Associates	American
Kuala Lumpur	1964	Kuala Lumpur Transportation Study	Crooks, Mitchell & Peacock	Australian
Calcutta	1967	Calcutta Traffic & Transport Plan	Wilbur Smith & Associates	American
Bogota	1970	Phase 1: Bogota Transport and Urban Development Study	Freeman Fox & Wilbur Smith & Associates	British/ American
Tehran	1970	Urban Transportation System for Tehran	Japan Overseas Technical Co-operation Agency	Japanese
Delhi & Madras	1972	Rapid Transit Studies for Delhi and Madras	Town & Country Planning Organisation	Indian
Manila	1973	Manila Urban Transport Study	Japan Overseas Technical Co-operation Agency	Japanese
Cairo	1973	Greater Cairo Transportation Planning Study	RATP Sofretu	French
Hong Kong	1973	Comprehensive Transport Study for Hong Kong I	Wilbur Smith & Associates	American
Singapore	1974	Singapore Mass Transit Study	Wilbur Smith & Associates in assoc. with Parsons Brinckerhoff Tutor, Bechtel	American
San Jose Costa Rica	1974	San Jose Urban Transport Study	Wilbur Smith & Associates	American
Bogota	1974	Phase II: Bogota Transport & Urban Development Study	Freeman Fox & Wilbur Smith & Associates	British/ American
Madras	1974	Madras Area Transportation Study	In-house Madras Metropolitan Dev. Authority	Indian
Kuala Lumpur	1974	Urban Transport Policy & Planning Study for Metropolitan Kuala Lumpur	Wilbur Smith & Associates	American
Lagos	1974	Lagos Metropolitan Area Transportation Planning Study	Wilbur Smith & Associates	American
Bangkok	1975	Bangkok Transportation Study	Kocks, F.H/Rhein Ruhr	German

Table 2.1 (Continued)

Place	*Date*	*Title*	*Consultants*	*Nationality*
Istanbul	1975	Istanbul Urban Transport & Land Use Study	Jamieson Mackay & Partners	British
Jakarta	1975	Jakarta Metropolitan Area Transportation Study	Arge Intertraffic Lenz Consult.	German
Tehran	1976	Tehran Urban Transport Project	Freeman Fox and Associates	British
Manila	1977	Metroplan Metro Manila Transport Land Use and Development Plan	Freeman Fox and Associates	British
Surabaya	1977	Surabaya Area Transportation Study	Freeman Fox and Associates (later Halcrow Fox & Assoc.)	British
Penang	1979	Urban Transport Survey in Greater Metropolitan Area	Japan International Co-operation Agency	Japanese
Jakarta Metrop. Area	1979	Jabotabek Metropolitan Development Planning: Report on Transportation	Staff of Jabotabek Metropolitan Development Planning Project	International
Metro Cebu	1980	Metro Cebu Land Use & Transport Study	REDECON	Australian
Sao Paulo	1980	Transport Study of Sao Paulo Metropolitan Area	NATO Research Institute Brussels	International
Davao City	1981	Davao City Urban Transport & Land Use Study	Japan International Co-operation Agency	Japanese
Johor Bahru	1982	Transplan: Urban Master Plan for the Johor Conurbation	Japan International Co-operation Agency	Japanese
Metro Manila	1983	Metro Manila Urban Transportation Strategy Planning Project	Pak-Poy & Kneebone Pty in Association with R.J. Nairn & Ptnrs	Australian
Jakarta Metrop. Area	1983	Jabotabek Traffic Management & Road Network Development Study	Colin Buchanan & Ptnrs in Assoc. with T.P.O. Sullivan & Ptnrs	British
Metro Manila	1984	The Metro Manila Transportation Planning Study	Japan International Co-operation Agency	Japanese

Source: Table 5.1, Dimitiou, 1990. Adapted from Table 1, Rimmer 1986 with additional information furnished by Wilbur Smith Associates, Hong Kong

Rapkin (1954) at Columbia University which presented numerous key hypotheses regarding the relationship of traffic and land use. The basic stages of the classical format of the process include:

1 the preparation of land use, transport and travel inventories of the study area;
2 the analysis of present land use and travel characteristics;
3 the forecast of land use and travel characteristics;
4 the setting of goals and the formulation of transport alternatives designed to accommodate the projected travel demands and land use changes; and
5 the testing and evaluation of alternative transport plans.

The above stages have remained the major corner-stones of conventional urban transport planning practice since the inception of the process in the USA during the 1950s. It has subsequently been applied world-wide in one form or other, to cities as diverse as London (Freeman Fox *et al.*, 1964–6) and Athens (Wilbur Smith and Associates, 1963) in Europe; Calcutta (Wilbur Smith and Associates, 1967) and Kuala Lumpur (Wilbur Smith and Associates, 1974a) in Asia; Lagos (Wilbur Smith and Associates, 1974b) and Cairo (1973) in Africa; and Bogota (Freeman Fox *et al.*, 1970 – 1974) and Sao Paulo (1980) in Latin America (see Table 2.1). In the industrialised world, the process (or modified versions of it) has been employed in every major urban area of the UK and in every metropolitan city of the USA.

Manheim (1978) has described the UTP process as:

> a large scale computer system, based on models involving large volumes of data collection, orientated around long range planning and analysis, and a small number of relatively large-scale comprehensive transportation land use sets of alternatives. Massive in its methodological scope, many people in transportation studies typically spend years to develop models and often do not have a chance to use them to understand issues.

The major features of this planning process, include (after Creighton, 1970):

1 an extensive dependence upon simulation and quantification;
2 a semblance of comprehensiveness;

3 a formality of approach, based on principles of systems thinking; and
4 a set of procedures akin to a scientific approach to problem solving.

The reliance of the UTP process and many of its constituent parts on simulation and quantification is most evident in the modelling of travel demand. This simulates the adjustment of transport demand and supply by modelling various factors believed to affect travel. The simulation exercise is represented by a set of interrelated sub-models which estimate: trip generation, trip distribution, modal split and traffic assignment. The extensive dependence on quantification arises from the ability of the transport analyst to measure vehicular flows, their speed, their origins and destinations.

The early concern of urban transport planning with highway engineering and design issues, such as road capacity problems, underlies the 'quantification tradition'. The need to cost proposed transport facility provision to assist investment decisions further emphasises the quantitative data requirements of the process.

The claim that the UTP process is 'comprehensive' in its concern, is derived from its attempt at providing a city-wide coverage of all types of urban transport modes. The semblance of comprehensiveness also arises from its incorporation of land-use/transport interactions as a basis for estimating future travel demand.

The formality of the process and its extensive reliance upon systems thinking as a prerequisite to formulating recommendations, emerges from the methodology's need to handle complex interrelationships and analyse large amounts of data. With the rapid growth in use of mainframe, and (more recently) micro and personal computers (as well as the reduction of computer operating costs), the format of the UTP process and its derivatives has over the years reflected a growing reliance upon the computer.

Principal components and assumptions

There is a great deal of technical literature which over the years has outlined and detailed various versions, aspects and derivatives of the UTP process (see Martin and Wohl, 1961; Creighton, 1970; Bruton, 1970; Lane *et al.*, 1971; Dickey, 1975; Morlok, 1978; Black, 1981; Blunden and Black, 1984; and Webster, Bly and Paully, 1988). The literature has been disseminated so extensively that it has done much to reinforce the conventional wisdom associated with the process. In the light of policy and other changes of the 1980s, reflections on the scope and content of these standard texts have subsequently been written by a number of academics (see Meyer and Miller, 1984; Jansen *et al.*, 1985; Nijkamp and Reichman, 1987; and Newman and Kenworthy, 1989).

Coverage of this literature will not be repeated here, but it is important before embarking upon a critique of the UTP process clearly to differentiate among:

1 the principal components of the process;

Figure 2.2 Principal components of the urban transport planning process

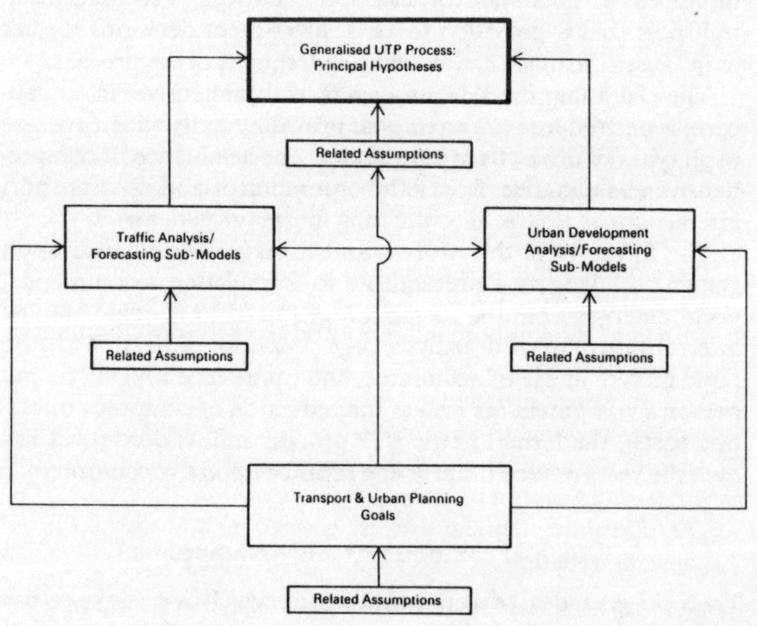

Source: Figure 2.2, Dimitriou, 1990

2 the various modelling procedures it employs;
3 its derivatives; and
4 its context.

Differentiation is essential if failures and benefits associated with developments in the field are to be disentangled. Making these differentiations is also a prerequisite to understanding how to dismantle and reassemble valuable components and techniques of the process for future use, in a manner which better serves differing development and institutional contexts.

For the purpose of this book, components of the UTP process may together be likened to a generalised travel demand model, based upon certain broad assumptions, incorporating a number of sub-models – each with its own related assumptions (see Figure 2.2). The three principal components are:

1 traffic and transport systems analysis and forecasting;
2 land-use based urban development analysis and forecasting; and
3 goal, policy and plan formulation for transport.

Before examining each of the above, it is useful to dwell a little further on the general assumptions that underlie the process. Although now somewhat dated, these are best expressed by Bruton (1970) as follows:

1 Decisive relationships exist between all modes of transport and therefore the role of a particular mode cannot be determined separately.
2 Transport systems both influence and serve the development of an area.
3 The transport situation in areas of continuous urbanisation requires regional treatment.
4 An urban transport study is integral to the overall planning process and cannot be considered in isolation.
5 The transport planning process is ongoing and thus requires constant updating.

If one looks back more than thirty years at the application of both the UTP process and its derivatives, it is apparent that the use of these generalised assumptions is more reflective of normative (sometimes wishful) thinking and the use of conveniently untested hypotheses, rather than based on well understood empirical evidence and practice. This and other criticisms, especially as they relate to Third World circumstances, were voiced by a number of academics and practitioners in the 1970s (see Viola, 1976; McNeill, 1977; Dimitriou, 1977, and Darbera, 1978). Unfortunately many of the criticisms remain valid today with regard to several of the newer transport planning developments, particularly in the modelling field. The employment of the same or similar generalised assumptions ignores major limitations of the process. Their use in urban transport planning is akin to an architect continuing to elaborate the interior design of a building, even though he knows its foundations are suspect.

Reservations about the conceptual validity and empirical evidence supporting generalised assumptions of the UTP process have received renewed interest (see Atkins, 1986; Supernak and Stevens, 1987; and Talvitie, undated) and are discussed at further length in Chapters 3 and 4 of this book. In the application of the process to other countries, this aspect is merely one of concern. Another dimension warranting serious investigation is the compatibility of the assumptions to the 'development context' and the related goals of settlements in different countries (see the latter part of this book, particularly Chapters 7 and 8).

The analysis of the evolution of the UTP process discussed in a later section of this chapter and in Chapter 3, confirms that the hypotheses and techniques it employs are primarily taken from experiences of industrialised countries. This is especially evident if one examines assumptions concerning the relationship of transport to urban development in land-use/transport integration models, and assumptions made about travel behaviour, as well as the value of travel time in discrete-choice modelling. This is despite the fact that it is widely held that assumptions about desired paths of urban development do not have universal application, in that the notion of what is desirable varies from place to place. Similarly, the use of assumptions about travel behaviour based on traditional market economics of industrialised nations can, it is argued, only be applied with caution to the Third World given the different cultural dimensions and economic priorities (see Banjo, 1982).

Transport systems analysis and forecasting

Within the general framework of the UTP process, a number of more specific concepts and assumptions are employed. These are

Figure 2.3 **The urban transport planning modelling process (also known as 'four-step' model)**

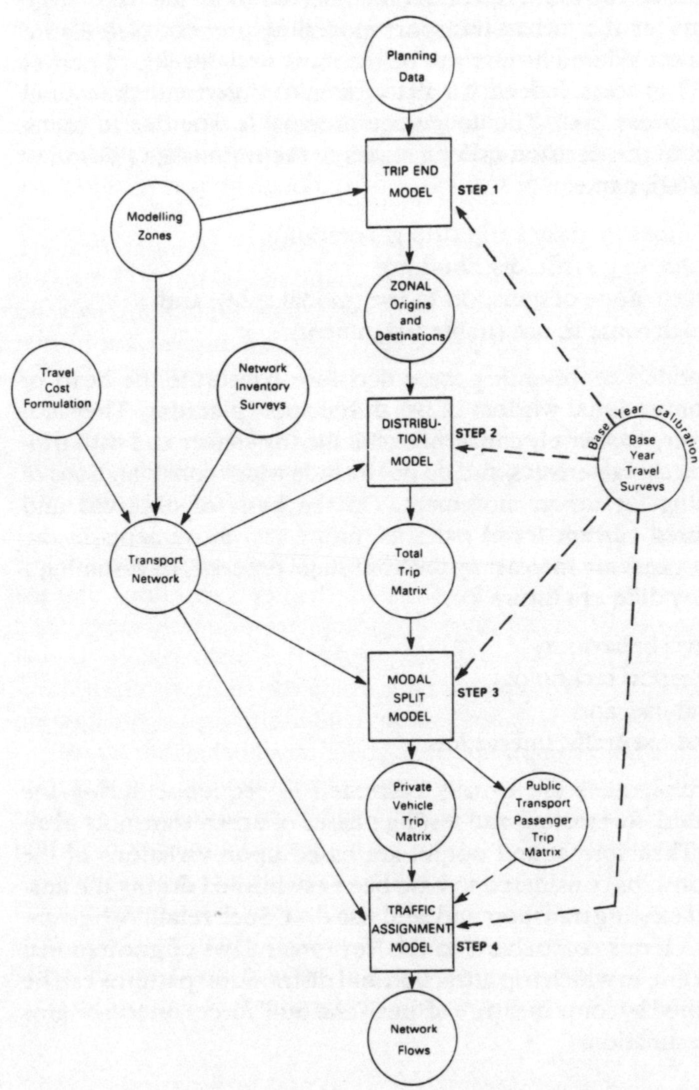

Source: Redrawn from Figure 11.1. 'Institution of Highways and Transportation and Department of Transport 1987', *Roads and Traffic in Urban Areas*, HMSO, London.

usually tied to a set of sub-models used to analyse, simulate and forecast traffic movements – movements which are seen to be a function of land use and socio-economic changes of an urban area. This set of sub-models, commonly referred to as the 'four stage process' or the 'urban transport modelling process' (see Figure 2.3) is considered by many to be the most well-developed part of the UTP process. Indeed, it is all too often confused with the overall UTP process itself. The 'four stage process' is intended to correspond to the decision-making stages of the trip-maker (Wilson *et al.*, 1969), namely:

1 whether to make a trip (trip generation);
2 where to go (trip distribution);
3 which mode of transport to use (modal split); and
4 which route to use (traffic assignment).

Sub-models representing these decisions constitute the heart of the conventional wisdom of urban transport planning. They are, however, exclusively concerned with the trip-maker and with trip-making characteristics, and do not include wider considerations of planning for urban movement. On the basis of observed and measured current travel patterns, future trip movements in the UTP process are forecast by the 'four stage process', by assuming a not very different future for:

1 travel behaviour;
2 transport technology;
3 land-use; and
4 land-use/traffic interaction.

The sub-models are usually calibrated in sequence during the analytical, forecasting and testing phases of urban transport planning. Their format and output are based upon variations of the relationships considered to have been established during the analysis of existing transport and land-use data. Such relationships are seen in terms comparable to the Newtonian laws of gravitational attraction, in which trip attraction and distribution patterns can be explained by some measure of 'push and pull' forces on trip origins and destinations.

Land-use based urban analysis and forecasting

Sub-models of urban development analysis and forecasting associ-

Figure 2.4 Stages, inputs and sub-models of the urban transport planning process

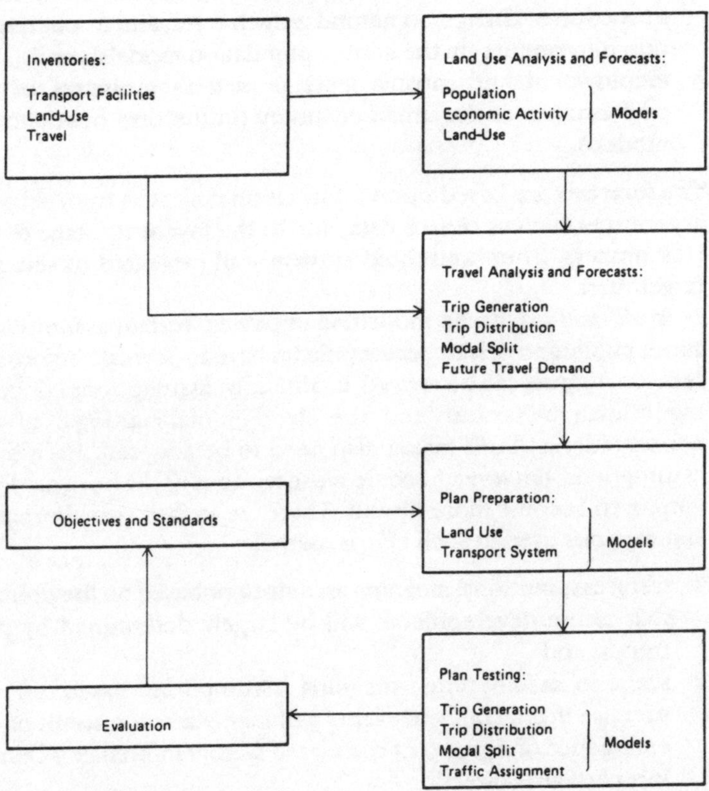

Source: Hutchinson B.G. 1974, ***Principles of Urban Transport Systems Planning*** McGraw-Hill, adapted from Figure 1.1

ated with the UTP process are much less clearly defined – some would say less well-developed than sub-models of the 'four stage process'. The models relate to: land-use changes, population growth characteristics and trends, as well as economic and employment features and forecasts. The purpose of these models in the overall context of the process, is to provide inputs (see Figure 2.4) to the traffic sub-models, seen as functions of:

1 proportions, densities and levels of availability of different types of urban land uses (in the case of land-use models);
2 population growth rate and distribution characteristics, being a function of changes in natural growth-rates, and in-out migration movements (in the case of population models); and
3 employment and income level as well as measures of the performance of the urban economy (in the case of economic models).

The forecasts are based upon information collected from secondary sources such as census data, and in the inventory stage of the UTP process, from household surveys – all projected to selected target years.

In all land-use based modelling exercises, certain assumptions about public and private sector policies have to be made before any realistic outputs can be arrived at. Similarly, assumptions concerning human behaviour and the decision-making logic of the householder and trip-maker also need to be adopted. Many such assumptions, however, become more tenuous as the horizon dates employed become more distant. There are in fact, two alternative assumptions used in such efforts, namely:

1 trend assumptions, meaning assumptions based on the premise that future developments will be largely determined by past trends; and
2 scenario assumptions, meaning assumptions based on the premise that a family of events will take place as a result of the emergence of a group of correlated factors influencing change in a particular direction.

On the basis of the above, projections derived from past trends may be seen as merely some of the numerous possible scenarios. To be consistent with the common use of trend assumptions in traffic sub-models, most land-use inputs to the UTP process have traditionally been based on trend analysis, rather than scenario-building exercises.

Many of the earliest, and subsequent models, owe their origin to Echenique (1975):

1 the emergence of large-scale urban land-use transport planning studies;
2 the advent of and later developments in computer technology; and

3 the success of modelling in other important fields, especially in management, industry and military areas.

Several of the underlying concepts and features of these modelling efforts mirror those of the UTP process in general, and those of its traffic sub-models in particular. These include: the use of systems thinking, the employment of laws of social (based on Newtonian) physics and the general concern for quantification. For a more in-depth exposure of these modelling concepts and features, the reader is referred to the works of Echenique (1975), Mohan (1979), Foot (1981), Putman (1983), Hutchinson and Batty (1986) and the discussion in Chapter 3.

Goal, policy, plan formulation and evaluation

Traditionally, urban transport planning has concerned itself with details of goal, policy and plan formulation *after* it has collected data relating to the current situation. From the information collected, emerging trends are identified, and are then projected to a given horizon date on both a city-wide, city-zone or other area-specific basis. Transport needs are subsequently identified and evaluated in response to which transport improvements are recommended within a strategy so as to meet anticipated changes in transport demand.

Although in this sequence of tasks the adopted planning process employs in its early phases some overall goals of transport and development, the major effort of their detailing usually takes place after alternative transport recommendations have been made, that is when it becomes necessary to assess specific alternative recommendations. In this way, the normative character of the process is limited. Further detailing occurs during the testing of the final short-listed alternatives, a process during which more specific ends are formulated and more detailed evaluation criteria are set.

Given the numerous stages in the UTP process at which goal and policy formulation exercises arise, it is useful to employ the following typology of urban land use and transport planning goals:

1 city-wide general urban development goals, such as those to stimulate the economic growth of the city;
2 city-wide general urban transport goals, such as those to provide an integrated multi-modal public transport systems coverage of the city;

3 city-zone specific urban development goals, such as to stimulate the economy of the central area; and
4 city-zone specific urban transport goals, such as to reduce traffic congestion levels dramatically in the central area.

Transport goals may, in turn, be subdivided into those concerned with:

1 transport systems operations – e.g. to reduce the travel costs and travel time of transport users; and
2 transport systems impact – e.g. to minimise the use of land in the provision of transport infrastructure.

These goals may be applied on a city-wide, area or zone-specific basis. In all instances they need to be associated with supportive strategies and policies; this is something that is often lacking because of a common confusion over goals, policies and strategies.[3]

The goal and policy formulation stages of the UTP process (which include strategy and plan formulation) are in fact the least formalised of the process. In part, this is because they incorporate the interaction of decision-making undertaken by both the professional and the politician, each of whom has different perceptions, priorities and time scales, and consequently tend to favour different actions (see Chapter 6). This has the effect of clouding over goal and policy formulation procedures, and limiting the degree to which they can be simulated in a formalised manner akin to other components of the process. Such circumstances prevail notwithstanding the fact that the possession of clearly articulated goals, policies and strategies is a prerequisite for the effective evaluation of urban transport planning proposals.

EVOLUTION OF THE PROCESS

Origins and periods of development

The true origins of the UTP process in fact pre-date the US pioneering work in urban transport of the 1950s. As early as 1920 the US Federal Government promoted (for the first time) the concept of a 'continuous' national system of highways (thereby identifying the need for a systematic approach to highway planning) which later provided the conceptual basis for the development of a standardised transport (highway) planning process (see Appendix 5).

This process was institutionalised in the USA by the introduction of the Federal Highways Act in 1962 which stipulated that highway and transport planning should abide by the 'three c process' which meant that they had to be 'continuous, co-operative and co-ordinated'. Subsequently until the late 1970s, urban transport planning proceeded in three major directions:

1 clarifying the central conceptual scope of the field of concern from what predominantly had been a single mode to a multi-modal transport perspective; which led on to
2 the conceptualisation (drawing from econometric methods) of the travel demand problem of both passengers and freight; and
3 the implementation of new methods in disaggregate travel demand analysis in a wide variety of styles (see later discussion on disaggregate modelling in this chapter).

Numerous papers have been written on the evolution of the UTP process – the majority of which refer to the USA experience (see Hillegass, 1973; Weiner, 1976 and 1986; Gakenheimer and Wheaton, 1976; and Jones, 1983). The most recent and extensive account is Weiner's (1986). One of the more interesting, however, is the analysis of evolutionary periods offered by Gakenheimer and Wheaton (1976), an expansion of which is outlined below in modified form to place the cited periods in a wider international context. These periods include:

1 Conceptual development (1946–55).
2 Operational development (1955–64).
3 Conceptual stability (1965–69).
4 Stalemate, critical review and revisionism (in industrialised countries) and widespread Third World application (1969–76).[4]
5 Conceptual *ad-hocism* and disarray (1976 to date).[5]

Period of conceptual development (1946–55)

This period began in the USA towards the end of the Second World War. It was characterised by widespread optimism and a strong belief in the use of science and technology to solve social and environmental problems. The faith in science principally emerged as a result of the technological advances achieved at that time by the military and later by space researchers. The optimism was further fuelled by the post-war US economic boom and political initiatives to stimulate other economies in the industrialised world.

The technological developments were accompanied in both the USA and other industrialised countries by urban authorities and governments experiencing rapid urban growth and extensive suburbanisation. At the same time, dramatic increases in car ownership, combined with declining public transport patronage, led to growing urban traffic congestion. In response to these conditions, local bypass schemes were developed and link-specific engineering improvements were undertaken in order to alleviate points of local traffic congestion. Professional thinking simultaneously moved away from simplistic travel surveys, towards the use of more analytical techniques for travel demand analysis and a greater interest in the impact of land use on transport and vice versa.

Given the embryonic state of professional thinking at the time, and the post-war preoccupation of the then colonial powers with reconstructing their own economies, little was done to transfer the technical and conceptual developments of urban transport planning to the Third World. Among the earliest applications and testing of Mitchell's and Rapkin's hypotheses concerning the relationship of traffic to land use was in San Jose, Puerto Rico in 1948 (Paddilla, 1978). Because the city at the time possessed urban development characteristics and problems more akin to those of the Third World than other US cities, one may in retrospect view the San Jose Transportation Study as the earliest application of the UTP process to Third World conditions.

Period of operational development (1955–64)

This period, Hillegass (1973) points out, brought to an end the manual procedures employed in the earliest efforts at urban transport planning and saw the advent of the use of electronic digital computers as foreseen by Carroll (1956), and as demonstrated by him in the methodologies developed for Chicago and other cities in the USA. By 1959, major advances had been made in the development of the constituent parts of the process for land-use forecasting (Hamburg and Creighton, 1959); trip generation estimates (Wynn, 1959); trip distribution estimates (Voorhees and Morris, 1959); and traffic assignment methods (Brokke and Carroll, 1959).

These advances were all achieved in the process of working on urban transport studies for US cities, notably Chicago, Baltimore and Washington DC. By 1961 the developments were further refined and resulted in the publication of the seminal work by Martin and Wohl (1961), *Traffic System Analysis for Engineers and Planners*. Operational land use models were presented at the end of the period. These included both the Lowry (1964) and EMPIRIC (Hill *et al.*, 1966) series of models.

Many of the above-mentioned pioneers in urban transport planning subsequently set up their own consultancy firms which later spawned the export of their planning techniques and the UTP process to countries outside the USA. Such firms at first concentrated on the demand for their services in the USA, later in Western Europe, and then in the Third World, as the demand for their expertise waned in the industrialised countries. Houston Wynn, for example, became a founder director of Wilbur Smith and Associates – a transport planning and engineering consultancy firm that has undertaken the largest number of urban transport planning studies in the Third World (see Table 2.1) and which recently experienced a senior management buy-out after Wilbur Smith's retirement. Alan Voorhees (later with Brian Martin as Martin Voorhees Associates) also established a consulting firm which became increasingly engaged in the export of the UTP process and its derivatives from the USA overseas, first to the UK, and later to Third World cities.

Period of conceptual stability (1965–9)

This period was greatly influenced in the USA by the federal government's concern with the US Interstate Highway System and the continuous financial support of the US Highway Trust Fund for the construction of highways. The adoption of the standardised UTP process was still largely an American phenomenon, and soon became the envy of many other industrialised countries. This was even more so after 1962, when federal legislation was introduced in the USA which obliged all counties before being granted federal aid to fund and construct highways in major urban areas, to have prepared (or be in the process of preparing) general transport plans, with associated land use and development considerations (Weiner, 1976).

The process that had evolved became even more firmly

established and formalised with the legislation's requirement that all urban transport planning studies had to demonstrate continuity in planning and co-operation between the agencies involved in planning transport and land use, as well as comprehensiveness in geographical coverage. This, in turn, led to a widespread demand for specialist urban transport planning skills throughout the USA during the late 1960s. To help overcome the shortage of skilled expertise, the American Association of State Highway Officials and the National Association of County Officials embarked on a programme to train its members to carry out urban transport planning studies, employing the standardised approach. The US Bureau of Public Roads (later to be called The Federal Highways Authority) also published guidelines defining the elements of the 'three c planning process', together with manuals for forecasting urban travel.

Such institutional support later became a feature of national governments elsewhere, as in Brazil (see Barat, 1990) and Britain. In the latter case, this manifested itself in the form of statutory Transport Plans and Programmes (TPPs) required by central government in the mid 1970s, as a prerequisite to their funding of local authority urban transport proposals. With the institutionalisation of the UTP process, came its increased standardisation and more extensive dissemination of its concepts and techniques through official and professional channels alike. By 1965 all the then 224 urban areas of the USA either had had an urban transport plan conducted or had one underway.

The increased demand for urban transport planning expertise meanwhile contributed to the further expansion of US transport consultancy firms, many of which, given the pioneering nature of the work, attracted professionals from overseas. After their apprenticeship in the US, many of these overseas professionals returned home to apply their newly acquired skills and techniques to their own environments. Some were astute enough to set up in their own country consulting services in association with firms already established in the USA and elsewhere in the industrialised world. On the basis of the USA experience, therefore, not only were the UTP process and its derivatives exported to other industrialised countries, but also to selected Third World cities. The stabilisation period of the process saw its application both to London (1964–6), and Calcutta (1967). The same consulting practice (Wilbur Smith Associates) was employed in each case.

Period of critical review, revisionism and wides Third World application (1969–76)

The years between 1969 and 1976 saw the most paradoxical developments in the application of the UTP process. In the USA and other industrialised countries, significant modifications to the process were made, particularly in associated environmental fields, the importance of which were first highlighted by British professionals such as Buchanan (1963). The organisation, methodology and procedures of the UTP process were increasingly critically viewed during this time, and public confidence in the capabilities of urban transport planners substantially declined as the transport planning environment began to alter significantly. The period was associated with a shortage of funds, an emphasis on local management approaches, the use of shorter-term horizon dates for planning, an awareness of the need to plan for stagnation or decline, and a greater interest in issues of equity and public participation (Jones, 1983).

In Third World countries, the same period saw the widest application of the UTP process. Studies in which it featured significantly were conducted for Tehran (OTCA, 1970); Kuala Lumpur (Wilbur Smith Associates 1974a); Lagos (Wilbur Smith Associates, 1974b); Madras (MMDA, 1974); Jakarta (ARGE, 1975); Istanbul (Jamieson Mackay and Partners, 1975); and Bangkok (Kocks Gk/Rhein-Ruhr Eng. Gmbt, 1975) – to mention but a few (see Table 2.1).

The growing disillusionment with the process in the industrialised countries was, according to Gakenheimer (1978), principally a product of the emergence of the 'highway revolt', the subsequent re-orientation to alternative public transport solutions and the growth of the environmental and conservationist lobby, especially after the 1973 energy crisis. In the USA, furthermore, most metropolitan urban transport planning studies had been completed by the mid-1970s, thereby limiting the 'hands-on' modifications to what had by then become well-established (if not entrenched) procedures. In the face of new issues, such procedures appeared increasingly inflexible and inappropriate (see Chapters 3 and 4).

Meanwhile the introduction of environmental legislation and community participation measures in the USA, and the evolution of similar developments in the UK, helped to create a 'shadow planning process', operating in tandem with the conventional UTP process (a development that has not yet occurred on a significant scale in Third World countries). In the USA, this 'shadow planning process' took the form of associated legislation, whilst in the UK, decisions could more easily be turned over through the public enquiry procedure. The net result of both developments was that environmental and political constraints were increasingly imposed upon the standardised procedures of the process, which in turn eroded its 'scientific' image. The combined effect in some instances was the emergence of a more 'open study' approach to urban transport planning. This reduced the pressures of the 1960s that had sought fully to institutionalise urban transport planning procedures and looked toward a greater role for public transport, supported in the USA by funds diverted from the highway sector.

The years between 1969 and 1976 saw the consolidation of transport planning expertise in other industrialised countries, notably in Denmark, France, Germany, Holland and Japan. The significance of this, apart from the impact on the urban transport sector of each of these countries, was that it contributed to the creation of additional foci in the industrialised world (both educational and professional) for the later export of urban transport planning expertise to the Third World.

Capitalising on the specialist developments in urban transport planning practice in their own countries, numerous North American, European and Japanese consulting firms more readily offered their professional expertise to Third World countries – often in association with technical assistance programmes. By the mid-1970s, certain of these countries had developed specialist fields. North American, German and British consultants became renowned for their highway expertise. At the same time, the French and Japanese developed a greater specialisation in rapid transit planning, benefiting from technological advances made in their own countries. The Japanese also marketed their expertise in transport planning for intermediate-sized settlements based upon minibus technology (Rimmer, 1986).

The focus on urban public transport during this period took on growing significance following the increased disenchantment in the industrialised countries with urban highway developments, and as the role of public transport began to be more appreciated by Third World governments. Urban public transport became so widely appreciated that numerous rapid transit, metro and bus transport feasibility studies were conducted.

The planning of many of these systems employed steps similar to those of the conventional UTP process or its derivatives, but were usually confined to a particular line-haul section of a city. Other types of public transport studies were a product of earlier city-wide analyses of movement patterns and needs in which a rapid transit/metro or other public transport component was proposed. These had the effect of accentuating the division of opinions between those favouring further urban highway investment and others preferring greater investment in higher capacity public transport systems, such as bus, light-rail or conventional rail-based systems. Such studies opened up the debate of the relative merits of high versus lower public transport cost options, as witnessed at the time of the preparation of the Singapore Mass Transit Study (Wilbur Smith Associates *et al.*, 1974–7). These events were the seeds of the more recent emphasis on improved public transport systems management.

Period of conceptual *ad-hocism* and disarray (1976 to date)

It is difficult to be precise about the commencement of this period, for there was no abrupt universal replacement of the highway planning tradition by another single professional ethos to mark the clear start of a transition. Rather, it became increasingly noticeable that urban transport studies failed to employ the whole UTP 'package' of standardised assumptions, concepts and techniques. Instead, a very much wider spectrum of approaches emerged.

However, the period of 'conceptual disarray' may be said to have started when many in the established professions in urban transport (i.e., civil, highway and traffic engineers) began to confess openly their own reduced confidence in the long-range forecasting capability of the UTP process, and subsequently advocated a return to traffic engineering and traffic management as the most 'practical' alternative to earlier city-wide transport planning studies.

Apart from the wholesale de-emphasis of long-term planning, this period saw a significant shift in transport planning methods and techniques away from the use of aggregate to disaggregate data. The period is also associated with the technology-transfer of conventional wisdom to Third World countries – both as a single package (with only minor refinements, as in the Second Comprehensive Transport Study for Hong Kong [Hong Kong Government

Transport Department and Wilbur Smith Associates, 1989]), as well as in the form of particular techniques and sub-models associated with the study of modal choice, as in Singapore (Wilbur Smith Associates *et al.*, 1974–7).

The period furthermore, has been associated with a growing divide between developments in transport planning research and practice, against a backcloth of major changes in urban transport policy directions. The major change in this regard has been the replacement, especially in many industrialised countries such as the UK, of the planned approach to transport provision with the market approach, highlighting privatisation of public transport operations, greater emphasis on cost-revenue options, and private sector funded infrastructure projects against a background of a resurgence of growth of the environmental movement.

The most important technical developments of the period include the greater use of micro-statistical disaggregate analyses to reformulate and extend traditional urban travel demand models, underpinned by a theory of discrete choice based on random utility theory (see Chapter 4). Modelling of this kind is seen as a means of better understanding different traffic flow and movement patterns, and represents a departure from the classical approach to travel demand analysis in that it adopts as its starting point the travel characteristics of the individual traveller (see Ben-Akiva and Lerman, 1985).

Some disaggregate models have involved the structuring of the motorcar ownership decision, together with the choice of mode to work, both of which are simultaneous decisions and functions of travel time, costs and income, as well as a stage of life cycle and other social and economic values. All such models employ descriptive variables of social and economic factors, together with descriptions of the transport services which are present throughout the whole transport system under consideration. They are estimated with standard econometric methods, and meet standard statistical tests to reflect high quality practices.

Among modelling developments in land use/transport interaction during the period when these disaggregate modelling developments took place, have been the work of Zahavi (1979), Brotchie *et al.* (1980), and Putman (1983). Of note for the Third World is the LUTO model, applied in Hong Kong (Choi, 1986) and subsequently in Beijing, and the later research of Zahavi *et al.* (1981). Zahavi's earlier work analysed urban travel patterns with a view to establishing underlying behavioural phenomena that could be used to describe travel without recourse to complex computer-based models. In his later work he related his findings to Third World cities and further developed the models to incorporate transport policy decisions influencing urban structural change. Concepts of travel time budgets figured significantly in Zahavi's latter research, as did activity-based approaches to urban transport analysis.

Advances in activity-based approaches developed at the Transport Studies Unit of Oxford University constitute another significant development in the field of urban transport planning during the late 1970s and early 1980s (see Banister, 1984). Such approaches are believed to offer a possible overall reorientation to transport planning, based upon travel behaviour analysis conducted within a household activity framework (Carpenter and Jones, 1983). They emphasise constraints rather than choice on locational and travel behaviour factors of transport. However, unlike advances in discrete choice models which have been used and further developed in practice, activity-based approaches have not been operationalised, nor applied to Third World situations.

Other developments in the urban transport planning field since the late 1970s include: efforts at improved valuation of project benefits, the re-examination of concepts such as shadow pricing, parking policy enforcement, and the provision of relevant comprehensible travel information (Jones, 1987). In addition to these, there has been: a call for a return to basic principles through the better understanding of human needs (see Dimitriou, 1982, and Banister *et al.*, 1984), a greater focus on particular target groups (Linn, 1983), a call for more attention to strategic and integrative planning (Dimitriou, 1977; Banjo, 1984 and Thomson, 1984), a greater emphasis on institutional building (Barrett, 1983), and the derivation of origin and destination matrices from traffic counts (Khan and Willumsen, 1986). Most approaches to urban transport planning likely to emerge from these developments – as in the case of activity-based approaches – are less formal in character and more 'open' than their predecessors. They are as a result less conducive to packaging and standardised use which calls into question the suitability of previous styles of planning for urban transport (see Chapters 3 and 4 for further discussion).

3

CRITIQUE OF THE UTP PROCESS

Functions, assumptions and concepts

INTRODUCTION

This chapter and the next principally summarise responses to major issues in urban transport planning in interview sessions with numerous notable theorists and practioners in the USA, including many of the initiators of the UTP process of the 1950s and 1960s (see Appendix 1). The questions were posed (see Appendix 2) with the intention of drawing out the respondents' views on the limitations and strengths of the UTP process and its derivatives to extract information about their personal involvement in the field that helped mould their views. Issues presented for discussion by the author in the interviews are shown in the text below in italics.

The chapter commences with selected comments from those interviewed regarding the evolution of the UTP process as outlined in Chapter 2. It continues by outlining and commenting on views expressed to the author regarding the assigned functions and employed assumptions of the UTP process since its inception. The chapter concludes by addressing the principal concepts relied on by the process, recounting selected impressionable comments made during the interviews regarding the validity of these concepts.

The interview material presented in this chapter and Chapters 4 and 7 has not previously been published, and offers a valuable archive of experiences of some of the best known and most experienced professionals in the field of urban transport planning. In the light of the more pragmatic responses to urban transport planning currently adopted and the recent greater understanding of the limits of 'scientific' approaches to transport planning, many of the views expressed can in many respects be better appreciated retrospectively. The interview responses provide a useful backcloth for the formulation of a more appropriate approach to transport planning for Third World cities outlined later in the book.

In this chapter, as in Chapters 4 and 7, where reference is made to one or more of the interviews conducted in 1978, no reference date is given. The reader is instead referred to Appendices 1 to 4 for further details.

EVOLUTION OF THE PROCESS

Origins

What are the main phases of development of the urban transport planning process since the Chicago (CATS) study?

Although many consider that the UTP process has its origins in the 1940s with the old Bureau of Public Roads when it surveyed people's movements in terms of travel patterns (to try to understand trip origins and destinations), and subsequently in the 1950s in the Chicago and Detroit transportation studies, Kornhauser claims that there was, in fact, a great deal of urban transport planning in the USA from the early 1920s. He cites, for example, a number of transport planning reports from the early 1900s of subway systems for Pittsburgh, New Orleans, Cincinnati and many other cities, in which a great deal of urban traffic analysis of people and of goods took place. Many of these studies are, he points out, now in a private library owned by John Kohl of Princeton University.

More interestingly, Kornhauser claims, between 1950 and 1955 there were numerous consultant reports for twenty cities throughout the US which looked at new urban transport technologies (including the monorail), that studied travel demand characteristics and site planning. Although there was not much discussion of models in these studies, some systematic modelling such as regression analysis was used. What these studies displayed, Kornhauser suggests, is that while the discipline of urban transport planning was not structured prior to the development of the UTP process, it was practised, and that as far as public transport planning is concerned, the field has come 'full-circle'.

Levinson believes these developments need to be understood in the light of the economic boom after the Second World War, when systems analysts were looking for a way to apply their skills in 'solving' social problems. They did this, he claims:

> in the belief that social engineering and the technology that had emerged from both World War II and the cold war, could be applied to problems of human existence, with the kind of rigour that was not previously possible by the 'soft social scientist' and 'philosophical' types.

The urban planning profession at the time, he argues, was looking for an acclaimed scientific approach to city problems. In this regard, the relationship between transport and land use proclaimed by Mitchell and Rapkin (1954) was seen to be a stimulating discovery for it made possible a more systematic approach to the planning of transport. Rapkin had this to say about the influence of his work on urban transport planning in the USA:

> in our book, what we tried to do was to move away from simple studies of traffic burden. We hoped that kind of direction would be picked up by both transportation and land-use planners, so that there would be co-ordination in large scale planning.
>
> For a while, we thought that there was interest in that direction. But there were a number of things that diverted the attention from this path. One was that there were huge sums of money available for freeways; the emphasis was therefore very much upon the expansion of the highway system – which it was expected would offer additional movement space. These sums were seized upon by the states because they could get 90 per cent or so funding for such highways from the federal government.

Mitchell and Rapkin wrote their seminal piece at Columbia University, whilst Carroll and Creighton simultaneously worked along similar lines at Harvard University. Recalling these times Levinson explains that:

> The whole process of punching land use on computer cards and developing concepts of travel demand were developed then... whilst down at the Yale Traffic Institute, where Voorhees worked with Wilbur Smith, travel demand concepts were further developed and later picked up by the Bureau of

Public Roads as part of the standard professional practice it later advocated.

The first major technical breakthrough in terms of the application of the most rudimentary basics of the UTP process, as it had then been developed, came in 1955 with the Washington Metropolitan Area Transportation Study which applied the first of the trip generation and trip distribution models (see Chapter 2). An earlier major landmark, however, was the Detroit Area Metropolitan Transportation Study (1955–56) directed by Carroll. This represented the first widely publicised and well-documented application of the ideas commonly associated with the UTP process. The study subsequently contributed not only to the development of travel analysis but to attempts to rationalise parts of the transport system configuration.

The Chicago Area Transportation Study (CATS) which followed (1959–62), also directed by Carroll, looked at the metropolitan scale of transport and examined some very significant examples of network concepts. In trying to arrive at least-cost highway and public transport solutions (one in a sense independent of the other), the study offered interesting advances in economic testing. It made inroads in the use of the 'opportunities model', rather than the 'gravity model' for trip distribution, as well as in the examination of least-cost solutions, in terms of minimum social and environmental impacts. The US studies subsequent to this, those of Pittsburgh (1958), Penn-Jersey (1959), Tri-State (1961) etc. were based on much of the work done in CATS or earlier work on the gravity model, with the difference that they incorporated advances made in the field of modal split analysis.

Interestingly enough, Carroll since claims that he and the team conducting the CATS study were not influenced by Mitchell and Rapkin as much as has been claimed. He recalls:

> they (Mitchell and Rapkin) articulated in a more scholarly and well written manner (in their book) what I came to totally independently.... We met somewhere in Detroit and traded ideas. I felt what they said was correct.... I never thought that the transportation system alone could produce the (forecast) outcome. But they did not either.

Gomez-Ibanez suggests that at least three major developments have taken place in the USA since the inception of the UTP process.

The first is the concern for transport interaction with land use, particularly in the early 1960s, incorporating the periods of operational development and conceptual stability referred to in Chapter 2. Second (correlating with the period of critical review and revisionism), were developments in the field of public participation, where he claims:

> it soon became clear that one could not do any major urban transport planning without involving citizens.

This was vividly illustrated by the experience in Boston in the 1970s when the city had a Transportation Planning Review that cost between US$ 3–4 million, very little of which was spent on technical modelling but a great deal on consulting with neighbouring communities to obtain a political consensus about what was acceptable (see Gakenheimer, 1976). The third development (equating with the 'conceptual disarray period' discussed in Chapter 2) relates to the collapse in the credibility of large-scale planning efforts which were replaced by more small-scale planning or limited short-term projects, often using techniques closely related to (or derived from) those of the Chicago study but of (in Gomez-Ibanez' words) a 'back of an envelope' sketch-plan character.

A very important early achievement in urban transport planning, according to Carroll, was to break away from simple traffic engineering to look at the urban transport system as a whole. In so doing, it is then evident that many current and recent developments, are, in urban transport planning terms, regressive.

Another major step in the evolution of the process cited by Levinson and others, was to give more attention to public transport systems. While the immediate post Chicago (CATS) study developments generated important advances in the work done, i.e., in the measuring of access of land use and increasing the understanding of the behaviour of metropolitan growth, the Chicago study particularly offered an explanation (though not in quantitative terms) of the potential feedback of transport system changes on land usage patterns.

These early studies in the USA, Heanue and Ettinger point out, were conducted by some of the brightest minds of their profession. Many such people (or their former students) are now in key positions in academia, international development agencies, consulting firms, and federal and state agencies, where they exert considerable influence in the developments of the field. Even in the late 1970s, these professionals continued working on refinements of the same UTP process and its derivatives, making certain aspects more institutional, while detailing others.

Standardisation and institutionalisation

The US Federal Highways Act of 1962, which specifically refers to the UTP process and calls for the application of a 'continuous', 'co-operative' and 'co-ordinated' effort, was perhaps the most important landmark in the institutionalisation of urban transport planning in the USA (see Appendix 5). The legislation decreed that the planning procedures that had at the time been developed (and were still in their formative stages) were to be adhered to by the states and the local agencies for the planning and design of the interstate highway system. This was done, Hillegass suggests, because at the time, the states were gaining too much control over this area of concern.

The legislation laid down criteria for the planning of roads under Federal Government control, thereby giving impetus to the further formalisation, computerisation and institutionalisation of transport planning. The Federal Highway Administration, which was controlled by engineers, was assigned the responsibility to administer the legislation. Because the Highway Administration, through its regional divisional offices throughout the country, was able to propagate the planning criteria and the UTP process, the period of the decade in which the legislation was introduced marked the beginning of a highly standardised dissemination of this process in the 1960s (see Chapter 2).

According to Hillegass, contrary to conventional thinking, the CATS procedure was not the one standardised by the Federal Highway Administration in its legislation but was rather derived from a variety of sources, of which CATS was just one. These included among others, the Up-State New York Urban Area studies and the Tri-State study of New York City, with the early Washington DC study being regarded by many as the one which brought together all the various elements into a packaged form as described by Creighton (1970).

Although some applications of the UTP process, as in California, were radical, their elements were the same. Hillegass argues that:

> The differences were more in the calibration, the parameters and variables employed, and assignments and adjustments used. But the basic assumptions were the same. The assumption for example that travel is generated by land use, that trip distribution is some function of travel time, that modal choice is some function of travel cost, time and income, and that one can reasonably plan some twenty years hence, were all important common assumptions underlying the process.

Kain argues that the Detroit study directed by Doug Carroll and John Hamburg etc., was more original and intellectually more interesting than the Chicago (CATS) study, described by him as:

> no more than a detailed improvement on the basics of the early approach.... The CATS study was, however, significantly, the first (at least publicised) example of the application of the computer to the field.

The principal methodological advances of the CATS study, Kain claims, had nothing to do with computerisation but with improvements in land use forecasting, to the extent that, some twenty years after its completion, he declared:

> in a lot of ways, it (the CATS study and therefore the UTP procedures associated with it) is still one of the best land use forecasting exercises you can find, at least as far as dealing with extensive metropolitan growth.

Others involved in the implementation of the study, such as Hills, however, claim:

> The CATS study was criticised by other agencies for its 'trend planning'... for being over-ambitious, in that the study planned/projected far more freeways than we can ever build, or that the public would ever permit us to build.

Post-Chicago study advances

The demise of long-range highway planning

What followed the CATS Study, with the exception of certain amendments and developments in network modelling, were further refinements on the same basic theme, with improvements in land-use forecasting and modelling that injected the UTP process with greater analytical capabilities in aspects of urban travel behaviour.

By 1975 the Federal Highways Administration had successfully spread this whole procedure of urban transport planning throughout the country, and to many parts of the world (see Chapters 2 and 7). The subsequent re-examination phase, however, saw certain fundamental questions raised, namely:

1 is it really possible to plan twenty years hence, and if so, how can this be done in the light of increased uncertainties; and
2 if not, what time period is reasonable and is it feasible to do contingency planning as well as to test alternative plans for flexibility?

The most disruptive aspect for the development of the conventional wisdom of urban transport planning was the period of 'highway revolt'. This was a time in the USA when, as Gakenheimer explains, the accumulation of *ad hoc* interests began to displace travel demand and land-use interests, with other interests such as public participation, which ultimately dismembered the apparent 'invincibility' of the technocratic rationale. During this period, referred to as the period of 'stalemate, critical review and revisionism' (see Chapter 2), community groups strongly expressed their opposition to the freeways the UTP process advocated, and especially to the associated heavy costs of their construction. Gakenheimer points out that the same people later complained about the high construction and operating costs of rapid transit systems which followed the highway building era.

During these developments, 'trends' were consistently projected and passed on as 'planning', future projections being extrapolated from past trends. This approach, still practised today in more conventional transport planning quarters, is denounced by Vuchic as:

> neither theoretically nor practically sound planning... merely the simulation of past trends. For although it makes sense to take into account what is going on at present in order to understand trends that have taken place up to now, judgements need to be made with regard to whether the trends are desirable, and where they lead. Whereas, in the 1960s and early 1970s, a situation had developed in the USA and elsewhere, whereby projections had been made to a point where

they not only became economically or socially unenviable but physically impossible.

Paradoxically, in the USA as the confidence in professionals waned, so the more conventional transport planning practitioner's own regard for their handling of vast amounts of data gathered and increased to unrealistic levels. This mechanically enhanced capability was, it is claimed by Vuchic, accompanied by a decline in innovation, as the degree of reliance upon data and repetitive procedures increased. He remarked: 'urban transport planning has been transferred (unwittingly perhaps) from philosophically based planning to extrapolation.'

Transport systems management

During the demise of the credibility of comprehensive long-range city-wide transport planning in the USA, short-range planning came into its own. It constituted a reaction to the limitations of long-range planning and led to the introduction and growing reliance upon transport systems management (TSM) (see Gakenheimer and Meyer, 1990), where the principal concept is to employ the comprehensive approach (previously applied to long-range planning) for short-range planning on a five year basis.

However, the multitude of different agencies, interests and political forces involved in TSM, made it very difficult to obtain an effective and co-ordinated effort at the project implementation phase. As a result, it took much longer for the approach to gain the influence it deserved. Nevertheless, TSM came to be seen as one acceptable alternative response to urban transport planning, and in the late 1970s, marked the beginning of a more open approach to the field.

Disaggregate modelling

The early studies contained modelling exercises which were extremely aggregated and it is not clear whether the questions answered were the right questions, or indeed, were all the relevant questions. As a result, one of the other most publicised post-CATS study advances, apart from TSM, has been the technical developments made in disaggregate modelling.

What has proved especially fruitful in such efforts at better understanding urban travel demand are the methods of estimating models of individual travel choice behaviour, using relatively small samples. The aim of such disaggregate modelling Manheim explains, is:

> not merely a matter of refining modal split models, but more of thinking through the process with which different sets of people with different cultural and economic strata characteristics make decisions to participate in activities, so as to arrive at their travel choices.

While Quarmby (1967) was the first to do such work, the re-emergence of his ideas in the form of disaggregate modelling in the late 1970s offers a rich set of methods which articulate the structuring of the choice process that individuals go through in the selection of transport modes and routes. Conventionally, urban transport models treat automobile and locational choice as separate exogenous predictions, and produce, therefore, very poor quality estimations. The worst element of these exercises according to Manheim, was the adjustment of the gravity models to fit future factors.

More recently developed disaggregate models involve structuring the choice of mode to work (involving simultaneous decisions), as functions of travel time, costs, income, the stage of life cycle, and other social and economic values. All such models employ descriptive social and economic variables, as well as descriptions of the transport services that are consistent throughout the whole system, on the basis of which one can design data collection systems to produce the small sample of observations necessary to estimate models for each different strategy examined.

Disaggregate modelling emerged partly from a concern for the distributional effects of transport planning, and has its origin in traffic clover leaf theory and behaviour analysis at intersections. Charles River Associates in Boston and faculty staff of the University of California, Berkeley, initiated much of the work in the field in the USA. Even though developments of this kind have not yet been well integrated into the overall process of urban transport planning (it has developed as a specialist area), it has generated sufficient confidence to be considered suitable for region-wide application, employing samples as representations of the population. It has also been claimed that disaggregate models provide a very quick tool (relying on simple techniques using pocket calculators) for the estimation of travel demand (Manheim, 1990). Manheim claims:

> there is, therefore, a spectrum of (urban transport planning) analysis styles available which range from the comprehensive, long-range, area-wide studies (which are heavily computer based) to hand calculations and programmable pocket calculator methods. At each level, you have different degrees of subtlety, detail and complexity, etc.

Paradoxically, while urban transport planning has seen, by the late 1980s, a proliferation of techniques, and a certain 'loosening-up' of the field with new ideas (see Williams, 1987), beginning with the concern for participation and openness, as well as a regard for policy matters and issues of investment, the period has also seen the increasingly confined use of these techniques on a project basis, outside a wider planned treatment of these issues, and within the context of a greater politicisation of the field.

FUNCTIONS AND ASSUMPTIONS OF THE PROCESS

Functions

What were and have become the main functions of the UTP process?

Historical perspective

The UTP process was originally conceived in the USA to help decide where to invest in new freeways and how to accommodate the transport demand in cities. Its orientation later moved towards a mixed combination of freeways and transit lines. By the late 1970s urban transport planning practice was described by Gomez-Ibanez as an exercise:

> where one tinkers with the system in modest ways which are politically acceptable to large numbers of people... representing a movement away from the accommodation of demand and growth of travel previously assumed to occur.

Gakenheimer describes the initial function of the UTP process as an explicit exercise in guiding the investment in highways where it was understood that large expressways were to be built by the USA

Highway Trust Fund and the interstate highway programme.[1] In Marxist terms, Ziv (1977) argues that mega-industries influenced and determined the function of the UTP process, but this view has no general consensus among those interviewed for this book.

In defining the functions of the UTP process, Shuldiner emphasises the need to differentiate between large-scale studies for cities such as Chicago, Detroit and the Tri-State Region, and much smaller metropolitan area transport studies that were required under the 1962 Federal Highways Act. He points out:

> they (the latter) were generally freeway network designs which really go back to the highway studies of the 1930s set up under the Cartwright Act (the Federal Highways Act of 1934) which initiated highway planning studies. Some of the techniques and tools learned in those days for motor vehicle user studies, O & D (Origin and Destination) studies, and the notion of freeway planning, for example, were merely transferred from non-urban area situations to urban contexts.

Rapkin explains that the functions assigned to the UTP process can in retrospect be said to have varied over time and geography in accordance with differing economic cycles and changing political circumstances. He cites the CATS study, during whose early phases of formulation the USA was experiencing economic growth, as being prepared in an environment where it was expected that infrastructure planners had to cater for the boom in automobile use and ownership. This contrasts with the late 1970s, when growth was slow or non-existent and the maintenance of the system was a problem. During the latter of these two periods, Rapkin claims there was a realisation that:

> we cannot build ourselves out of problems anymore... but instead have to sit down and cope with them. We have now to treat them with imagination and use better management techniques.

Observations of the changing use of urban transport planning exercises over the last three to four decades, suggest that while the principles of transport systems analysis employed in the USA were the same, the specific tools (and technology) utilised, and the political environments in which they were adopted, have altered significantly. This was especially apparent in the late 1970s when the phase of large-scale highway and rapid transit projects came to an end, and when, as Rapkin put it:

> we entered into the situation whereby the use of smaller pliers instead of big hammers, and a lot more paint and much less concrete became necessary.

Rapkin recounts these differences by recalling that in the 1950s, unlike the late 1980s, given the financial incentives from Federal Government, it seemed cheaper to build a new road rather than repair an old one. He concludes that although these past practices and attitudes may have been wrong, the expertise to go ahead on this basis in the highway sector was, in the 1950s, readily available, whereas this was not the case at the time in the public transport industry. Although still lagging behind highway and traffic engineering expertise, skills in transport systems management in the USA public transport industry have since been greatly developed.

In the latter part of the 1980s, however, the industrialised world in general and the USA in particular, saw a rise in highway building – partially as a result of growing affluence but more because little new highway capacity had been provided since the early 1970s. The demand for additional capacity and the declining urban transport system travel speeds over time began to lead to the challenge of earlier public resistance to new roads on the grounds of environmental protection (Gakenheimer, 1989).

More recent perspectives

Investment programmes in urban transport were originally formulated for 20–30 years ahead, whereas the planning process is now seen by many as merely a means of setting a scenario within which to look at the immediate investment programme. As Hillegass succinctly puts it:

> they (urban transport studies) have changed from the production of a plan to the production of information to support (shorter term) decisions.

The emphasis of the functions of the UTP process has now conspicuously altered from a long-range planning function to one more orientated toward day-to-day support for decision-making.

In the early days, the UTP process was aimed especially at

adapting the capacity of channels of transport to the volume of traffic. It was, in Rapkin's words:

> directed by desire lines, so that origin and destination surveys were merely devices which were employed in order to enable the engineer to route the highway rather than to determine whether he wanted to encourage movement between two points or not – or whether he wanted to use the transportation system as a (planning) tool.

These efforts at optimising the freeway network and a dozen or so alternative configurations, were tested elaborately in the UTP process. According to Shuldiner, however, no one asked how efficient the network would be if the total system was *not* constructed and/or when one or more critical links were *not* built; despite the fact that for a variety of reasons such situations often occurred. Yet circumstances of this kind not only produced sub-optimal results but often created worse traffic conditions than had existed previously. Optimisation efforts of this kind contrast greatly with the approach advocated by Mitchell and Rapkin (1954). Rapkin recounts that this:

> saw urban transport planning as a device to minimise the transportation movement which was unnecessary in the city, so that activities which had a high degree of interaction were located close together and (activities) that we thought should not be encouraged were made less accessible, instead of more accessible.

He concludes that what is needed is for urban transport to guide growth and development, rather than to accommodate the impulse for further mobility generated by market forces. Rapkin claims that many of those who employed his and Mitchell's ideas, used them to suit their own interpretations of the urban transport planning problem.

The theoretical basis of the UTP process, even as early as 1970 (see Chapter 2 and Bruton, 1970), was not intended to support any one transport mode but to deal with the provision and distribution of transport facilities throughout urban areas. Despite this, Hillegass and many others concur that in the late 1970s there was still a highway bias in the approach. Hillegass says:

> Certainly that (the emphasis on highways) was definitely what

> many people had in mind when employing the package... but only the naive can believe that traffic congestion may be solved through additional supply (of road infrastructure)... for as long as we have a fairly affluent country (travel) demand will (always) expand.

Manheim suggests that a cynic would argue that the main function of the UTP process has been to keep the real issues from being debated, in that much of its application resulted in the use of a set of models which avoided key political issues (see later discussion in this chapter on role of models); and that the longevity of the process can be accounted for in these terms.

Pushkarev, on the other hand, suggests that the major function of the UTP process is bureaucratic and institutional, i.e., to fulfil the requirements of federal law. This view is shared by Levinson who argues that the process

> constituted the rationale for obtaining federal funds and support for a planned transportation programme.... in some cases, studies were done in order to get federal certification.

Assumptions

What are the main foundation assumptions of the UTP process?

Interrelationship of assumptions

Carroll maintains that layer after layer of assumptions may be revealed in the UTP process. One of the most important assumptions is that a human settlement is an orderly phenomenon that can be described and quantified. Other principal assumptions, cited by Mitchell, include:

1 that one can make a plan that will have some validity (as a static plan) for the future;
2 that the UTP process is a valid intellectual exercise of analysis and design, even though it omits an interaction with implementation;
3 that one can make a sufficiently reliable forecast of land-use, independent of transport (technology) changes, and use this as a basis for future land-use pattern forecasts;

4 that patterns of human behaviour as affected by life styles, etc. will remain the same for the next 25–30 years;
5 that one can optimise transport services without adverse effects on other sub-systems of urban life;
6 that one can employ evaluation criteria based on aggregate information, whereas the range around the average is much more significant;
7 that the major concern is for the movement of people (not goods) in vehicles;
8 that 'desire lines' represent where people want to go, as opposed to the transport facility provided; and
9 that one is planning for land transport rather than water transport.

Also important to the assumptional baggage of urban transport planners is that the belief of the 1950s and 1960s that the public's demand for more highways was well known, and that instead the delivery (of services and infrastructure) was the problem; has given way to the recognition that the problem is now much more one of defining what the public wants.

Hence, although the adoption of assumptions is inevitable, it is according to Carroll, increasingly apparent that it is essential to investigate and extract the truth out of these assumptions. He explains that although what is believed to be the truth at one time may change in another, assumptions are still needed. Carroll continues:

> When I think of those assumptions I was attracted to then, I am much wiser about them now. However, I do not think that anything could have been done without the energy of 'true belief'. You do not put energy into things that you do not believe in. That is one of the difficulties of the more sophisticated society; there is too much disbelief! There is nothing to replace belief and the glow of hope that can get you to the end of the rainbow.

Travel demand assumptions

Central to the UTP process are the travel demand assumptions. These are well described by Stopher who has claimed that many of these assumptions are so inexact and their related models so detailed that to standardise them (which is common) is unrealistic.

He argues the most important underlying assumption of travel demand analysis is that one has the capacity and ability to simulate the travel behaviour of transport users.

Other important travel demand assumptions (also see Chapter 2) include:

1 that the impacts of changes in travel demand on the transport system are region-wide – an assumption that is not always upheld, for most effects are often very localised;
2 that one can handle all these phenomena by studying aggregates of households, person trips, etc. – a claim that is seen as suspect, as illustrated by the increasing use of disaggregate data;
3 that the interacting forces at work affecting changes in travel demand are adequately represented by the process and that these are stable and can be used for forecasting; and
4 that no major unexpected changes affecting the (land-use/transport) system will take place during the period planned for – in that it is impossible for models to have built-in an accommodation of the sudden effects of the Arab oil embargo, for instance, or in Britain's case, the discovery of North Sea oil.

Of the more recent applications of both the UTP process and its derivatives, Gakenheimer (1989) has expressed the view that these are distinguished by a movement towards the use of more pragmatic assumptions. This is in contrast to the classical form of the process employed by early transport planners who believed it was possible to serve all travel demand, forgetting that reduced travel times would attract more traffic, and where it was believed that the process could provide all the transport infrastructure necessary to service the travel demand. This (utopian) assumption, he points out, was a key assumption that guided the traditional approach to urban transport planning that gave rise to a family of collaborative assumptions, which (as in the case of environmental protection) experienced a general adjustment over time.

Also regarding travel demand assumptions, Levinson argues that the UTP process assumes people make trips to achieve objectives in a particular way, and that this is related to:

1 their socio-economic status;
2 the type of land-use (and level of density) of areas in which they both reside (origins) and travel to (destinations); as well as
3 the geographical patterns of activities in the metropolitan area.

The process, he claims, also assumes that one can revise current relationships that relate trip-making both to human behaviour and to land-use patterns, which can then be projected into the future, as they relate to:

1 land-uses;
2 populations; and
3 economic activities.

Within this set of assumptions, Levinson believes there are three additional travel demand assumptions, all of which dramatically affect the results of the UTP process. These relate to:

1 the future population;
2 the activities of the future; and
3 the economic level of the future population.

Land-use/transport assumptions

Perhaps one of the earliest and most fundamental assumptions of the UTP process relates to Mitchell and Rapkin's (1954) premise, that:

> travel is a function of land-use, whilst land-use is a function of, among other things, the availability of transport, and that this functional relationship exists not only in the minds of planners and analysts, but also in the real world.

Shuldiner's view, however, is that this connection is not so strong and direct as has been thought.

The second land-use/transport assumption, is that one can measure and perceive enough of the above-stated relationship to model it in an urban transport planning exercise. The third related assumption is that one can predict the state of the independent variables of the UTP process, and have a sufficiently firm understanding of the structural relationships to be able to predict travel demand.

The above three assumptions have characterised the UTP process and its derivatives in the USA up to the late 1970s, and later in other countries, with the difference, as Shuldiner puts it,

> that we (the professionals) are now just far less confident of our abilities – in many respects because we have to work within a much wider scale. We are now much more con-

> cerned with people movements than we were when the process was first conceived.

Heanue and Ettinger argue that each urban transport planning approach was predicated on a land-use inventory basis, whether or not they used land-use area measures or population indices. The approaches went through a process of trip generation and a separate trip distribution procedure – which is the gravity or opportunity models or growth factor model. They then went onto assignment, and depending upon the size of the city, adopted some transport mode choice procedure.

Travel behaviour assumptions

According to Manheim, the classical UTP process as regards its treatment of travel behaviour, reflects 'an aggregate, mechanistic search for statistical regularity, without a thoughtful treatment of behaviour', whereas the neo-classical models which were primarily used in the late 1970s represented an explicit behavioural hypothesis from an economic perspective. One can conclude from this that the treatment of travel behaviour assumptions differs according to when they were developed.

The real challenge, Manheim argues,

> comes with the development of the next generation (of models) which is particularly important for Third World countries. These will (or ought to) draw from the insights of anthropologists, psychologists and sociologists, to produce quality hypotheses that then would be translated into qualitative policies.

While partially reflected in advances in disaggregate modelling, this optimistic view is clearly very far from having matured in the practice of urban transport planning in the 1980s, anywhere in the world.

Forecasting assumptions

Another assumption of the UTP process, despite the wide range of divergent views obtained from those interviewed for this book, is that it (the process) was reasonably good at travel demand forecasting. Modellers, such as Gomez-Ibanez, for example, perceive the UTP process positively, as illustrated by his following statement:

> it is easy to make cheap shots about the (UTP) model, but what you essentially have to do is to remind yourself of the problem that the model is trying to solve, i.e., that you are in a situation where you have to worry about building very durable and long-lasting facilities that may take ten years to build... you do not have a lot of alternatives in demand forecasting to the standard UTP procedure.
>
> People bitch and carp about how many arbitrary assumptions are made, and it is easy to see how one can tinker with the model to modify it and alleviate some of these bad assumptions. However, when you come down to it, there are a lot of problems inherent in an exercise which tries to simplify a very complicated process to a point where it is analytically tractable, and can say something useful. Whilst there is a lot of error in the basic model, it is the best method we have got to do this long term (forecasting) task.

Hillegass claims that the travel demand forecasting side of the process has in fact, received too much attention in relation to other components, and is, furthermore, too deterministic. He emphasises that this deterministic side is itself subject to a variety of assumptions that are themselves not necessarily deterministic. Put simply, he explains:

> People make trips. The more people – the more trips! You tell me how many people there are, and how much affluence they have, and I can tell you how many trips they make, and how much travel they will generate.... what is needed, is a very good and systematic look at metropolitan change from a planning perspective before getting into specifying the quantitative parameters that you build into the (urban transport planning) process.

However, it is because conventional methods of the UTP process assume travel demand to be inelastic, and fail to bring out the differences in travel behaviour of different social groups, and because they are so insensitive to issues other than matters of increased capacity provision, that disaggregate travel demand forecasting became important.

Other assumptions

The assumptions which follow represent the remaining breadth of assumptional baggage that has been called upon in support of the UTP process and its derivatives over the last three to four decades of their development.

One of the early general assumptions of those using the UTP process was that there was no distributive effect of the urban transport system, and that, therefore, there was no need for a redistributive concern. This assumption was rectified, however, in earlier adaptations of the UTP process, when as Gakenheimer recalls:

> there was in a sense, a discovery that you could not do a cost benefit analysis of the transport system simply because the costs were sustained by one sub-group of the population while the benefits were enjoyed by another. As a result, the balance between costs and benefits cannot be taken as an indicator of project quality.

There is also the long-standing assumption that urban transport planning enjoys (or rather should enjoy) a positive relationship with urban planning. This is assumed, despite the considerable evidence which shows that in practice the relationship between urban and highway planning is weak. Altshuler, for example, points this out by claiming that when the interstate US highway programme was enacted in 1956, there was almost no recognition of urban problems. Most urban planning at the time, he claims, was notorious for paying attention to engineering considerations alone.

According to Banfield, it is even debatable if urban highway planning took place in the USA as early as has been claimed. He argues that President Eisenhower (in office between 1953 and 1961) opposed the construction of urban highways on the grounds that it would be disruptive to urban settlements. Banfield claims:

> the state planners pulled a 'fast one' on him (Eisenhower) – he did not realise until it was too late that urban freeways would be built.

With regard to another assumption, namely that both urban planning and transport planning can be managed at the same time – this being inherent in and necessitated by the land-use/transport interaction assumption – this is according to Gakenheimer, an expectation that grew out of necessity rather than normative thinking. He describes the assumption as:

> unrealistic because the characteristics of the two are widely different. One of them (transport planning) is very 'lumpy', the other (land-use planning) is very incremental. One is done by central and state government, the other by local government. One (namely land-use planning) can be normatively assertive, the other (namely urban transport planning) is conservative.

Assumptions about public participation in the UTP process are rarely mentioned in early urban transport planning literature. According to Gakenheimer, there appeared to be

> an implicit assumption held by many laymen that the technocrats had rational answers that did not bear discussion, and that society should accept that.

As urban transport planning developed, some later claimed the encouragement given to non-professionals to participate in transport planning exercises was in fact an overreaction. Picarsky, for example, declares:

> many of us who have been involved in citizen participation more deeply are of the view that a citizen who allegedly represents a group often represents no one but himself, and the accountability of the citizen or group is really transitory to the person who acts as spokesman (i.e., they may be here today and gone tomorrow), and may in fact represent a very small portion of the population... so that only elected people are accountable and responsible.

There is also a general assumption (substantiated by research findings) that travel is related to levels of affluence – something especially manifest in the trip generation model of the UTP process. Hillegass argues that this has led forecasting exercises to become self-fulfilling, in that they tend to lead to a greater provision of transport services for higher income groups than for lower income groups. This assumption, *vis-à-vis* affluence and travel demand, is, according to Hillegass, based upon a propagation of the past. The question to be posed, he suggests, is:

> if one provides the same level of service to both income levels, would some of the lower income individuals then not be low income for quite so long?

Some have argued that the long-range plan component of the UTP process was often not dependent on the ability to implement it but rather, as Picarsky explains,

> more a wish that the plan could be implemented – for as new funding sources emerged and as other concerns of society came up, these came into play in a form that altered the priorities for plan implementation.

In Gakenheimer's view, this has encouraged those implementing transport plans and projects to do their own planning, usually in a manner which under-emphasises the normative controls that are both expected and needed of planning. In circumstances where one pays too much attention to long-run considerations, there is a tendency to believe that the more difficult problems are long term, and the more easily solved are to do with existing capacity problems whereas, as Gakenheimer points out, the opposite is the case. A final note of concern raised by Mitchell regarding implementation, is his observation that many of the proposals emanating from the UTP process have been excessive to the extent that they are impossible to implement.

PRINCIPAL CONCEPTS

Land-use/transport system balance

What constitutes the land-use/transport system balance?

Although attaining a balance in the land-use/transport system is presented as one of the main conceptual planks of the UTP process (see Webster *et al.*, 1988), the ideal state for this equilibrium depends on cost considerations and requires a great deal of careful study to ascertain. Many urban transport planning professionals, however, have their own notion of the 'correct balance' and employ the concept primarily to support their own beliefs.

Stopher, for example, describes the concept of a land-use/transport system balance as:

> a situation where the development of land use and transport

> are mutually supportive, and where one does not undermine the development of the other.

This is, in fact, one of the principal objectives of urban transport planning: harmony between land use and transport. If, however, as Shuldiner points out, one begins to think of the concept outside the traffic peak problem – one then comes up with unreasonable answers.

Hillegass regards a land-use/transport system to be 'in equilibrium' when the density of land development is in proportion to the transport system. Heanue and Ettinger, on the other hand, emphasise that the concept is merely notional, for since change is constant, a state of equilibrium will never last for long. More simplistically, the two DOT officials explain:

> If you have heavy congestion at some point, you are 'out of equilibrium'! In some areas, proposed pricing is used to renew the equilibrium. At any given time, we are in a state of equilibrium. How growth (either planned or unplanned) and investments can help us to arrive at a renewed equilibrium then becomes a main issue.

Gakenheimer echoes the point made by Heanue and Ettinger, emphasising that while in theoretical terms the equilibrium concept can be explicitly defined, in practical terms, it is virtually never reached. In the context of planning, he suggests:

> a balance between a land-use plan and a transportation plan would exist when land development is at its long-term peak density. At that point, the related transportation system was operating at its practical capacity – but not exceeding it... nor operating below its practical capacity. At that time you would have designed a transportation system which is perfectly workable, in that you have neither squandered money by providing excess capacity, nor created congestion by providing too little.

Reiterating the above, Manheim explains:

> for every land-use plan, there is a transport plan that is the best way of serving its needs... one has to ask, what are the assets and liabilities of alternative mixes of transportation and land-use actions that can be taken?

Hillegass claims that one of the best illustrations of disequilibrium in the land-use/transport system may be seen in the US suburban street system which at one time was the county road system. When major developments are built along these streets they create an imbalance between the road system and land development. At the level of the specific site, therefore, the concept implies, for planning purposes, that transport infrastructure and service capacity must match the density of land-use development. This suggests, according to Levinson, that one not only has to look at a particular traffic/land-use zone but also at the ideal distribution of activities within that zone.

Picarsky claims that while professionals see the balance in technical terms, such as desired residential densities, certain prescribed land uses and the ability of providing the relationship with particular types of transport systems (see later section on land-use development control and transport in this chapter) the political decision-maker is the one who ultimately determines the relationship. This is done, he argues, through financial (funding) means and not by technical exercises alone. He explains:

> as an entrepreneurial nation, we (US citizens) are not able to control land use as other countries are able to do. So that whilst there are goals and directions toward which we strive, they are constrained by market forces. The process does not accommodate market force 'compromises' or 'bargaining' in the use of land. One can therefore talk of a 'balance' determined by technical notions as well as by political/financial forces.

Internal operational transport systems efficiency

How important is the concept of 'internal operational efficiency' of transport systems in urban transport planning as opposed to the concept of associated 'externalities'?

Operations efficiency

The emphasis on the internal efficiency of transport system operations is fundamental to the thinking associated with the UTP process. Creighton (1970) emphasises this when he suggests that the evaluation criteria used for the CATS study are best summed up in terms of 'minimising' total transport costs. Referring to this point made by Creighton, Shuldiner makes the following comment:

> truth and beauty could not be measured, so they were subassumed in what you could measure. But that is not really the direction in which we should go. What we should do is to look at what we want the (urban transport) system to achieve, not in terms of input, but in terms of outputs.

Here Shuldiner is echoing a view first presented by Webber (1969) who argues for a more normative approach to urban transport planning from which to define evaluation criteria. Such criteria, Webber advocates, should be linked to a hierarchy of objectives, rather than left outside it as constraints, so as to record tertiary, secondary and primary impacts. Leaving criteria of this kind outside the objective hierarchy, he claims, is to leave problems to the end, and to build up a situation which makes the community (especially those affected by proposals) resentful. Shuldiner reiterates this view somewhat more graphically:

> If you do not state the question and objectives from the outset, so that you can start looking for the answers, the answers are always going to be unduly and prematurely constrained... (otherwise) what you are doing, is acting like the drunk who has lost his keys in the bushes, and is looking for them by the lamp post, just because there is more light there.

Although in the classical UTP process there was a planning framework with the objective of maximising travel time saved, in the mid-1970s this premise was challenged as people became more interested in creating travel opportunities. By the mid-1980s, however, saving travel time appeared to resume its earlier dominance in the evaluation of plans and projects, both in the USA and elsewhere, primarily as a result of the rising concern for the increase in congestion. This development, plus the tendency for urban transport planning studies to focus excessively on line-haul travel led, according to Gakenheimer, to inadequate attention to the detailing of the next level down of the urban transport system (i.e., that part servicing the neigbourhood). Efforts at maximising the operational efficiency of transport systems were thus, Gakenheimer explains, in effect confined to major routes and not applied to the hierarchy of the transport system as a whole.

Heanue and Ettinger in part attribute this inadequacy to the fact that the US Congress voted for the development of the interstate highway system before city planning was ready for it. The opposition the interstate highway system generated from many cities – particularly with regard to their indiscriminate building through urban areas, encouraged Congress and the administration to shift the decision-making authority for urban transport from the state level to local elected officials who were believed to be better able to plan sensitively and participate in dialogues with representatives of citizens' groups. Gakenheimer (1989), on the other hand, merely sees these developments as part of a general decentralisation of responsibilities away from the federal level introduced by the Reagan administration.

It has been argued in retrospect (Dimitriou, 1990) that the concept of maximising the operational efficiency of transport systems has excessively dominated developments in the evaluation of urban transport planning studies, and that costs and benefits external to the system have as a result been under-emphasised. This is despite the fact that in some instances the externalities could become so great as to override any benefits enjoyed within the system. According to this argument, too much emphasis is thus placed on direct 'transport user benefits', as against impact effects. This view is supported by Kain who believes:

> Transportation investments are determined almost entirely by the evaluations of user aspects... in terms of formal evaluations... they tend to concentrate almost exclusively on user benefits.

Manheim is also of the view that there is a common over-emphasis on transport operational considerations:

> Whilst people have placed priority on link capacity, they have not really placed priority on service delivery.

Externalities

Concern for externality considerations of urban transport systems began to emerge in the early to mid-1970s. By the late 1980s, externalities featured much more than ever before in urban transport planning; but some would argue still not enough. As much of the preceding discussion implies, a great deal of transport planning addresses the overall question of how the transport system works, and while this entails a great deal of quantification and the digesting of much information, it is apparent that many issues regarding externalities remain unresolved, primarily because they are more political than technical.

Part of the greater concern for externalities is for differential impacts on different geographical areas and groups of people. It is well known that the issue of equity in transport is hard to evaluate and was not seen as an issue until the late 1960s – because highways were seen as being provided for everyone! The inequities, however, became prevalent then because of the scale of the highway programme and the institutional machinery associated with the Johnson administration which was concerned with equity in health and education. That this concern did not at first relate to transport or produce legislation in the USA dealing with urban transport equity issues, is thought by Gakenheimer, to have provoked the first flush of 'highway revolt' in the late 1960s and early 1970s.

By the mid-1970s, the need to improve the mobility of the urban poor, the elderly and the handicapped began to emerge. As Rapkin explains:

> We discovered, to the middle class amazement, that poor people rarely moved outside of a very constricted radius.

This discovery led to an attempt to 'humanise' the transport planning response and enlarge the horizons of the disadvantaged. There was subsequently an attempt to overcome some inequalities associated with the highway programme by introducing more timely compulsory purchase notices on land, by conducting more public hearings, and by providing more protection for people who might be displaced (both owners and tenants).

It was inevitable, Shuldiner believes, that this earlier neglect would make environmental matters of urban transport an emerging concern, which it was in the late 1970s, and (after a certain lapse of concern in the early 1980s) was even more so in the late 1980s. He explains:

> once you look at and/or deal with one externality, you automatically become concerned with another, and whether you

class it an 'externality' or a 'distributional effect', is a matter of taste.

Environmental issues in the USA became important to the US Department of Transportation (US DOT) in 1968, when wholesale adaptations of the UTP process were attempted in order to cater better for public transport. The National Environmental Protection Agency (NEPA), first established in 1969, became the agency responsible for conducting environmental impact assessments of transport and other studies. The Clean Air Act of 1970 addressed air quality planning issues associated with motor vehicle travel, adding to the already mounting pressure on aspects of environmental externalities of the transport sector, while air quality conformance and priority procedures were introduced in 1981.

From 1975 onwards, there was a move towards short-term planning and low capital transport projects, as well as energy saving approaches, which lasted until the early 1980s. By then, renewed affluence in many parts of USA bred a more carefree attitude regarding issues of energy consumption and equity. Environmental matters, however, have since grown in importance. In the course of the 1970s, urban transport agencies in the USA turned into multi-discipline bureaucracies which by the 1980s became less able to assemble the sort of data previously collected for earlier city transport studies. As a result, short-cut, low-cost models and techniques of transport planning became increasingly acceptable.

The highway planning ethic was popular in the early years of the UTP process because roads produced considerable employment and opportunities for investment. Highways increased the accessibility of outlying lands and in some instances, in so far as the slums were literally removed by the rights of way, made slum clearance possible – although this was never explicitly stated. At a later stage, it became increasingly clear that new highways made it easier to move into the city and *also* to leave the city to live in the surrounding areas. This generated a great deal of concern, since an increasing number of these highways were beginning to exhibit unintended and undesirable impacts on land use and the environment. It helped, for example, to drain industry from the City of New York in the late 1970s (the vacant land-use being replaced by office and commercial activities in the 1980s). According to Rapkin, what is interesting, is that transport was not identified as the culprit –

instead, attention was directed to other forces such as the in-migration of Puerto Ricans.

According to Plant (1988), the outset of the 1980s saw in the USA certain changes in its urban transport systems, as a result of: problems of capital formation, an imbalance between investments in highways and other modes, a declining public perception of the system's performance, the inability of the government to provide city transport facilities in a timely and proactive manner, and the lessened financial support of urban transport by the Federal Government authorities. In response to which, a great deal of discussion took place, and in the mid-1980s action taken, regarding how public-private co-operation in the funding and operation of US city transport could take place (see Appendix 5).

Comprehensiveness of coverage

How comprehensive is the UTP process?

The extent to which the UTP process provides a comprehensive treatment of the area it claims to cover has long been under debate. This matter has been highlighted by the author in past publications (see Dimitriou, 1990) where it is argued that the preoccupation of the UTP process with detailed modelling of traffic movement and selected transport user aspects has led to an excessive in-depth concern for transport user matters, and an inadequate examination of wider contextual policy issues and non-transport user considerations. A graphic representation of this imbalance is given in Figure 3.1 where reference to 'comprehensive vertical analysis' refers to the former and 'comprehensive horizontal analysis' to the latter.

Discussions between the author and Stopher suggest that the initial studies employing the process were essentially comprehensive from a standpoint of measuring highway travel demand but not in other aspects; while developments since then have led elements to be added to it. He explains:

> The (UTP) process, as we still use it, remains a long way from being comprehensive, although we have added on various things in an attempt to try to make it more comprehensive; such as: public transport planning, environmental impact analysis, short-term investment analysis, etc.... but by and large, I do not think these aspects are handled very well. So I

Figure 3.1 **Vertical versus horizontal analysis in urban transport planning**

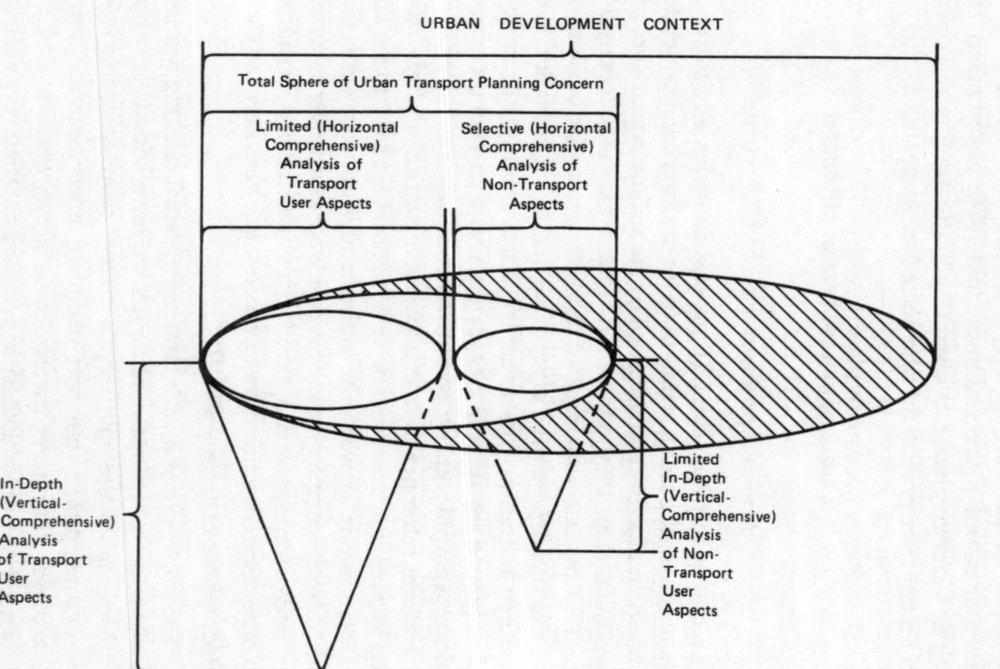

> suppose the process is marginally better and more comprehensive but not much more....
>
> It has become rather like a 'life-size clothes hanger', upon which various garments are hung... it is just that the shape of the hanger is wrong, in that it is lop-sided, and some clothes keep on falling off.

In retrospect, the perception of the UTP process as comprehensive can be associated with the idea that by taking into account both the land-use and transport system in a single methodology, one was in effect adopting a two-sided 'comprehensive' process. Mitchell, however, claims that a comprehensive urban transport plan has never existed, and that efforts at integrating planning studies with other planning, as well as efforts at co-ordinating the execution of proposed action, led many planners mistakenly to believe that they were preparing a comprehensive study.

Certainly, when the UTP process incorporated transit options into its methodology, after dealing mostly with highways, the process for a while took on more of a semblance of 'comprehensiveness' than it had ever done before. But this development ignored other sector and smaller scale issues, such as local environmental impacts and small-scale land-use changes. Levinson explains:

> We were led to believe that the process was more elaborate, systematic and comprehensive than it was... the emphasis though of the process was more on (travel) demand and the quantification of transportation usage. Costs were also included in the process, but inadequate attention was paid to direct impacts. With regard to indirect impacts, the real questions of: whether we are spending too much on transportation, do we really need to spend so much, is it going to help the community, is it in scale with the way we are about to change – we are really rather lost about all this.

Heanue and Ettinger warn planners of spending too much time on secondary (impact) issues, claiming that the UTP process has the ability to answer almost any question, or at least provide insights into any (urban) transport issue. Altshuler, however, takes a different view. He argues that while agencies preparing transport plans in the USA have claimed they were 'comprehensive' in their approach, he does not think people (especially politicians) really care whether this claim is valid (see later discussion in this chapter on planning styles and politics). He explains:

> There were certainly a few people who believed it (i.e., the claim of comprehensiveness) but my reading of the history is that very few of the studies had any impact on what subsequently happened, except at levels of technical detail e.g., precise location decisions and how many lanes to build.... In terms of how much money to spend and what types of facilities to spend it on, I do not think those plans had much influence. Yet, they (the highway planners and their plans) consumed (relative to other non-construction costs) a lot of resources!

Altshuler argues, that such resources, however, were trivial in comparison with the cost of construction. This led him to confess that when he was Secretary of Transportation for the Commonwealth of Massachusetts he preferred to study rather than to build, since it was cheaper. Gakenheimer (1989) claims nevertheless, that these studies had profound effects on the transport system in that they concluded not to build additional highways and resulted in the building of other transport infrastructure such as transit extensions.

Altshuler also points to the fact that by utilising current land use, population characteristics, etc. as a basis for projecting travel demand, the urban planner is assumed by the UTP process to have a more exact knowledge of the physical and socio-economic environment than he himself would like to accept. In support of this view, he explains:

> He (the planner) certainly is in a situation beyond his capabilities. The question is whether that is inherent in the task (of planning)?... the problem of planning lies in the efforts to be comprehensive, i.e., if you choose to be the expert in comprehensiveness, in some fashion you are always having to use inferior technical rationale. You are always going to be arbitrary in what values you adopt in a given situation. You are also always going to want to pull considerations from where you have insufficient data and skills.

On the basis of the above, he concludes that one inevitably pays a price for moving from specialisation to comprehensiveness, in terms of a loss in precision of technical rationale – and urban transport and city planners are an extreme case of that. Conversely, it has been stated in conversation between the author and members of the Chicago Rapid Transit Authority, that:

> it is both a great shame and dangerous when specialist analysts, because of their good reputation in one field, are then asked to become planners. The transit planning field (in the USA) went through a stage like that – but then it had to because there was (then) no outside money.

Shuldiner claims that those who developed the UTP process and advocated its use, wanted it to be *seen* as 'comprehensive'. In the final analysis though, he argues, it is a very narrow exercise which has led to several positive spin-offs. For example, much of what is known in the urban transport planning profession regarding land use, Shuldiner points out, comes in an objective and measured way from the energies invested in, and the funding and organisation of, the UTP process. He concludes:

> We have become more comprehensive now by de-limiting in a sense, what transportation planning really is and can do.

Making the same point from a somewhat different perspective, Stopher comments:

> The only claim to comprehensiveness (of the UTP process) was the fact that it was in the past a very new thing to try and deal with an entire metropolitan region in one go.... it is still a long way from being comprehensive. I have a strong feeling, from what I see going on in this country (the USA), that public transport planning is very much an add-on aspect to the process, undertaken very badly. The process still provides little or no understanding of what is going on with regards to travel behaviour.

Carroll, on the other hand, argues that urban transport planning can be as 'comprehensive' as one likes – but with related pitfalls:

> there is a point where you begin to forget transportation planning and deal with social planning, which in itself is not bad... but I think that there is a particular discipline and role of transportation planning, and it ought not to get too far removed by becoming more comprehensive and not do a good job on the system at hand. We are so far from optimising

some vague social integral, that I believe much more in sub-optimisation – i.e., take on what you can and do it well.

In addition, Gakenheimer claims that the levels of comprehensiveness incorporated into the formal methodology of the UTP process and some of its derivatives, have in fact been greatly reduced since the mid-1960s, whereas the level of reality has grown. He suggests that there are other issues that have come into play since the late 1970s (particularly to do with environmental and social impacts) which have required highway planners to be more disciplined and to become more sensitive to the priorities of comprehensiveness than before.

Among the notable deficiencies of the UTP process as applied in the USA and other industrialised countries, is its lack of coverage of pedestrian needs. Another area belatedly brought into the agenda before the introduction of TSM was the better use/management of existing transport capacity. The history of the process is one that primarily concentrates on providing additional capital investments without first examining whether existing transportation resources are used efficiently. It is in fact because these resources are *not* used efficiently, as Kain points out, that the process and many of its derivatives embody the biases and inefficiencies that they do.

The level of comprehensiveness the UTP process offers has also partly to do with how it has been used. With the general heavy emphasis on the quantification of transport-user aspects, Manheim argues, the differential incidence of impacts on social, economic, aesthetic, environmental and developmental aspects of transport (on different groups of users, their destinations and trip purposes), are often more relevant, even if they cannot be quantified, than those that can be quantified. He concludes:

> My view is that I find 'economism' (the values of and techniques of economists) as a major tool for quantitative analysis, a powerful concept in demand analysis, but in evaluation, to be extremely limited.

The reason for the quantitative bias of the UTP process, according to Picarsky, is in its orientation toward making a huge ('up-front') capital investment in something which may or may not pay dividends to the community in ten or more years hence. Politicians in the USA (indeed almost anywhere) he argues, rarely adopt a perspective of more than two to six years (according to their term of election). They are, as a result, extremely reticent about making judgements on long-term issues and investments. To protect themselves, therefore, they seek as much quantitative data as possible in the decision-making process – simultaneously warning of the dangers of the long-term economic viability of such projects.

Travel demand

What are the major parameters that control urban travel and efforts at meeting travel demand?

Work on travel demand aspects of the UTP process has proceeded in three major overlapping directions (Bell, Blackledge and Bowan, 1983):

1 attempts at clarifying the central scope (what has been termed transportation systems analysis) from predominantly a single mode to a multi-mode perspective;
2 a conceptualisation of the demand problem of both passengers and freight in a way that draws from modern econometric methods; and
3 the implementation of new methods in disaggregate travel demand analysis in a wide variety of styles.

Each of these aspects are touched on below.

Derived travel demand

An underlying fundamental concept of the UTP process is that urban travel is a 'derived demand' rather than a direct demand, since the vast majority of trips are made because people wish to move to a place to carry out some further activity. This does not diminish the importance of the nature of urban travel demand, but rather acknowledges two things:

1 the demand for movement is generated by forces at play both outside and within the transport sector; and
2 transport is a means to an end.

The demand for urban transport services and infrastructure is in fact derived from work, recreation, professional and other activities.

The best way of simulating such demand for forecasting and planning purposes is to establish the individual's propensity for travel, differentiate between travel needs and wants (aspirations), and identify other characteristics affecting the level of trip-making a person is likely to make (see Chapters 4 and 7). While the level of trip-making is expected to vary from city to city, and from culture to culture, certain common factors are believed to influence urban travel more than others. These include the now widely accepted considerations (see Chapter 2) of income level, age, sex, etc. of the trip-makers, as well as other aspects found to be linearly descriptive of differences in trip-making characteristics.

Travel demand parameters

Urban societies have what appear to be unlimited wants with regard to transport services and infrastructure, but limited resources with which to satisfy those wants. To disentangle and understand the factors which influence urban transport demand, and cause demand levels to fluctuate, one therefore needs to appreciate a number of other aspects apart from derived demand. These include the 'elasticity of demand', principles of resource allocation (including issues of equity), and options for measuring travel demand.

The first expresses the rate of change in demand in response to a rate of change in a factor which affects travel demand. The second refers to a spectrum of resources, including financial, manpower, environmental and energy resources, the availability of which can act as stimulants or constraints to travel demand. The third aspect refers to measures of the quantity (volume) of transport usage and extent of usage in terms of distance travelled (for passenger and/or freight movement) by mode.

Also of importance to urban transport demand analysis is the concept of 'marginal utility' – i.e., where decisions are made at the margin and are seen as the satisfaction derived from possessing one extra unit of a commodity or (transport) service, or the satisfaction lost if it is given up. Associated with 'marginal utility' is the assumption that the more one consumes of a commodity or a service, the lower will be the utility of an extra unit consumed.

The most important factor influencing transport demand, is the price of the transport service, as it is believed that the higher the price the lower the demand will be. Other factors affecting demand in addition to cost are 'transport demand conditions', which include (after Bell, Blackledge and Bowen, 1983):

1 the price of other (comparative) goods and services;
2 the influence of taste, fashion and changing attitudes;
3 income levels and distribution of income of the consumers of the service; and
4 population characteristics reflecting the dynamics of population changes.

Regarding the last of the above, it is particularly necessary to look at market segments of travel demand, for in some sections of the population there are significant differences in their characteristics. These differences generate different responses to deterrents of trip-making (alternatively referred to as costs), such as fares, tolls, journey times, ease of access considerations to transport systems, reliability of service, probability of gaining access to service, comfort of service, excess travel time, the number of interchanges that have to be made, etc.

In practice it is the quantifiable aspects that are most commonly included in transport planning exercises, while generalised costs are usually made up (e.g. for passenger travel estimates) of fares, excess travel time, and some kind of transport interchange penalty.

Travel time valuation

To assess the impact of these generalised costs on travel demand, one of the main planks of travel demand analysis in the UTP process and its derivatives is the use of a monetary value of travel time, so as to relate the cost of fares to other components of generalised cost. In conventional transport planning exercises, travel is considered to be a disutility on the assumption that time spent in travel has an 'opportunity cost' that may be related to either the value of working time or non-working time when leisure activity is foregone.

There is much debate as to how to value travel time of the journey to work. Some transport economists, for example, argue that travelling to and from work should be assessed on the basis of non-working time, since it is leisure activity which is sacrificed. More conventional analyses, however, rely upon economic marginal productivity theory which suggests that the wage rate of employees will give the value of time (in working time terms) and that the non-working time can therefore be valued in relation to this as an opportunity cost of the value of working time.

This method, which is widely used for forecasting and evaluation purposes, has however associated problems, namely (after Bell, Blackledge and Bowen, 1983):

1 the wage rate may not reflect the true opportunity cost of the resources used, as wage rates are sometimes strongly influenced by other factors such as a sense of equity;
2 there is the assumption that individuals are indifferent between work and travel – if there is a greater disutility attached to travelling then perhaps the value of travel time savings needs to be increased; and
3 there is also the assumption that travelling time is wasted – which in many cases is not true.

With reference to the above, Manheim points out, it is not merely travel time, travel cost or distances travelled that are important in transport demand analysis, but socialisation and other attributes of travel and associated activity patterns which also significantly affect specific sections of the travelling community and their travel habits. Stopher, more controversially, argues that the major factors which control urban travel demand are not well understood, despite the volumes of literature on the subject. In support of his views he cites the experience of recreational travel which he suggests is too readily dismissed as insignificant, even though research in the USA in the late 1970s indicated that as much as 30 per cent of trips are made for leisure purposes; a proportion which by the late 1980s increased to a point that in some congested segments it represents the bulk of trips.

4

CRITIQUE OF THE UTP PROCESS

Issues and performance

INTRODUCTION

This chapter continues the critique of the UTP process commenced in the preceding chapter but with a more specific focus on emergent issues and the overall performance of the process as judged by the objectives it set out to achieve.

As in Chapter 3, where reference is made to persons interviewed, the reader is referred to Appendices 1 to 4 for further details.

ISSUES OF THE PROCESS

Travel needs and aspirations

What constitutes the difference between 'travel needs' and 'travel aspirations'?

The debate

The terms 'need' and 'aspiration' are normative terms which cannot be satisfactorily quantified. Despite this, they are widely used (especially the former), implied (in the case of the latter), as well as abused in transport planning literature. Clearly they warrant discussion. Indeed, Manheim argues that had these terms been more clearly defined and more thoughtfully used, alternative ways of solving urban transport problems might have been arrived at. This is particularly the case had some clear differentiation been made between needs of survival and other kinds of transport needs.

Gakenheimer claims that it is very difficult to define a 'travel need' beyond which one could define a particular aspiration as a single variable, unless one decides that something such as 'comfort' is really an aspiration and not a need. He explains:

> it ('the term travel need') ultimately is a very qualified concept. Government may define a travel 'need' it can fulfill, strongly influenced by its perception of available budgets and technologies. The individual's sense of 'need', however, reflects a different optic on intuitive feasibility, such as the return to a prior, less congestion state of the system.

Vuchic claims that there is no absolute 'travel need', though he emphasises that people travel for a particular purpose, which means there is obviously a 'need' or 'desire' to travel. Some travel, he admits, is a question of survival, in that on occasions people must make a trip and will thus pay a very high price to do so. Vuchic suggests that travel needs and aspirations can be listed and ranked on a scale (excluding emergencies) as advocated by Gakenheimer. For example, to go to work and back, and to have access to schools may be seen as 'travel needs'. With recreation trips, the ranking becomes a little less basic in that the trip could be postponed or replaced by other trips.

According to Picarsky, the difference between a 'travel need' and a 'travel aspiration'is that:

> the former is more likely to be translated into an actuality, depending upon the ability to achieve this. Once accomplished, it (the 'aspiration') becomes a 'need'. There are many perceived 'needs' today which may be translated but which in turn create conflicts. Over time, technological developments may make some 'needs' obsolescent and in turn, generate new needs.

Pushkarev accuses many professionals of using the term 'travel need' as a 'Trojan horse' for other meanings, very often intentionally so, because:

> when you start saying the problem is that there is too much travel, and that planning should really be directed toward reducing 'travel needs', rather than satisfying them – in 97 per cent of the procedures this is considered heresy...

He goes on to argue that the use of the term 'travel need' as a statement of 'aspiration' is a major problem of urban transport planning, and of the perception of movement problems in cities. He contends that every 'need' is contextual and that this fact is not sufficiently appreciated. It is because such differentiation is not made, he claims, that self-fulfilling forecasts duplicate efforts at meeting non-essential travel demand before basic travel needs are met.

Travel aspirations

The term 'travel aspiration' is not explicitly used in transport literature, although in the late 1970s in the USA, some would say that the lengths gone to to meet the transport requirements of the handicapped and elderly, as in the case of the Washington DC metro, constituted an effort at 'aspiration fulfilment'. With reference to this, Gomez-Ibanez suggests:

> we have gone a little overboard on this. It is a nice example of the mal-use of the term 'need'.... they (the handicapped, elderly and poor) are very ambiguous about what their minimum level of mobility is.
>
> It is implied, whatever 'a travel need' is, that it should be provided for whatever the cost, and that this is a basic obligation that the society has. If you look at the cost of doing this, i.e., of providing the handicapped with lifts and bus services, it is quite clear that you could buy cab fares for the next 30 years for all the wheel-chaired people of that city (Washington DC) for the price of maintaining and providing all the elevators. The handicapped people would perhaps have preferred the money. This then is a case of a 'transportation aspiration' being called a 'transportation need'.

Because the term 'travel aspiration' implies a futuristic notion, Levinson suggests 'travel preferences' might be more appropriate, reflecting the type of travel some would like to make. He emphasises that housing and lifestyle are two of the most compelling aspiration-generating characteristics of travel. For him, 'travel aspirations' represent:

> aspiring after a level of accessibility and a quality of (trans-

port) service that is perhaps much greater than is actually needed.

Attitude surveys can provide some very useful insights into 'latent travel demand' and the 'travel aspirations' of some urban inhabitants. However, differentiating between 'needs' and 'aspirations' is crucial, for according to Levinson, it leads on to the deeper matter of how transport needs of an urban area will change over time. An examination of this, he explains:

> requires standing back and looking at people and activities, and examining what their requirements are, how they can be served, trying to provide facilities to do that, and comparing the results of this approach with those of simulation.

Travel needs

As already emphasised, the only real 'travel needs' are those of 'survival'. What someone wants, needs or aspires to, therefore, depends upon the perceived attributes. From an economist's point of view there is no such thing as a 'travel need'. It is, as Manheim points out, rather a question of costs satisfying different levels of desire, although of course, it is necessary to establish the policy position as to what the levels of 'travel preference' and 'aspiration' are that should be aimed for.

Kain suggests therefore that the term 'transport need' is a dangerous one. He is, furthermore, of the view that it is a common fallacy that people with lower incomes ought to be able to travel as much as people with higher incomes, or will otherwise be considered 'disadvantaged' or deprived. As a result, he claims there is a tendency to look at the behaviour of higher income groups and suggest that this represents the difference between what the lower income people have and 'need'.

Stopher argues that 'travel need' is bandied around in the USA as a 'travel desire' – i.e., what a person would like to do, not necessarily what he has to do! The problem with this he explains is:

> when one comes down to try to define a 'travel need' one has to adopt a kind of 'god-like' position, and start stipulating what people must do and what are their options. There (in

> such circumstances), I suppose one would have to start relying upon the economists' notions of what are necessary things to provide.

Stopher's observation is supported by Altshuler who claims:

> I have purged the term 'travel need' from my own vocabulary and I try to purge it from the vocabulary of my students... it is a term that emerged during the period of highway engineering as a way of persuading people that there was somehow an 'objective need' (for travel and thus transportation facilities).
>
> I know what it is to say that a person 'needs' a certain amount of food or they will die – you have to have so many calories per day. I never hear that (qualification) in transportation. I never hear the statement 'if you do not want your city to die, then you must do these things'. So whenever anyone talks to me of 'needs' I always ask the question, what are the consequences of not providing for this need? When I hear of the consequences, it becomes clear that it is not a 'need' they are talking about but a preference.

The way 'travel need' has in reality been used is in terms of 'unconstrained transport demand' or travel demand as a function of prices and level of service, incorporating considerations of changes in income and related expectations (see Chapter 7). Gomez-Ibanez points out, one would not talk about 'travel needs' if they were met. The term thus combines a notion of:

1 Travel demand in the economic sense, as well as incorporating notions of 'latent demand' – in which there are some unrealised requirements or benefits to segments of society. However, because the provision of transport has not taken place (or because the cost of its provision is too high) that demand is not generated.
2 Suppressed demand – this is a 'travel need' which exists but where a person cannot travel. Such reasons may be tied to the price, availability and/or attractiveness of available transport services, or a set of other factors which may affect a person's decision to travel.

There is, therefore, ample distinction between 'travel needs' and 'travel demand'. The former is a term which can be operationalised and analysed, i.e., it can be quantified. The latter, however, is politically defined and a more loaded term.

Land-use control and transport

What extent is the capability of controlling urban land-use a significant factor in determining the success of an urban transport planning approach?

Land-use control and effective urban transport planning

The belief that the capability of government to control land use is a prerequisite to effective urban transport planning is a view long held by many planners, especially those from the UK and Scandinavia. In effect, it represents a postulation that government policy can influence the pattern of urban development which in turn is a major determinant of urban travel patterns.

There has been a long-standing split in the professional community of transport planners in the USA as to the possible impact of transport on land use and vice versa. Attempts to arrive at macro-relationships of urban densities and transport system types (see Zupan and Pushkarev, 1977 and Newman and Kenworthy, 1989) have made a valuable contribution to the field of urban transport planning, particularly in instances where too many traffic assignment studies have been conducted, and where the overall picture of the attempts to relate development to transport systems is lost.

Many, including Kain, argue that the real experience of countries such as the UK, suggests that government policy is not so influential as it is made out to be. In other parts of the world, the significance of land-use control on urban transport seems to vary according to the characteristics of the government involved. In Singapore, for example, Levinson points out that the success of the Traffic Restraint Scheme is largely attributed to strong central government. Where central planning is effective, therefore, it seems one can conclude that there can be meaningful ties between land-use control and the transport planning process. Where it is not, one has to plan with a greater degree of flexibility so as to accommodate unexpected variations in factors affecting urban development.

In the USA, Levinson recounts that the population projections made by the Regional Planning Association of New York between the 1920s and 1960s of its metropolitan area revealed some degree of accuracy, but estimated four to five million people living in Brooklyn and about 50,000 living on Long Island. These projections totally underestimated the subsequent dispersion and spread of the population. The fact that there were to be two million people on Long Island and that the population of Brooklyn would decline, merely confirms for Levinson that the USA does not have the instruments for, or public acceptance of, urban land-use controls. A disparity between desired development patterns and what could have been a very limited but easily managed land-use control has instead emerged. These events transpired because the urban planning process in the USA is not run by technocrats but by those who make investment decisions, i.e., private investors and politicians.

Nevertheless, some transport planners such as Shuldiner believe that a stronger control of urban land use would greatly change the way urban transport planning is practised in the USA. He and many others argue that a capability to control urban land use would have an effect on the time scale adopted by planning studies, the relevance of long-range plans, and the extent to which large capital investments might make sense.

To date, there have been a number of ways by which certain aspects of land-use control have been crudely represented in urban land-use/transport plans in the USA. These include (after Gomez-Ibanez):

1 the use of indices representing land availability and various types of residential and industrial land-use for each traffic zone; and
2 the incorporation of an assessment of the degree to which the urban area in question is likely to react under economic pressures from developers.

But as Gomez-Ibanez and others have pointed out, these tools have essentially been weak. Although they represent the only means of controlling urban land-use in the USA, they are seen in the conventional wisdom as a very important part of the practice of urban transport planning.

To the extent that US city government agencies have the desire to develop a plan and enact zoning measures, in Picarsky's view urban land-use controls cannot but help shape urban development and related transport infrastructure. However, to echo Levinson's earlier observations, Picarsky recalls that in Chicago in the 1970s, the city centre (as in other metropolitan areas in the USA) was alive only between 8 am and 5 pm. This led to government planning efforts at mixing residential land uses with employment areas, an idea made possible, he emphasises, because:

> the people who were making judgements were those who were investing the dollars (i.e., not the planners or anyone else with land-use control powers).

The power of the investor led in many US cities to what were seen as 'safer investments' on virgin territory in outlying urban areas, where it was believed that since continuous appreciation in central urban areas was guaranteed, more attractive returns were obtainable from developments on the urban periphery. Gakenheimer (1989) claims that politically this decentralisation served the Republican Party well in its attempts to gain support outside the central cities, particularly so during the Reagan administration, in that it led to the devoting of central government funds to the development of the outskirts of the city. This strategy was made workable Picarsky claims:

> only so long as the central area survived in its own right. But when they (the inner cities) began to decline rapidly, the danger of the umbilical cord being cut with the financial institutions, the city's communications network, etc., led to re-investment in the central areas.

This account verifies the traditional view in the USA, that despite zoning and the various types of land-use controls, city and regional planning agencies cannot do very much of significance about urban land-use control. The negative outcome of the absence of such control, however, particularly on the environment, has slowly begun to reinforce the belief (even in conservative quarters) that something has to be done urgently to restrain the worst effects of *laissez faire* land-use developments. Although the powers have not changed very much, the perception of the need for more urban land-use control has altered considerably and become very much more normative.

One of the biggest problems for transport and urban planners in the USA, according to Levinson, is that the urban transport plan has been specific and the urban land-use plan general; and while the latter has led to some action, the urban plan generally has not.

Confirming a view later argued by Newman and Kenworthy (1989), Rapkin claims that planners in the USA are trapped:

> For so long as they feel (or indeed are) compelled to meet the needs of people who want to have their nice single family homes on a half acre lot – but also want to be able to get into the central area easily – they are setting the stage for the creation of an increased demand for transportation facilities and associated pressures which begin to build up in the form of smaller lots, more intensive uses of land, higher buildings, etc.

Transport technology and urban land-use development

Banfield argues that the fundamentals of urban development have much to do with economics and changes in technology, especially changes in transport technology and communications, none of which, he emphasises, are planned by governments. So that although the ability of government to control urban land-use is often presented as an important prerequisite to effective urban transport planning, operationalising this is a very difficult matter.

The concept presented by Carroll (Chicago City, 1955–61), as well as Mitchell and Rapkin (1954), that land-use and transport are in fact so intimately related that they are almost the same thing, has encouraged some to advocate that transport facilities should be planned and used to create particular land-use patterns. In response to such an approach, Carroll has remarked, :

> that to try to achieve a desired land use by altering the transport system is like... trying to twist a bull by its tail.

Nevertheless, in US cities in the late 1970s, the Federal Government encouraged urban areas to use new transit lines to re-shape their urban development, the most dramatic case of which perhaps was the BART project in California.

Rapkin, however, no longer sees transport in the USA as an instrument to open up new territory in the way the city fathers did in the past. He explains:

> It (urban transport) is rather seen as a sector in need of a planning and management response in its own right – as in the case of public housing, whereby the municipality has an 'obligation' to improve upon the current situation but not

necessarily to think whether or not this is appropriate for the city's development as a whole. So that if the market place has in some way expressed a strong demand for a particular transport facility through the construction of new roads, for example, the municipality is expected to go along with the trends that this additional investment has generated.

Heanue and Ettinger claim that housing developments are far more influential than transport technology and infrastructure in moulding urban areas, given the ten year lag which is common between the planning and construction of highways and other major urban transport facilities. The two US DOT officials argue, with some justification, that impacts of transport on urban land use thus tend to be somewhat belated, although transport systems probably affect land-use patterns more than they are affected by them.

Land-use/transport simulation

The employment of simulation models of land-use/transport interaction in the UTP process (also see following section on role of models) is widely recognised by planners as one of the least mature elements of the process. As Heanue and Ettinger readily concur, their use has not met with a great deal of success, partly because most of the work in this area is research rather than operationally-orientated. They recount that many of the major efforts at simulation concerned with urban land use and transport interaction commissioned by the US DOT up to the late 1970s, missed the deadline for completion. As a result, much of the output of this programme of research was never utilised. Instead, more subjective inputs were used. Land-use patterns were, for example, assumed to match a transport plan and then tested, rather than simulated with a knowledge of growth estimates.

An important criticism levelled at the UTP process by both Kain and Stopher is that the process conveys almost nothing about the land-use development process, in that (see Chapter 2) land-use projections are used as an input to the UTP sub-models and do not have adequate feedback between transport investments and land use. This is partly, as Hillegass explains, because:

> many land development decisions in the USA are taken privately and nobody ever consults the planners.

Where urban land development is controlled publicly, however, Hillegass argues there is much more likelihood that the planner will be consulted.

Even in circumstances where control over land-use is possible, Stopher is still doubtful that the technical ability to incorporate this aspect exists. The fact that other countries with a greater ability to control urban land use, such as the UK, have employed simulation exercises to establish the land-use/transport interaction originally formulated for the USA (see Webster *et al.*, 1988), and despite possessing a greater capacity to control land use through their own planning controls, suggests that this is indeed a very weak aspect of the UTP process. It is thus evident according to Manheim (1990), that the process needs to be made much more responsive in nature and especially to take into account feedbacks between transport investments and land use.

One of the most basic of philosophical questions associated with the land-use control issue, is whether appointed public officials and politicians should make certain decisions on behalf of society and government, or whether land-use developments should merely follow market forces. To facilitate the latter, Vuchic explains:

> this is not planning but borrowing, and slightly adjusting an economic system which by definition and long experience is very effective in some ways and quite ineffective in other ways, in that it is also a generator of problems.... We have an obsession in the USA with market forces which is especially influential in the urban transport field.

He furthermore argues that the extensive reliance upon the 'willingness to pay concept' in urban transport, as supported, for example, by Kain, Roth and Walters, is an extended part of this same problem. In this regard, Vuchic claims that the excessive adherence to this concept as an expedient mechanism for 'managing' development is merely part of a passing fashion – albeit a long-lasting one which has lasted more than a decade since Vuchic made this remark. As he predicted, the approach has caused a great many problems. Vuchic concludes:

> even discussing matters on their own grounds with the most ardent supporters of the 'willingness to pay principle', their views on market forces are actually indefensible, simply because one can only successfully apply market forces where

market conditions exist. But it is the political forces and the policies, etc. that ultimately decide the outcome of events – and these are not always synonymous with market forces.

Transport consumerism and the motorcar lobby

Is there a significant element of 'transport consumerism' within the UTP process?

Transport consumerism

The idea that the process fosters 'transport consumerism' i.e., the indiscriminate abandonment of older transport technologies such as the tram, the bus and railways, for newer modes of transport, namely the motorcar, thereby generating more 'automobile dependent settlements', can in part be traced back to the environmental and consumer movement of the early 1970s. A movement which in the late 1980s has experienced a resurgence of support and which believes in the notion that public sector investments are made for the public good, from whom the resources have come. This being a notion that has in the past had a considerable disruptive influence on the UTP process, as most aspects of it have *not* been absorbed by or incorporated into the process – partly because the process itself is no longer a single entity.

Both Carroll and Gakenheimer believe that an ingredient of the indiscriminate abandonment of old transport technologies for new is inherent in the UTP process, in that, overall, it tries both to anticipate the future and speed up these developments. Confirming this, Carroll explains:

> it (the process) tends to wear out what you have and speed up those things that you try to get. It is a very obvious characteristic, although I am not very sure it is economical.... I also would have to take the view that finally, it must be as expensive as hell! You would therefore have to put me down on the side of people who look toward a change in the process.

Expanding upon the above standpoint, Gakenheimer claims that the UTP process aids obsolescence to the extent that the classical land-use/travel demand model encourages the use of new line-haul technology because that is what the model shows is necessary. Its use, therefore, tends to disadvantage relatively short distance travel, informal sector travel demand, as well as related technology. This characteristic, he argues, was particularly evident in the early years of applying the UTP process, where one was in effect accommodating consumer travel preferences (aspirations even), almost regardless of costs. On the same theme, Ibanez-Gomez comments:

> You drew these desire lines and you built the roads to fit them. You did not question what those desire lines were accommodating, or whether there were alternatives to them. We over-built our roads, I do not think there is any question about that. In the peak hours in the urban areas, that demand could have been choked a little bit by tolls, for example, instead of accommodating demand by providing the eight lanes.

Other transport specialists, such as Heanue and Ettinger, have a different view. They believe that the process has resisted the abandonment of rail transit, as well as supported the efficient use of the automobile, although they claim this has been so since the 1970s rather than before. Heanue and Ettinger point out that the rate of buying cars is increasing (with a more recent upsurge particularly since the mid 1980s) and that highway investment lags far behind this rate of growth (see Plant, 1989), so that the high rate of car ownership merely reflects the affluence and life style of the USA.

Pushkarev has similarly argued that most of the abandonment of past transport systems in the USA was in the street car industry (between 1947 and 1956) i.e., before the UTP process, and that, therefore, any 'transport consumerism' was purely an economic outcome for the transit operators. Indeed, he claims, part of the stimulus for metropolitan transport planning was an effort to preserve existing modes. Pushkarev cites an example of this in the transport planning work started for New York in 1960 and which continued into the Tri-State study during the late 1970s that very much favoured saving the railways from collapse.

Where the UTP did foster transport consumerism, Vuchic feels it did so unintentionally, except that planning agencies encouraged the continuation of past trends. These trends often led to a vicious circle where people who switched from the bus to the car, indirectly reduced the level of transit services and thus increased the demand for highways. As the building of highways continued and in turn failed to assist public transport, the vicious circle of transport consumerism continued.

Picarsky presents changes in transport legislation and transport finance as the underlying factors that encouraged the indiscriminate abandonment of old transport infrastructure and hardware for new, particularly as regards rail transit. He claims that the two major developments in the USA that both caused and accelerated the reduction in the use of public transport, and simultaneously, the 'love affair' with the motorcar, were:

1 the Federal Highway Act which for the first time in 1956 provided and ensured a continuous and reliable source of funding for highways; and
2 numerous Housing Acts since 1947 through to the Federal Home Insured Mortgages Act of 1961.

The former enabled planners and implementors to provide for projects some twenty years in advance, knowing that the money was there to execute them with the modifications that might take place. The latter offered a greater level of federal support to cities after World War II because of significant population movements to them from rural areas. Since it was less risky to invest in virgin territory along transport corridors (which were being built with highway money), shopping centres and residential areas developed in outlying areas, both producing and accelerating the urban sprawl that the UTP process was deemed unwittingly to serve.

As people left the central area served by public transport, residential densities were reduced. Fares subsequently were raised or bus service frequency intervals were decreased, thereby encouraging people to use motorcars. As a result, the cycle of the demise of public transport continued. As Picarsky explains:

> Whilst these (the above) factors were not incorporated as part of the UTP process, they were factors which influenced the process (and its ethos *vis-à-vis* changes of technological emphasis in transport facility provision). The economic and political interaction of events and circumstances influenced the process so much that the process then served these developments.

However, Shuldiner warns:

> When talking about technology, one must realise that part of the process involves an industry that is anxious to enjoy as much of the advantages it brings to it as it can... and the US automobile and highway industry has enjoyed perhaps a disproportionate share of support over the years.

He explains that since the mid-1970s, the public transit industry has worked very hard to increase, in both absolute and relative terms, its share of public support. How much of these efforts are, however, related to the issue of consumerism within the UTP process (as opposed to outside it), is, Shuldiner emphasises, difficult to ascertain. Stopher, however, presents a notion that is well worth investigating: namely, that the process itself does not encourage technological obsolescence but that those who administer it find it very difficult to handle the introduction of new transport technology.

Influence of the motorcar lobby

There are several groups in the USA who have a vested interest in the provision of highways. They include the Associated Contractors and Builders, the Highway Users Federation, the American Association of State Highway Officials (which has a transit component), the Concrete Industry (including Portland Cement Association) and of course, the automobile industry – all of which are multi-million dollar industries.

In response to the accusation that the UTP process and some of its modelling constituent parts reflect the interests of the motorcar industry (see Ziv, 1977), Kornhauser reiterates that the link between the motorcar industry and the construction of highways pre-dates the process. For example, the Ford Motorcar Company became involved in the legislative interests of funding the construction of highway facilities between 1915 and 1919. General Motors (GM) has in the past retained research teams which have conducted basic research that included the application of sophisticated transport planning software and land-use modelling systems at their technical centre in Michigan. Gakenheimer concludes though, that there is little evidence to suggest these teams have or had any substantial influence on the UTP process (or any of its parts). He explains

> For one thing, the extent to which this calculus (the UTP

> process) tends to sustain a highway and automobile dominance was rather a retrospective discovery. It was not a big concern before the early sixties, at the earliest. So there is no reason to believe that there was a conspiracy to bias the system.

Carroll shares the view that there were no 'behind the scene' activities involving the automobile lobby in the development of the UTP process or its constituent parts. He argues that the lobby had no reason to enter this arena as a sly way of promoting more highways and selling more cars, since motorcars sold well anyway. The closest Carroll detected to any effort by the lobby to exert influence on the process was when some of its members argued in Philadelphia that because land use was an important outcome of transport investments, one should mould the transport network to achieve predetermined land uses. In response to this, Carroll claims that the transport system has its own integrity and that the notion of making it a tool for the land-use outcome is a dangerous one. On this same subject, Manheim adds:

> From the little I know about automobile manufacturers, I find it hard to believe that they can be effective 'Machiavellian' manipulators of this low key set of issues. This game of urban transportation planning is 'small potatoes' to them and almost irrelevant. The only 'Machiavellian' element is in the cultural biases of the professionals.

Supporting the above views, Shuldiner claims that the work of the technical groups within motorcar manufacturing, was carried out *after* specific aspects of urban transport planning were looked at. While some of this research made excellent contributions to the field, he argues that it did not influence the UTP process because it was not where the real influence lay. According to Levinson, who had at one time worked as a consultant to the motorcar industry and was the principal author of three publications produced for the automobile manufacturers,[1] any influence was exerted indirectly and extremely subtly, through, for example, its support for single family developments, the highway development programme, and other conditions that were conducive to selling cars.

Stopher, one-time consultant to General Motors (GM) Research Laboratories in Michigan, explained that GM became involved in research because of pressure from urban interests. The government was concerned at the time with GM's massive size and their monopoly, and as a result, more or less obliged the company to reassess what it was doing as a corporation, compelling it to consider making some contribution to the general welfare of the country. The corporation's response was to set up research laboratories in which they considered various aspects of vehicle design, and conducted research on travel behaviour. The latter area, Stopher emphasised, had clear links with marketing the car. Nevertheless, he points out, it led to the better understanding of travel behaviour, which in some cases provided major contributions to the state of the art of urban transport planning in the USA and elsewhere.

It has also been claimed that particular automobile groups were trying to undermine certain street car and rail public transport operations in numerous cities throughout the USA (see Snell, 1975). Again this issue pre-dates the UTP process, for the controversy regarding this arose in the early 1930s when investments were made by the Firestone Tyre Company together with GM in the purchase of bus companies in 45 cities, until they had monopolised the public transit industry in these settlements. Instead of repairing the transit systems in these cities, the investors decided to introduce buses i.e., ***petrol driven vehicles with rubber tyres***.

While Kornhauser argues that it is in retrospect unclear to the observer whether the investors in this US example believed that this was superior technology of benefit to the cities, or whether it was merely an example of the industries colluding to invest in that conglomerate, other industrialised countries have experienced similar conflicts (see Hamer, 1987 for an account of the UK experience and Neutze, 1977 and Beed, 1981 for an account of the Australian experience). More optimistically, however, Newman and Kenworthy (1989) claim there is nothing inevitable about the power and influence of the road lobby.

Role of models

Have UTP models been developed to answer design rather than strategy or policy questions?

Differentiating between design questions and policy issues

The general ideology of road building prevalent in the USA at the time of the early development of the UTP process is behind the claim that the process employed models that were intended primarily to answer road design questions, rather than strategic transportation and policy issues. An important matter to appreciate in this context is that the interstate highway programme was adopted before any of the urban transport planning studies were set up and that therefore these studies were conducted within the framework of this programme.

Any discussion regarding the question of the role of models cannot be satisfactorily undertaken without first differentiating clearly between transport policy and highway design questions in urban transport planning. Gakenheimer argues:

> the design issue is where to put highways when you have decided that you are going to serve the travelling population by highways; and the policy issue is whether you are going to provide that many highways, or whether you are going to provide highways and something else?

As it has been employed to date, Gakenheimer claims there is no doubt that the process tackles design questions better than policy issues. Although, as he confesses, it would be unjust to conclude that the second question has been entirely ignored – it is rather that the first is easier to solve. On this matter, Gakenheimer advocates that:

> it is necessary to keep the use of modelling systems for design, and make very apparent that the policy issue is not addressed by them. That is hard to do because the arsenal of analytical tools for the design question cause it to supersede the policy question. The risk in using them is to get consumed in the design problem... forgetting that it is difficult to get from there to policy.

The reason for this highway design bias, according to Carroll, is that up to the late 1970s in the USA, there were no clients for policy models in urban transport. To be more precise, he argues that the demand did not manifest itself adequately, whereas:

> the use of the models as aids to design, with a view to relieving the professional of tedious repetitive analytical tasks, and to analyse many more alternatives over a specific period of time, was and still is in great demand.

Heanue and Ettinger claim that the over-emphasis on design rather than policy was inherited from the early application of the UTP process, when it aimed at providing a more orderly integration of the interstate highway system into cities. They argue that these same models can, however, still be applied in a policy planning context by testing alternatives. This is a claim others fear is suspect, on the grounds that it fails to take into account the fact that policy models need to look into scenarios, rather than predetermined forecasted futures.

In support of the UTP process being capable of tackling policy issues, Kain argues that since the process was developed as a long-range forecasting tool, at one level it automatically addresses policy questions. However, in terms of examining the efficient use of existing transport facilities (which is a policy issue in itself), the UTP process has only in the last fifteen years or so addressed the issue. Before that, the process was more concerned with future investments and less interested in systems management (see Chapter 2).

Levinson, among others, suggests that the fault of the design bias in modelling is more in the application and interpretation of the models, than in the their capabilities. Whereas, for Manheim, there has always been a schizophrenic tension between design and policy aspects in transport planning. He explains:

> on the one hand, the design engineers and planners rejected models when they started spieling out a mass of computer output. They (the engineers) then wanted to know to the force of four or five significant digits, the number of cars making left or right-hand turning movements...

The now long-standing call for models more sensitive to policy in urban transport planning is perhaps best summarised by Shuldiner:

> What we need are more policy-sensitive models... recognising that policy questions are several, continually changing, and ill-defined, we must provide the answers today, since we do not have the luxury of time to come back to them later. We must know what the risks are and in what direction to go.

Manheim welcomes the increasing tendency in some quarters, to influence the design of models according to the policy issues being considered. He advocates this, provided one always critically appraises the models and in this regard, suggests different types of models for different types of analytical situations (see Manheim, 1990).

Planning without models

A most important question arising from the preceding discussion is the extent to which urban transport planners can operate without models, and to what degree transport models are used largely to justify policy decisions (or 'non-decisions') already taken?

Carroll and Stopher are of the view that leaders of many societies use models for their own ends, and that this practice is no more prevalent today than before. Put more candidly, Stopher confirms:

> The main use of (urban transport) models in the USA is to justify policy decisions already made and/or non-decisions.

Carroll reiterates this view more provocatively by adding:

> There were periods when the 'black box' kept the public out of the 'ring' – I think that is indecent! But that is always there in any society of professionals who bury themselves in the professional lease. But as you know, if it (the model) cannot be transmitted, it is only privy to the intellectual or the technician. Anybody therefore who deals with computers and data and uses them to demonstrate a morally determined position is a charlatan – and it is done every day.

While crediting some of the more famous north-eastern universities with the development of numerous early and very useful models in urban transport planning, from a political perspective, Picarsky is dubious of the relatively more recent (post 1975) modelling developments. He expresses his concern as follows:

> We came to believe in some cases, that modelling techniques can be used far beyond their real abilities... We encouraged the use of some modelling, but we feel that a lot of the work done in the field is beyond the sophistication of reality.

Although Heanue and Ettinger also agree that models are often used to substantiate policy decisions already made, they emphasise that this is to do with the application of models rather the modelling itself. What is not always appreciated, they claim, is that:

> most models are in one's head and not (in) the computer, and that subsequently one cannot build and operate a computer model without a mental model.

Kain makes the point that everyone uses models for planning, often without recognising that they do. The real issue is how formal and how elaborate the models need to be. Carroll emphasises that model building with integrity is not an easy task:

> Finding something out and being objective is damn hard work! You have to be heavily motivated and you have to persevere. The notion that you can deduce your way to the best solution is completely untruthful. Yet by accident you can come up with something much better.

Altshuler, as one of the few planners in the USA who has held both senior academic and government posts in urban transport planning, remarks:

> I am not sure that simulation and modelling has had a great impact on (urban transport) planning. They (the models) certainly have absorbed a lot of resources... but their influence has been more apparent than real.

While he concurs that models are used partly to justify political decisions, he also makes the point that they are employed in part to carry out political decisions in technical detail. This is done on the grounds that it is politicians who make the big decisions. Altshuler claims politicians do not really care about details (see later discussion in this chapter regarding planning styles and politics, and Chapter 7). Those that do, he argues, are officials who are both technical and policy-makers, such as Highway Commissioners, Secretaries of Transportation and their staff. These persons need initial proposals provided by technical personnel. Within these proposals, models play an important role for some technocrats, although even here, Altshuler claims, it is surprisingly limited. The technical views of technocrats are, as a result, often able to prevail because of the politicians' indifference to technical detail.

The degree to which technical arguments, backed up by modelling, have changed what might have happened, is a moot point in urban transport planning in the USA. In his book on the Boston Transportation Review, Gakenheimer (1976) focused on cases where decisions were measurable and conducive to the use of modelling. He concluded that if one considered highways to be the solution, there were only a few alignments to choose from, and that the selection probably does not require a great deal of quantitative sophistication to determine which to use. An indication of this in Boston is supported by the fact that suggestions made in the 1920s for the proposals for major transport routes are much the same as all links that have been proposed since then, even though eight or nine major transportation studies followed.

While there are safeguards against technical decisions being used to justify political decisions already made, Altshuler points out that these are within the political process itself. So that rather than being concerned about model-makers being constrained by politicians, he argues, there should be a greater concern about model-makers *not* being constrained by politicians. The more expensive type of modelling, often a product of unconstrained model building, has frequently proven not to be very useful. This has led to much less money being spent on such models since the late 1970s. Altshuler comments:

> forecasting which is policy sensitive, is a valuable exercise which can on occasions inform the policy process. However, it is not worth while spending enormous amounts of money to get to the last refinement, because you do not always know what to do with it.

He goes on to argue that the real need is to employ an inexpensive approximate forecasting technique that can be utilised fairly rapidly (see Chapter 8). This is in contrast to older practices where, as in the 1968 Bay Area San Francisco Transportation Study, they took ten years because of problems with the modelling, to get the models put into practice, by which time their outputs were too late to be included in the plans.

Caution regarding the limited value of modelling in transport planning for decision-makers has also been reiterated by Banfield:

> Transportation models are used in planning, but whether they are used by people who make decisions is another matter... transportation planners, and other planners, would feel naked without a computer to hide behind.

In support of his views, Banfield refers to the research of two economists, Howard and Janet Pack, at the University of Pennsylvania in the late 1960s, when modelling was at its zenith. They published an empirical study based on visits to various cities and interviews with numerous planners, investigating the use made of models and the problems encountered. Similar findings to this research culminated in a book entitled ***Politicians, Bureaucrats and the Consultant*** (Brewer, 1973) which again indicated that the influence of models and other simulation techniques on decision-makers was minimal.

While Shuldiner suspects that the more astute policy-maker and politician is likely to use models only to his/her own advantage, he believes that in certain limited cases, models are an important part of the UTP process. In most instances, he argues models do not do too much harm, as long as they do not impose decisions on the basis of the rationale of the models.

However, a number of transport planning specialists, such as Levinson, Manheim and Gakenheimer, believe that urban transport planning is possible without (mathematical) models, i.e., the problem can be treated purely by the ***ad hoc*** use of data analysis. All acknowledge, though, that the exercise can be made more effective with the selective use of models. For although a non-modelling approach might consider a wider selection of alternatives, it would be difficult to select rationally among alternatives, and in Pushkarev's view this approach would be too intuitive.

Gakenheimer welcomes the more adventurous solutions likely to emerge from such an approach because:

> the (conventional) modelling system tends to dramatise the growth of demand in such a way as to make it seem irresponsible to undertake any effort which changes the system in any way but adding more of the same highway capacity.

Shuldiner too has suggested that the UTP process might operate as well, if not better, without the use of models. He recalls the following experience:

> there was a Conference in Williamsburgh, Virginia, on demand modelling (in 1972). Hanson was there as luncheon speaker, and was at the time active in the Boston Transportation Review. He was talking about the study in general, although the theme of the conference was demand modelling. I asked him: 'suppose you had a demand model, i.e., one which gave you the correct answer, as disaggregate as you

> chose, with quick and inexpensive procedures – would it have made a difference to the outcome of the study?'. The answer was 'no'.

Commenting on Shuldiner's quote, Gakenheimer (1990) points out that the case referred to is rather exceptional, in that it was an extremely controversial study of past commitments when, the issues were more qualitative than usual (see Gakenheimer, 1976).

Stopher suspects that the truth lies somewhere in between, so that the planner with a good sense of what to propose and how to use the model can better organise data for the decision-maker. He also claims that while urban transport planners can function to a degree without models, given that a model should provide more information, in the event such information is not available, one is obliged to make intelligent guesses.

Dependency upon quantification

To what degree have the quantitative inputs to the UTP process determined its design?

Origin of bias towards quantitative data

As already indicated in the preceding discussion, it is very clear that the quantitative requirements of the highway designer i.e., information about daily and hourly traffic volumes, etc., has had a major determining impact on the UTP process. As Stopher explains:

> quantitative data requirements of the process got transport planners believing that they had to get a very broad data base and obtain random samples of an entire metropolitan region... that has continued to influence the way the process has developed.

Carroll suggests that the over-dominance of data needs in the process is also partly based on the fact that there are many in the profession who cannot free themselves of data, and as a result, allow it to play too great a role in their planning. However, he claims, it is the ability to assess the data, and put this assessment into perspective that is most important. Some of the historical problems of data collection for urban transport planning are explained by Carroll in these personal reflections:

> When I started in this (transport planning) business in Detroit, I felt at the very least, no one knows what the hell is going on – so let's get some information.... we decided to gather information on a very carefully selected sample and interview basis, and put them together to see what happens. The next question was now what the hell do we do with it (the information)?

Levinson confers that a quantification bias does exist in the UTP process and its derivatives. He claims, however, that it was only in the late 1970s when the process was in effect cut into two (into the long-range and short-range planning process), that the emphasis shifted from data-based approaches to more open ones. Pushkarev is of the view that the criticism of excessive dependency upon quantification was especially true of the earlier urban transport planning efforts of the 1950s and 1960s which by and large, adopted simple-minded mechanistic models and steps which were incapable of adequately incorporating feedback effects.

Other personalities in the field, such as Kain, disagree that data has had an excessive impact on the process. Instead, he sees the UTP process as a relatively objective framework for analysing a lot of data and organising a great deal of material on travel behaviour in cities. Picarsky as a politician, however, somewhat counteracts this view and points out that:

> information contributes to decision-making, although I am not sure that all quantitative data is necessarily objective.

Manheim points to another concern, when he confesses:

> I would rather see people making judgements from the seat of their pants, than make them in a more rational manner and not do anything...

In his statement, Manheim is simply implying that too much data sometimes leads to inaction because of either the excessive time needed for its collection and analysis, or the high costs of these tasks.

Shuldiner believes that criticism of the reliance on quantitative data misses the point. The 'real issue', he claims, is the type of data collected. Without good disaggregated data, he argues, one cannot undertake effective analytical based planning. Earlier modelling exercises of the UTP process relied too much on aggregate data, whereas relatively more recent derivatives of the process focus on disaggregate data – be it outside of any real coherent policy and planning framework. Shuldiner claims:

> We can, however, avoid some of the naivety that characterises some of our earlier efforts and perhaps be somewhat less concerned with larger-scale systems of planning, and instead orientate our efforts to shorter-run and smaller-scale problems.

Importance and limiting effects of data

The value of data to the UTP process is clearly illustrated by Carroll:

> the extent that it (the data) can give a picture that you could not otherwise get, and to the extent that you can make that talk back to you... can give a real feeling of what you are trying to do. I do not know how to describe that – it is artistic.... It is often referred to as a 'science' I know, but it is when you put this into practice that you realise it is more of an art.

Regarding the data implications of many efforts at improving urban transport planning methodologies, Heanue and Ettinger claim:

> Further improvements of the transportation planning methodology will strain the limits of data availability... data is thus a constraint on the further refinement of the process.

Vuchic maintains that to have more data is an extremely important asset and the more (good and relevant) data one has, the more one can judge that. However, he warns, many come to urban transport planning believing that if they know the models and how to handle data, they then know how to do transport planning. This attitude, he claims, led to the devaluation of the appreciation of experience in urban transport planning.

Gakenheimer suggests that the particular form of data requirements associated with the classical UTP process, especially regarding travel demand and land development analysis, has induced a line-haul perspective of transport infrastructure provision for tackling transport problems. The process, as a result, provides relatively little visibility of other (especially more immediate) problems. This was very apparent he recalls, in the Boston Transportation Study where some of the more observant participants of groups fighting the highway proposals complained that there was too much quantitative analysis directed at the line-haul situation. They requested more attention be paid to smaller scale equity and environmental problems, about which Gakenheimer claims that:

> the elaborate calculus associated with the UTP process tells you very little.

They furthermore claimed that the money and effort required to collect and analyse the vast volumes of data might have been better spent elsewhere.

For these and many other reasons, Gakenheimer prefers a far more 'open framework' for planning urban transport than that associated with the conventional process:

> I have a predisposition to prefer fairly open kinds of study, in which some form of the formal quantitative travel demand modelling is accomplished – but in a sufficiently abstract way to firstly, warn the user of its limited value and secondly, to leave resources for doing other things.

The reason the classical (more quantitatively orientated) UTP approach gave way to the neo-classical approach in the late 1960s and early 1970s (see Chapter 2), in which a set of *ad hoc* elements was introduced, was, according to Gakenheimer, simply because the large-scale data for the grander models had already been collected in a previous iteration of studies. It was, as a result, possible to renew data by updating it through various selected sampled means and have a reasonable transport database without spending large amounts of money on it, as previously was necessary. This in turn made it possible for studies to enter into much wider territory, so that, he explains:

> people were able to say – look we have got all the basic data, so we do not have to hire a lot of systems analysts and statisticians. We need only hire a few of them to up-date what was collected and put it into shape and then hire people to study the *ad hoc* elements of environment and social impact and so forth, i.e., architects, social scientists and natural scientists.

Planning style and politics

How important is the systems approach to the urban transport planning profession?

Technical rationale

Altshuler claims that while a technical rationale is not always required in transport planning exercises, it also does not necessarily determine the outcome of decisions. He cites the findings of his research into the reasons why highway officials tended to win their battles against city planners in the USA. The research attributed the success of engineers over planners to the fact that the former have a library of well-defined technical terms and standards in support of their rationale. The research findings, however, also showed that such groups (i.e., highway planners) often in the end lose their case to political arguments. From this, Altshuler, concludes, the 'technical rationale' can only be viewed as one among many factors in influencing the outcome of an urban transport planning exercise.

What one is in reality therefore talking of in these situations, is an 'ideology' of the profession versus the politician (or pressure groups). Altshuler explains:

> The ideology may be based upon claims to technical skills or on other types of claims – e.g. equity claims, justice claims or claims as to how the society is – and if those are widely believed, then they triumph.

He argues that the citizen participation experience in the USA during the late 1960s and 1970s demonstrated how ideology can triumph over technology and a 'technical rationale'. Likewise, Altshuler continues, one can trace some of the arguments about the environment (which in the late 1980s has once again attracted political attention), and the increasing instances of its beginning to carry more weight than the highway argument, to the rise in the 'green ideology'. The question in this latter example is not that the environmentalist has a better technical rationale, but simply that the prevailing ideology of international politics towards the environment has changed in its favour.

Banfield believes there has been a deliberate effort on behalf of the upper middle class to promote 'rationality', 'order' and the absence of politics in the planning process so as to sterilise it. This he claims, has resulted in a history of attempts to 'popularise' planning on the grounds that it is the very antithesis of politics. He argues:

> A politician in America has the task and skills of making compromises on an *ad hoc* basis, to pull together informally dispersed elements. His job is to create a temporary central basis, sufficient to get something done and/or get himself elected. This is hardly ever compatible with the nature of (urban transport) planning.

Banfield, furthermore, points out that while there are thousands of planners in the USA who employ a highly-structured technical rationale (many of whom occupy government positions), and although there are numerous Metropolitan Planning Agencies (MPOs), there are *no* metropolitan governments in the country. This, he claims, is almost akin to making plans for a non-existent government. With the dismantling of metropolitan planning authorities in the 1980s in the UK by the Thatcher government, similar conclusions may be arrived at for Britain.

The ethos of transport planners

Many political scientists, such as Banfield, view the planning style that is represented by the UTP process and its derivatives as one which overestimates the extent of the planners' understanding of the dynamic interrelationships involved in urban transport planning, and the planner's ability to modify events, particularly in the long run. He argues that planners in the USA fulfil no other purpose than to provide technical data which is mostly ignored, since the influences of political forces are far beyond this comprehension. This is aggravated by the fact that:

> There is a self-selection of people into the planning profession, i.e., those who find the very notion of political wheeling-and-dealing unacceptable, and morally obnoxious or even irrational.

The transport sector has been artificially carved out as a separate area of study, with its main claim to separateness being its very high cost and its long-range planning needs. Without these, Gakenheimer believes urban transport decision-making would be more readily recognised as part of a general political process that is characterised by the dangers typical of all political decision-making. Not recognising this, many urban transport planners have become disillusioned by the influence of politics and operational transport considerations on planning. Public transport operators (previously alienated from the UTP process), who are typically more orientated towards greater cost-recovery considerations of their operations, now, however, enjoy more influence than they ever believed they could. Unlike most public transport operators, who in the USA have had to run their transit systems with scarce resources for many decades, urban transport planners (with a relatively recent history of ready access to capital funding) have been accused of not being able to recognise a scarce resource when they saw one. Hill explains:

> There has been an embedded ethos (even in planning education) among (transport) planners that we should provide more of what we have – it was almost a planning philosophy for a time in the 1960s... related to the 'big is better' idea.

The interface of politics and planning

Picarsky considers that elected officials should become involved early in urban transport planning, so that they are exposed to the work of the professionals, their ethos and their thinking. Although Altshuler attempted this in Massachusetts, such involvement is rarely pursued in full. It should be noted, that in reflecting upon his past experiences, Altshuler confesses that his experience at attempting to bring elected officials into the urban transport planning exercise at the earliest possible phase, taught him that mixing the two aspects of the political and technical process was too debilitating.

In an interview by the author with various members of the Chicago Rapid Transit Authority (CRTA) the following comments were made with regard to the relationship of technocrats to the politician in urban transport planning:

> There are occasions when only parts of the technocrat's work is utilised at the convenience of the politician. These are often used indiscriminately, i.e., they are used in parts in an unrelated manner. The technocrats are now having to learn a 'new ball game'.... At least, the successful ones are developing a new skill to deal with such instances – i.e., that one cannot

> formulate a technical plan in a vacuum. On the other hand, politicians too are learning more and more of the technical realities. So that there is a two-way educational process.

Carroll claims that since a city mayor is concerned with his election to office he is not likely to support a plan or project whose political returns accrue only in the months before the elections. He continues:

> whatever planners may think of this... this is what much of planning is all about... planning proposals must be sensitive to political issues.

This makes financial sense, in so far as the cost of money has today become so much dearer that long-run commitments by politicians to macro-projects can prove much more expensive than expected. In this regard, Hill believes that many major mistakes in the transport sector of US cities in the past have been made in resource allocation exercises, because:

> Too often, mayors want to look at the transportation pie baked last year, and wish to adopt the percentages shared out last year as a basis for their decisions. But to increase the transportation pie, one invariably has to take money from elsewhere.

It was not until the late 1970s that there was a growing recognition of the need for more cost-effective approaches to urban transport provision, forcing people to be more realistic. This paved the way in the late 1980s for the aggressive efforts throughout USA and elsewhere in the world towards maximising cost recovery.

Independence of planning stand

Another important aspect connected with politics and planning styles in the urban transport field, is the issue of how independent a transport planning consultant ought to be of a project. It is an issue that has seen a considerable change of attitude over the last two decades. In the 1980s, and now in the 1990s, there are increasing instances of turnkey packages being offered in the urban transport field which include subsidised if not 'free' feasibility studies conducted by consultants in association with transport hardware manufactures and/or construction companies. Given that there are enormous profits to be made in the design and construction of urban transport systems, it has been up until relatively recently, conventional practice for the consultant to stand outside vested interests. This is, as Altshuler points out, because:

> the potential for corruption is overwhelming – and it may be subconscious corruption, i.e., a man may think he is honest but if he stands to make a million dollars if he comes down on one side of a question as opposed to another he may be subconsciously influenced.

Having a non-independent consultant, therefore, makes sense only if the policy-makers have decided what they want, and the consulting report is merely to confirm it. Altshuler argues, however, that in the many circumstances when the politicians do not know what they need:

> the political process wants an honest answer to its problems. It requires honest men to do that. The politician then, when he hires expertise, wants it to work for him and not any supplier such as a rapid transit manufacturer.

Trends versus policies

The issue of whether the UTP process relies more on projected trends than policies[2], which in turn, would lead to the implementation of trends as policies, has important implications for urban transport planning.

Banfield rather contentiously claims there are no urban development policies in the USA:

> We have government programmes that have effects – most of them unintended. It is, however, a mis-use of the word to call them 'policies'. They are (financed) events that have outcomes but to think that out of intention, planners had anything to do with them (the events) is preposterous. Practically everything that has happened (in the USA), the government has affected but almost all has been contrary to its intention, in so far as there was any intention. There are a thousand intentions – most of them are more or less at odds.

Taking a somewhat different perspective, Altshuler maintains that trend projections are very important restraints on policy-making. How much one wishes to go against/fight the trends or to steer them, is a central policy question not adequately addressed by most urban transport planning exercises. He explains:

> Planners have rarely been particularly articulate about which strategies they should implement. They just let the trends realise themselves, steer them or fight them. Quite understandably so, since 90 per cent of what is going to happen is a function of trends over which we have little control, and all we can hope to do is to steer certain kinds of developments within that onrushing stream. To do that is not necessarily a criticism, it may in fact be a far more intelligent strategy than saying that we will somehow fight those trends and turn them around.

Banfield's response to the dilemma is well illustrated by his following remarks:

> if politicians paid any attention to trends and what the planners came up with, or rather what the planners allege to be the trends, then trend planning might be a problem. However, there is one thing we know for sure, and that is that the future is not going to be like the past!

Treatment of uncertainty

Critics of the UTP process and many of its derivatives have claimed that in instances where uncertainty is high and penalties for errors too costly, the highly structured systems approach of the UTP process is unsuitable. Banfield on the other hand, has argued that it is not a question of whether the process is suitable but rather whether it and its assumptions are compatible with the nature of the 'real world'. He explains:

> there is the premise in the approach that there is (in the political system) some capacity to carry out plans, whereas in the real world in the USA, there is not – the treatment of risk is almost academic.

Others have rather cynically argued that the major function of planners is the legitimation of government decisions, i.e., to provide a rationale for decisions already taken or for decisions to take no action. Banfield concurs with this conclusion and claims:

> It (planning) is a form of window-dressing of government. It is essentially an adjunct to the political process. As far as planners are used at all... they are used to confirm decisions already taken... Too much importance is attached to the planner. Politicians are rarely in need of so much justification.

One may conclude, therefore, that the limited influence of the planner is not necessarily a failure of the profession but a product of the unrealistic set of aspirations he values.

Interdisciplinary planning

It has been argued (Dimitriou, 1989) that the internal specialist disagreements which commonly take place within an urban transport planning exercise that involves an interdisciplinary team, leads to ambiguities in the planning style adopted which merely add to the problems of tackling real issues.

While university teaching programmes in policy sciences and urban planning are intended to overcome this problem by increasing interdisciplinary interaction, Banfield concedes that those not trained in this manner, such as engineers, economists and political scientists, find it much more difficult to perceive problems from other standpoints. He also claims, that many of the policy science programmes in the USA (at least in their early days) were in reality treated almost as economics programmes. Such programmes, he explains, were:

> like the old recipe for the rabbit and the horse – i.e., equal parts, one rabbit and one horse; the economist being the horse. They (the economists) have the intellectual tools to dominate and preserve the predominance of economics in the field.

Altshuler adds:

> There is always a certain amount of tension between people of different mandates. The main thing is that transportation planners are more likely to value transportation objectives more highly than people who have broader mandates. Moreover, historically in the USA, the transportation planner has

> had more money than all the planners put together which has led to a certain amount of dominance on the part of the specialised group of planners over those who had broader mandates and who should, in theory at least, have had much larger budgets and technical influence. In that sense, there have been certain practical tensions whenever you have people with two mandates trying to get the other to comply.

Altshuler is, however, of the view that engineers became powerful, not necessarily because of their superior technical rationale but because, for a time, their values coincided with the dominant political values in the USA. He subsequently claims:

> The way to beat that... was not to try to convince the engineers but the politicians,... you do that by changing the nature of the political system, i.e., by mobilising a lot of people who vote and then the political tide begins to change, and it has changed quickly.

Much of the tension also has to do with the perceptional baggage that each professional group takes on board (see Chapter 6). Land-use planning is in essence, a specialty within comprehensive planning (development planning), whereas, historically, city planners have inappropriately tried to define their field as comprehensive planning/urban development planning. Since the transport planner is concerned with access and mobility, there is a clear functional role for his efforts. Whereas, the land-use planner is more likely to be concerned with land-use consequences of improving access and transport links, and the health and environmental planner with air and water pollution. The role of the comprehensive (development) planner is to be concerned with the balancing of all these, as well as many other elements.

Public participation

Given that many amendments to the UTP process result from issues which surfaced from public debate, how much more socially orientated has this made urban transport planning?

Decline of belief in professionalism

In the early days of the UTP process, it was widely recognised that there was a certain professionalism and belief in professionalism in the urban transport planning field. By the mid-1970s, however, this belief had been significantly eroded (see Chapter 2), partly because public participation was expected in most major urban transport planning exercises in the USA, even though it may not always have been welcome.

Although participation was widely seen as a healthy development, it brought to the forefront the problem of how to take (or sustain) 'planned action' given the delays often caused by public involvement. For according to Hillegass, the issue of public participation and its incorporation into urban transport planning is closely associated with the growing concern with whether the resultant planning process is both implementable and sufficiently dynamic. He explains:

> We talk a lot about changing factors that need to be considered and that as a result, the planning process must be continuous. We talk about changes in land use development, car ownership changes, etc. – but at the bottom of the list is a passing reference made to the changes in public values.

Hillegass argues that public values typically change much faster than other variables and that the reason that many of the plans are not implemented is because of unanticipated changes in these public values. He believes the outcome for urban transport planning would have been radically different in many cities throughout the USA if public values had not changed in the last 20 to 25 years. There would have been more freeways, for example, in San Francisco and New York, and the attitude to the authorities would have been much more subservient.

Heanue and Ettinger claim that the incorporation of public debate into urban transport planning was inevitable, and that the very fact that the US Congress had been sensitive to this issue from the 1970s merely formalised what would have happened anyway. The outcome of this, they suggest, was significant for it accommodated opposition viewpoints, and provided useful information that was very influential in changing the shape of decision-making in urban transport throughout the USA. In response to these developments, individual urbanised areas were permitted by Congress to indicate whether they wanted a freeway built or whether they wished to use the same funds for rapid transit.

Without the public debate and the changed investment decisions stimulated by it, Kornhauser is of the opinion that there would not be the current co-ordination in urban transport planning that one now finds in the USA. Levinson, however, believes that the values and inputs that were necessary to make the UTP process socially more responsive in its early form, were omitted by the process itself. He recounts:

> From a very parochial perspective of a consultant, we (at Wilbur Smith Associates) were so busy producing and verifying the numbers that we lost many of the basic social issues. Very often, one was not even able to find out what was (socially) important, who the important people were, and how one could bring all these factors together...

Premise of public participation

Although the public debate on highways started out as a public outcry against building more roads, the premise upon which the debate was based was, according to Levinson, very wide. On the one side, there were those who believed that the plan which destroyed the least, constituted the 'best', and on the other side, there were those who believed that the best plan constituted the one which provided the most mobility. The outcome of the debate not only changed the scale of urban road construction, but, in Levinson's view, also introduced greater sensitivity. The debate though, he insists, did not change the process itself, but merely broadened its scope. The importance of contributions from the community in urban transport planning rests on the belief that the locals from a particular area, know where, how and why it is going to change, and from this one can surmise what the effects of transport investment are.

Taking a different tack, Picarsky argues:

> there is a mistaken notion that the change in the (UTP) process came about as a result of public involvement. It really came about, in my opinion, as a result of political concerns and because we were moving in a society orientated to the automobile in a direction which could not endure success on a long-term basis. So the political process had to find a satisfactory political approach.

In arguing the above, Picarsky suggests that it is abundantly clear that the political support received by the public accelerated this political development – in some cases to the extreme. It was, he claims, convenient for the Federal Government to develop the Environmental Protection Agency (EPA) with which to try and slow down some of the problems. In support of this view, Manheim explains:

> It is my judgement, however, that these changes (to the UTP process) did not emanate from the public at large, but from the decision-makers and their advisors.

On the basis of the Regional Planning Association's experience in New York, Pushkarev claims that the 'opening-up' of the UTP process would definitely not have taken place without public pressure. Stopher concurs with this view. Substantiating this, Pushkarev explains:

> After all, we (the Regional Planning Association of New York) are part of that public debate. Until 1973/4 we still had 800 miles of freeways on the regional plan. We were saying that this is ridiculous. But more importantly, there were inadequate roads locally. As a result, some things became politically unacceptable. The plans were then modified so that the amount of roads were reduced to more modest dimensions... that was not because any planner decided that, but because the political opposition in the neighbourhoods was so strong that it was just not viable....
>
> One day, Mayor Lindsay just threw it (the large scale proposal for highways) out of the window, without asking anybody. For he felt that there was too much opposition from the neighbourhoods.... The planning agencies merely adjusted themselves to this political reality.

Vuchic shares these views of the significance of the political dimension and the importance of public participation as instrumental in 'opening-up' the UTP process. He sees the role of citizen participation groups as keeping in contact with planners, so that they (the planners) have an idea of what is being done. On this basis, he claims that citizen participation came in a form which did far more good than one perhaps expected, especially because the whole participation process later became institutionalised.

PERFORMANCE OF THE PROCESS

To what degree does the UTP process achieve the tasks it set out to perform?

Historical perspective

While a number of those quoted in this publication – especially engineers and economists – express a qualified confidence in the performance of the UTP process and its derivatives, they also emphasise that the political and bureaucratic context in which urban transport planning has taken place makes the process (however it may be modified), ultimately constrained. Pushkarev, for example, remarks:

> the intellectual potential is there. Whether it (the UTP process) is made effective, given the politics and that the Governor's office is rather remote from any of the planning agencies, is difficult to say.

Others – particularly planners and political scientists – claim that the process did not achieve the tasks it set out to, and thus the process cannot be seen in the positive light in which it has often been presented. Mitchell, who shares this view, argues that there is in fact, some mileage in looking at several of the short-cut techniques employed in the pre-Chicago and Detroit Study days for possible re-application after some refinement.

However, a general consensus which did emerge from those interviewed, is that by the late 1970s the UTP process had been stretched to its limits in the USA – both in terms of technical and political viability. This is primarily because the Federal Government had adopted a more stringent set of environmental laws which contributed significantly to the extensive revision of the original process and created a 'shadow transport planning process' (see Chapter 2).

The harsh criticism of the process in its failure adequately to take into account environmental considerations is more valid than is generally credited. This is evident from information arising from interview sources quoted here which indicated that opponents of the interstate highway programme, even at the time of its earliest implementation, were unhappy because of its negative environmental consequences (largely in terms of the number of displacements) which were inadequately taken into account. It was not until there was a general change in attitude in the whole country, several decades later, that one saw a gradual more positive re-focus on environmental considerations. From this, Heanue and Ettinger conclude that:

> the process *did* achieve its tasks, it is just that attitudes were meanwhile changing.

In later correspondence with the author, Heanue (1989) reiterates his confidence in the UTP process by stating:

> One measure of its overall success is the fact that we now have on the ground over 11,000 miles of completed interstate in urban areas. Several hundred miles were not built but the resolution of the controversies surrounding those miles including the decision whether or not to build transit in their place was accomplished through the process.... Virtually every interest group that has taken a position on the post-Interstate (Highway) Program has called for a continuation of the process or a strengthening of the process.
>
> You can see from my comments that I use a very broad definition of the 'word' process. I consider it to encompass not only the technical analysis but also the interaction between the professional staff and the policy committees that are composed principally of elected officials.

Gomez-Ibanez suggests that the UTP process might have been good at certain tasks in the past, particularly at getting things done, whereas later, it became less effective. He explains:

> it (the UTP process) dealt with the problems it was faced with.... The early process thus fulfilled its purpose, for it classified streets, it dealt with (transport) systems, it was systematic, and it programmed capital investments. Whether in hindsight, it did this in the most economic way – I would have to say that it did not.

While Levinson also perceives the UTP process as reasonably successful in achieving its initial objectives, he like Mitchell, points out that, had it been expanded to include more land-use alternatives and development strategies in a much more integral way, it might have achieved more. He furthermore argues that while the process (and its derivatives) have probably achieved certain savings in transport investment and helped to arrive at better designs in city-wide transport systems, many of these developments might anyway have taken place without the process.

Although, given the changed circumstances and current socio-economic and political events, the UTP process in its traditional form is now considered in certain quarters to be 'off-stream practice' – if not downright discredited – many aspects of the process survive and are still utilised (see Hong Kong Transport Department and Wilbur Smith Associates, 1989). This is especially true of many of the derivatives currently used in traffic management schemes, transport systems management efforts, corridor planning studies, public transport developments, and *ad hoc* road improvements (including maintenance).

Elements of the process also percolate through updating exercises of old transport plans in many cities of the USA and elsewhere. This is especially apparent in New York, which having had earlier transport studies based on the UTP process, often re-addresses old issues and resurrects old planning principles and assumptions. Carroll who directed the Tri-State study confirms this, commenting on the fact that New York city in 1978 still faced infrastructure proposals first forwarded in the 1920s and 1930s.

Objectives achieved

The performance of the UTP process and its derivatives can only be accurately assessed against the stated intentions of their use. If one returns to the testimony in the brief to the US Congress in 1961, which indicates rather modest aims for urban transport planning, then within its limited remit of better planning of the interstate highway system (as it affected urban areas), one can argue that the process *did* in fact execute its tasks very successfully; especially in terms of quantifying the transport demand that would utilise the transport system. Indeed, Shuldiner claims that many of the early urban transport studies employing the UTP process met their respective objectives better than more recent studies, although he concedes, this is mainly because most of the highway networks that were contemplated have now already been built.

Taking a contrary position, both Mitchell and Stopher argue that the process has not proved very successful in achieving the tasks it set out to perform. They attribute this, on the one hand, to the fact that in many respects the process has been 'out-of-date' for a long time, and on the other hand, because many of those using the process tried to make it produce things it was not capable of producing. Mitchell explains:

> I see the current process (and its functions) as a modification of what it was originally. It is not a new process, nor has a new one emerged.

Attributing the UTP process with the successful building of urban freeways, as Heanue does, needs to be tempered with the knowledge that an important factor in attaining this aim was the availability of the Highway Trust Fund and its continuous funding of the construction of the interstate highway system. Mitchell, furthermore, claims that many studies contained highway proposals which were never carried out, as in the notable case of Philadelphia. In these terms alone, therefore, he believes the process was less successful than has been claimed.

If one considers that another of the stated tasks of the process is to make reasonably accurate projections, and provide a basis for doing good planning, Stopher argues, the UTP process has not proved as effective in achieving its objectives as many have believed. He claims that on comparing traffic predictions that have been made in the 1950s in the USA (when the first urban transport studies were conducted), to what has actually taken place at the horizon years some 20 to 30 years later, the process has *not* accurately predicted the current situation (see earlier comments by Pushkarev).

What needs to be appreciated, however, in making these kinds of judgements, is that the objectives of urban transport planning in the USA of the 1970s and 1980s are less clear, in that they are intended to accommodate much more of the dynamic characteristics of urban and transport developments and related policy-making, in comparison with those of the 1950s and 1960s. Developments have changed so much, that by comparing the performance of the process over the various decades, one is, in Heanue's words (1989) critiquing a moving and evolving target.

Public participation

Where the UTP process has especially proved weak has been in the field of public participation (see earlier discussion on public participation). Modern society is basically pluralistic, containing multiple interest groups with different goals and objectives. Gomez-Ibanez argues that if the UTP process set out to implement policies about which there is a democratic consensus, then:

> the process does a better job than before.... It previously ran 'rough-shod' over groups that did not have a lot of political influence, in that they were not politically active and were thus not used to participating.

Having said this, he concedes that certain public participation practices in the late 1970s led to situations where numerous transport projects were critically needed but because of extensive public participation, they were never implemented. This contributes to what Gomez-Ibanez describes as:

> a very delicate kind of pendulum that has perhaps gone slightly too far... although those whose homes are going to be taken, and who are going to have to breathe the fumes and suffer the noise created by proposed transport projects should have a say in whether the project ought to proceed. Whether they ought to have a veto or the last say over the decision to go ahead is another matter!

Transport planning in such circumstances can be said to possess a great deal of vetoing power, but an insufficient capability to 'buy-off' the costs of those most negatively affected. Gomez-Ibanez claims this has:

> created a situation whereby, although action ought to be taken for the good of society as a whole, this often cannot be achieved because a mode of planning has now evolved which has given the people the veto power but does not allow the general public to 'buy-off' some of these groups that obviously have a right to be outraged about how they are (or are likely to be) affected by new projects.

In the light of the above, Manheim (1990) has argued that urban transport planning must therefore become much more of a 'technical support'. It should provide an input to a more pluralistic conflict-laden decision-making process regarding investments in urban transport as well as their impact on cities and their inhabitants. The main issue then becomes a matter of what technical tools to use to help transport planners and engineers to become more useful in this conflict-ridden process.

Transport facility provision

Notwithstanding the influence and importance of the Highway Trust Fund in providing the financial means to construct so many highways in the USA, Rapkin believes the UTP process has been *enormously* successful in justifying the building of roads in urban areas, even though this has detracted from the development of railways. Very many of the urban transport planning studies employing the UTP process, he argues, did in fact assemble a good body of data – some of which was still in use some twenty years later – for there was no other compatible database available.

However, in Pushkarev's view, many such studies were under-exploited, despite the rich source of data they offered. For although they were attributed with a good methodology for data collection, their planning methodology was too deterministic, and in his own words:

> came up too often with over-blown highway schemes which collapsed under their own weight.

He claims that, very often this did not lead to their implementation but merely confirmed that some of those highways were to go ahead.

As Pushkarev's views and earlier statements by Heanue, Rapkin and Stopher suggest, there is a certain amount of disagreement as to whether the UTP process led to the construction of urban highways in the USA, or whether the highway proposals had already existed and would thus have been carried out anyway. Given that there are no statistics on this and because the rationale upon which these road building decisions were initially founded are now in most cases lost in history, this issue can never be cleared, except perhaps on a project-to-project investigation basis.

Hillegass emphasises, however, that it should be appreciated that technocrats have always had a naive view regarding how long it takes to integrate something into the political decision-making process. He explains that the interstate technical proposal system, for example, had been discussed since the mid–1940s. If, on this basis, the UTP process in the 1960s (when it was only five years old) was expected to have had some effect on the huge political interest in the interstate highway system, then according to Hillegass, this demonstrates a consistent level of naivete by those technocrats who expected this. One cannot, he claims:

> create a new procedure, process or organisation, and expect five years later that it will somehow have had an impact in a significant way on the political process. To expect then the UTP process to have affected the interstate highway system, which was the last big freeway building effort in this country, is not realistic.

This is not to say, he continues, that the planners who were producing the new process did not believe it would have an impact. Indeed, in many cases, they certainly tried to ensure that it did. But in general, the process had a much more limited impact than some believe, principally, because when a planning process such as the UTP process gets too far ahead of the political process, it tends to encounter insurmountable political rather than technical problems.

Even over a longer time-span, what also has to be appreciated is that to achieve any deep-rooted change in planning practice, such as the effective integration of the various elements that make up the transport planning task, takes many years. Hillegass argues it takes 15 to 20 years in urban transport planning in the USA, from the inception of a concept to its clear-thinking execution on the streets. This has been apparent in the case of traffic management schemes which it can be said have been conceived in the USA within the Transport Systems Management framework. This framework originally took projects which traffic engineers and public transit specialists had already developed, and put the parties together to formulate (and subsequently submit) a prioritised programme of projects. Its developments, however, (see Gakenheimer and Meyer, 1990), have yet to make TSM into a substitute planning process for urban transport which some mistakenly have claimed it could become.

Part II

A DEVELOPMENTAL APPROACH TO UTP FOR THIRD WORLD CITIES

5

TRANSPORT AND THIRD WORLD CITY DEVELOPMENT

DEFINING THE THIRD WORLD

Problems of definition

Although the 'Third World' is now a widely used term, it is employed in so many different ways that one cannot assume a universal definition.[1] As Worsley points out (1980), this is not merely due to a lack of intellectual rigour but is also the result of various historical conceptions of the term that evolved at different times in response to different situations. According to the same source, the term, was first used by the French demographer, Alfred Sauvey, who in 1952, in the title of an article, applied it to those countries which were outside the two international power blocks, and also, at the time, outside the communist world. In this paradigm, the 'First World' refers to the capitalist industrialised countries; the 'Second World' is made up of the centrally planned economies;[2] and the 'Third World' represents the remaining 'developing' countries.

The initial use of 'Third World' as a term was, therefore, closely associated with the 'Third Force' concept, coined by French scholars in the late 1940s and early 1950s, to denote a non-aligned force. In the late 1960s, newly established African countries employed a similar non-aligned interpretation. When East-West tensions declined, and more colonies emerged as new countries, the connotations of 'Third Force' with non-alignment altered. The term re-emerged in the 1970s, to connote development with common characteristics. The notion of confrontation, however, was transferred to the North-South dialogue (or rather, lack of dialogue), as summarised by the Brandt Report (Independent Commission on International Development Issues, 1981).

This later paradigm presents the 'North' as containing all the capitalist countries of the Western world (the majority of which, apart from Australia and New Zealand are located in the northern hemisphere), as well as the centrally directed economies of the Comecon Countries (excluding Cuba and China); and the 'South' as including the majority of the poor nations, also referred to as the 'Third World' or the 'developing nations' (see Figure 5.1).

If the three-world paradigm is too simple, then there are obvious objections to an even more simplified view of the world as two broad camps. This is particularly so since the 'South' includes affluent newly industrialising countries (the NICs) such as Korea and Taiwan, at one end of the scale, and poor nations such as Bangladesh and Chad at the other. The division becomes even more misleading if one focuses on per capita GNP figures. Some countries in the 'South' (mostly oil-exporting nations such as Saudi Arabia and Kuwait) have higher per capita GNP figures than many countries of the industrialised 'Northern World' (see Appendix Table 6.1).

Despite these limitations of definition so well articulated by Harris (1986) in *The End of the Third World*, the term 'Third World' still has a substantial degree of conceptual validity in its representation of countries with a common past or present set of development experiences. For this reason, this term rather than 'developing country' is used by the author throughout this publication. To use the latter would erroneously imply that only so-called 'developing countries' are making 'progress', and that there is a universally known and accepted form of 'development' to progress toward.

The latter presumption is seen by Bauer (1980) to encourage the imposition of indices of the industrialised world as international standards of development. Countries that do not meet or share these standards are then by implication considered 'backward'. Bauer goes on to argue that the use of either of the terms – 'underdeveloped' or 'developing' countries – suggest that their conditions are not only abnormal but rectifiable.

Many Third World specialists believe that the real chances of improving the situation of many Third World countries are few, given that the industrialised capitalist and Eastern European countries enjoy more than four-fifths of the world's income. On this

Figure 5.1 The North–South divide

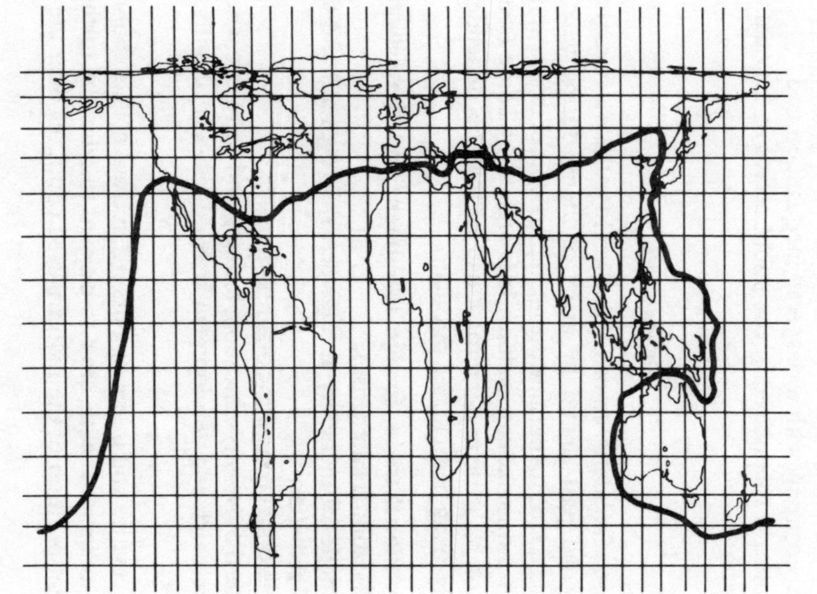

Source: Redrawn from book cover, *Independent Commission on International Development Issues*, 1981

basis, Bauer concludes that in reality, it is the 'Northern Nations' that are 'abnormal' in as much as they are exceptional.

Third World characteristics

The case for referring to a block of countries as the 'Third World', despite all the dangers of over-simplification, arises from their shared socio-economic features (some past and some present), and the international sense of solidarity their common experiences have generated. Such shared socio-economic characteristics can be summarised and discussed under the following headings:

1 dependence on the industrialised world, combined with a shared perception of their historical development experiences;
2 rapid growth phenomena in major socio-economic trends affecting development;
3 a dual economy with widespread inequalities; and
4 a dominant role played by the public sector in national development.

Dependency

The sense of solidarity among Third World nations is reinforced by the colonial past shared by many of them, during which the colonised countries became the main providers of raw materials to the then industrialising nations. It is argued by some (see later discussion on structural-internationalists) that this dependency is currently being perpetuated through:

1 international trade, foreign investment and the activities of multi-national enterprises;
2 international monetary arrangements, foreign aid and the related activities;
3 international consulting organisations;
4 Western university education, training and literature; and
5 the research and development activities associated with all the above.

These activities and interests, pursued in close collaboration with a small indigenous elite, are also claimed to reinforce further the dominant position of the industrialised countries over the Third World.

Shared perception of historical development experiences

An increased sense of common purpose in the Third World has, according to Mabogunje (1980), arisen out of the realisation (substantiated by development planning failures) that the aid and loan policies of capitalist countries with their associated development strategies are not necessarily the 'effective medicine' they were thought to be. In certain instances, this realisation has led to a search for new and more appropriate development strategies.

Rapid growth phenomena

None of the numerous indicators representing the common plight of Third World countries is more striking than their high population growth rates (see Appendix Table 6.2). Associated population characteristics include:

1 A high participation of the total labour force in agriculture, generally between 72 per cent (for low-income economies) and 48 per cent (for middle-income economies), compared with an average of 7 per cent in the industrialised countries (World Bank, 1988).
2 A significant proportion of the total population residing in rural areas, averaging between 65 per cent (for low-income economies) and 42 per cent (for middle-income economies), compared with an average of 22 per cent in the high-income economies (World Bank, 1990).
3 A relatively low per capita GNP, ranging from an average of US$ 320 (for low-income countries) to US$ 1,930 (for middle-income economies), compared with an average US$ 17,080 for the high-income economies (World Bank, 1990).

A feature of Third World rural populations is that their social and cultural values are in direct contrast to (if not in conflict with) urban values. The life-styles of Third World city-dwellers, on the other hand, are greatly influenced by industrialisation and modernisation, both of which are commonly associated with trends of rapid urbanisation.

Average annual urban population growth rates, though declining in many Third World countries, have generated population levels that are now critical (see Appendix Table 6.3). In middle and low-income economies, respectively, urbanisation has increased by an annual average of 3.3 per cent between 1980 and 1985 (World Bank, 1988) and 4 per cent per annum between 1980 and 1988 (World Bank, 1990). In the high-income oil exporting nations, it rests at a level of 6.1 per cent per annum between 1980 and 1985 (down from 9.5 per cent between 1965 and 1980) – compared with an average of 1.5 per cent per annum in the industrialised countries (this in turn, having increased from 1.4 per cent between 1965 and 1980) (World Bank, 1988).

The absolute increase in urban population has taken place because, as before, of the fast-growing population movements from rural to urban areas, and an over-concentration of new employment opportunities in the cities, added to which, natural population growth rates are rapid within many such settlements.

Together, these growth phenomena have created a lethal combination of interrelated and self-generating urban problems of enormous proportions. Problems of urban transport associated with the rapid growth in vehicles, are but one integral component of the wider urban development situation of Third World cities. The backcloth to these circumstances in most of these countries consists of (World Bank, 1990):

1 widespread under-employment;
2 a lack of skilled manpower especially at managerial levels;
3 occasional high rates of inflation (a 66.7 per cent per annum average for middle-income economies between 1980 and 1988, compared with 4.9 per cent per annum for high-income countries during the same period);
4 higher birth and death rates of 31 and 10 per thousand average, respectively, for low-income countries, as against comparable figures of 14 and 9 per thousand in the high-income nations;
5 shorter life expectancy levels at birth with an average of 60 years for low-income countries and 66 years for middle-income economies, as against 76 for high-income nations;
6 higher illiteracy levels, with an average 44 per cent in the low-income countries and 26 per cent in middle-income nations.

Dual economy

Third World countries are also characterised by an internal dual economy; a domestic economy in which a ‘superior’ (advantaged) and 'inferior' (disadvantaged) economic system co-exist. A dual economy manifests itself in the co-existence of: modern and traditional methods of production; 'formal' (registered and taxable) and 'informal' (unregistered and illegal) economic activities; as well as extreme poverty and affluence. Although these inequalities exist in various parts of the world, they are particularly widespread and indeed on the increase in many Third World countries.

Recent developments

The last decade for lower-income countries of the Third World has been described in an editorial by *The Economist* (Crook, 1989) as 'a cruel disappointment'. Confirming this view, the World Bank reports that some sixty low and middle-income economies have suffered declining real GNP per capita in constant prices during the 1980s (World Bank, 1990). These trends have taken place principally, because most such countries have been burdened with heavy debts and have seen living standards that were already below unacceptable levels, fall further.

This has contrasted with a rise in per capita incomes in the industrialised countries from US$ 11,000 in 1980 to US$ 13,000 by the end of the decade (Crook, 1989). While the World Bank (1990) reports per capita levels in the high-income countries reaching US$ 17,080 in 1988. One cannot but conclude from this that the poorest of the Third World are not sharing in the globe's increased wealth but instead experiencing an economic decline – something that is particularly apparent in Africa. In this context, Crook (1989) comments:

> If prosperity in the rich north does not automatically trickle down to the south, as conventional economic thinking predicts it should, perhaps the poor countries are simply condemned to stay poor... the temporary setbacks of the 1980s will seem as nothing beside the prolonged stagnation that awaits poor countries in the 1990s and beyond.

Answering the questions and predictions he himself posed in the editorial, Crook, drawing from the findings of an *Economist* survey of Third World countries, concludes that even the poorest of the low-income countries are capable of development if the example is followed of the 'super-achievers' of East Asia (namely, Taiwan, Hong Kong, Singapore and South Korea). For this to happen, however, the editorial argues that governments must 'learn their place'.

What Crook (1989) appears to be advocating in the *Economist* editorial is a fundamental change in one of the main characteristics of Third World countries, namely a reduction of the dominant role of the public sector and associated government intervention, in order to 'free-up' market forces.

Without wishing to pursue this debate too much further here, the author wonders, given other facts presented in this and the following chapter, how Crook can present such a simplistic view, when the evidence of other successful Third World economies, such as Indonesia, has had government playing a critical role in the guidance and motivation of overall national development thereby *enabling* market forces to flourish. A related issue is what impacts will a market-led economy have on income distribution and the environment, given that many Third World countries are typically controlled by a small elite who have an influence out of proportion to their numbers and often push their vested interests almost at any cost.

Typologies of Third World countries

Although in the 1950s Third World countries shared more characteristics in common than today, their taxonomy has always varied according to the principal development interest of those drawing up the classification. The categories employed in this publication to cite illustrative development characteristics have as a matter of convenience been based on the classification employed by the World Bank which has provided the source statistics.

The World Bank classification discriminates among Third World nations on the basis of their gross national product (GNP) per capita, and in the past (see World Bank, 1988), according to whether they are importers or exporters of oil. On the former basis, the three major categories of Third World nations (excluding 55 economies with populations less than one million and 9 non-reporting countries to the World Bank) are those with (World Bank, 1990):

1 a gross national product per capita less than US $545 (referred to as 'low-income economies', estimated at 42);
2 a gross national product per capita in excess of US$ 545 but

below US$ 5,999 (referred to as 'medium-income economies, estimated at 54);

3 a gross national product per capita in excess of US$ 5,999 but rising to a ceiling of US$ 27,500 in the case of Switzerland (referred to as 'high-income economies ', estimated at 25).

Estimates indicate that 151 countries make up the Third World. This compares with 21 nations in the industrialised world and eight East European countries either with non-market economies or with non-market economies currently in transition.

A review of other literature suggests that there are at least four kinds of typologies of Third World countries, namely:

1 economic and resource-based categories, e.g. those based on some measure of GNP or GDP, or estimates of national export and import levels of natural resources, particularly oil (of the kind referred to above);
2 politically defined categories which differentiate among centralised economies, mixed economies and market economies (albeit that the first are currently rapidly dwindling in number);
3 historical development categories, e.g. those based on stages of growth (see Rostow, 1961), concepts of colonial and neo-colonial models of development, and some measure of industrialisation; and
4 international development agency categories employed by agencies such as: the International Labour Office (ILO), United Nations (especially UNDP), World Bank (IBRD), and the Organisation for Economic Co-operation and Development (OECD). These are drawn up for the agency's own purposes, and therefore often constitute a mix of the above categories.

Definition and measurement of development

Before effective action can be taken to redress or alleviate development problems one first needs to be clear about how to assess progress so as to formulate useful measurements of development. One way is to employ development goals, targets and indicators which governments and/or international development agencies adopt and which facilitate the measure of change and progress arising from development efforts. This in turn, requires that those in a position of power who formulate the policies in the light of their own values, have a clear understanding of 'development'. Much ambiguity, however, surrounds the term.

The concept implies an 'advance' on the past or 'progress', usually through progressive growth in the various factors that contribute to the improvement. 'Development' signifies movement towards a pre-defined set of ends considered to be 'modern' and economically healthy, promoted, as a rule, by government and/or international agencies. However, development has been perceived by too many and for too long as synonymous with economic growth alone. In part, this is because politicians have found economic indicators, such as national income measures, politically useful.

Whilst economic progress is clearly an essential component of development, it is not the only one. Development is a phenomenon comprising many interrelated and inseparable components. Those who now subscribe to this school of thought have, however, had the benefit of reviewing ideas and debates contained in the literature of development economics and planning over the last thirty years. According to Todaro (1981), this literature has by and large, focused upon 'economic growth' theories, first articulated by Rostow (1961), and later 'structural-internationalist' models of development, including the work of Seers (1969 and 1977).

In the former, the process of development is regarded as a series of inevitable stages whereby the correct combination of economic ingredients such as: savings, investments and foreign aid, ultimately enables Third World countries to progress along the economic growth path of the more 'developed' nations. Among academics (but not international bankers), support for this perception has now largely been replaced by an increasingly widespread subscription to structural-internationalist views on development, in which the predicament of the Third World is seen as a product of dual economies and dual societies, both within nations and among them. In this school of thought the response to the plight of the Third World is seen within a context of economic growth and emphasises the eradication of poverty and inequality, the meeting of basic needs and the redistribution of wealth.

Todaro (1981) differentiates between two groups of 'structural-internationalists', namely, between those who subscribe to:

1 The 'neo-colonial dependence' model where the circumstances of the Third World are a consequence of the unequal relation-

ships formed between rich and poor countries during the development of international capitalism.

2 The 'false paradigm model' where the Third World's current predicament is largely attributed, on the one hand, to the well-meant provision of sophisticated but inappropriate kinds of expertise by international development agency advisers, and on the other hand, to the overseas training of Third World public officials. Both are often seen merely to support the existing interests of the domestic and international powers, which in many cases, perpetuate the current inequitable system.

FEATURES OF THIRD WORLD CITY DEVELOPMENT

Urbanisation and city population growth

Urbanisation is the process whereby a settlement's land use, and the activity patterns of the inhabitants shift from dependence on a rural-based economy to a predominantly urban one. Its population characteristics are measured (see Appendix Table 6.3) in terms of:

1 the number of urban inhabitants as a percentage of total population;
2 the growth of urban populations; and
3 the percentage of the total population in cities of given sizes.

The phenomenon is associated with population transfers from rural areas to cities and the inter-sectoral reallocation of resources from subsistence agriculture to the production of non-agricultural goods in urban areas (Richardson, 1977). Trends of urbanisation are therefore directly correlated with a nation's economic development, as many of the changes have led directly to increases in GNP and are closely associated with the development of urban-based industrialisation.

World trends in urbanisation have been increasing extremely rapidly. In the Third World, urbanisation has doubled since the Second World War; since the 1950s it has reached levels at least equal to those in the industrialised world. Third World city populations are currently increasing at almost twice the rate of overall populations (see Appendix Table 6.4). According to the World Bank (1984) half of this increase in the past is attributed to the balance of births over deaths within urban areas, and the remainder both to migration from rural areas and the re-classification of rural areas to urban status.

World Bank sources indicate that Latin America, two-thirds of whose population is urban, contains the largest and the greatest number of urbanised areas in the Third World. Cities such as Sao Paulo and its metropolitan area, and Mexico City are likely to attain populations in excess of 20 million by the end of the century. In contrast, Asia and Africa are still predominantly rural with approximately 25 per cent of their population in urban areas. In Asia, it is anticipated that jumbo cities such as Tokyo, Shanghai and Beijing, will join the league of cities of over 20 million inhabitants by the year 2000.

The largest cities, therefore, will be in Third World countries. Indeed, of the 24 cities which will have populations in excess of 11 million by the year 2000, only four will be in the industrialised world (see Figure 5.2). Nevertheless, it should be emphasised that the proportion of urban to rural inhabitants in the Third World has not dramatically risen, principally because rural populations are also increasing.

Cities, particularly those in the Third World, have been classified in a variety of ways. Stretton (1978), for instance, distinguishes among poor capitalist, poor communist, rich capitalist and rich communist cities. Mabogunje (1980) differentiates among colonial, traditional, and (pre-and post-colonial) industrial cities; while Galbraith (1974) refers to political, household, merchant, industrial and polyglot cities. Since cities are made up of many parts, those in the Third World (especially the largest) do not fit neatly into any one category. Even the type of city currently having the most visible impact on development – the post-colonial industrial city – is quite different from its contemporary counterpart in the industrialised world.

Urbanisation and industrialisation

Urban-based industrialisation as a vehicle for national development, particularly the kind based on 'import-substitution' policies, has become an increasingly dominant economic force in many Third World countries, especially Latin America. The relationship between 'industrialisation' – i.e., the building up of a country's capacity to 'process' raw materials and to 'manufacture' goods for consumption or further production (Todaro, 1981) – and the city,

Figure 5.2 Urban agglomerations with more than ten million inhabitants: 1950, 1975 and 2000

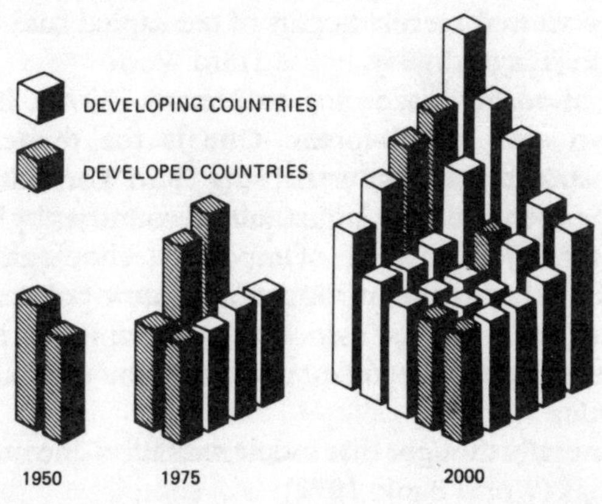

1950	(millions)		(millions)
New York, northeast New Jersey	12.2	London	10.4
1975			
New York, northeast New Jersey	19.8	London	10.4
Mexico City	11.9	Tokyo, Yokohama	17.7
Los Angeles, Long Beach	10.8	Shanghai	11.6
		Sao Paulo	10.7
2000			
Mexico City	31.0	Sao Paulo	25.8
Tokyo, Yokohama	24.2	New York, northeast New Jersey	22.8
Shanghai	22.7	Rio de Janeiro	19.0
Beijing	19.9	Calcutta	16.7
Greater Bombay	17.7	Seoul	14.2
Jakarta	16.6	Cairo, Giza, Imbaba	13.1
Los Angeles, Long Beach	14.2	Bangkok, Thonburi	11.9
Madras	12.9	Delhi	11.7
Greater Buenos Aires	12.1	Paris	11.3
Karachi	11.8	Istanbul	11.2
Bogota	11.7	Osaka, Kobe	11.1
Tehran	11.3		
Baghdad	11.1		

Source: Redrawn from Figure 4.3, World Bank, 1984

is a long-standing one. It was first forged in the nineteenth century in the UK, during the Industrial Revolution. Later, urbanisation was used by some as a surrogate measure of 'industrialisation', and cities were viewed merely as part of the capital base of industrial production (Harris, 1984).

The relationship, according to Roberts (1978), has today released two sets of sub-forces. One is the tendency for the semi-industrialised and industrialising Third World city to accentuate its dependence on the industrialised countries by becoming an increasingly major consumer of imported technologies and luxury goods. The other is the introduction of new political and social influences (and conflicts) associated with capital-intensive industrial activities, and the resultant changes in the economic structure of such cities.

It is generally thought that industrialisation encourages among other things (World Bank, 1972):

1 increased technological innovation (and transfer);
2 the development of managerial and entrepreneurial talent;
3 the improvement of technical skills;
4 increased standardisation in production;
5 a rise in consumerism; and
6 additional demands for urban infrastructure.

Urban industrialisation also contributes to:

1 dramatic changes in urban structure, land prices, and the predominant patterns of land use and tenure;
2 extremely high rates of unemployment and under-employment;
3 increased migration of persons from rural to urban areas; and
4 widespread technology dualism, especially in the sectors of transport and industry.

Characteristics of technology dualism are particularly spectacular in the transport sector of many Asian cities and are well described by Rimmer (1986). Here, traditional and modern modes of transport operate side-by-side, sometimes complementary but in many instances in conflict. Similar features of technology dualism may be noted in the manufacturing sector of these cities. The technology of motorised transport has in fact, had an immense impact on the Third World city. Planners and politicians alike have had great difficulty in coping with the complex ramifications affecting almost all spheres of urban development associated with this kind of movement, as explained by Thomson (1977) in his book *Great Cities and their Traffic*.

These, if not more complex implications for Third World urban development have long been foretold by planners, as a result of the anticipated 'speed-up' of communications and information systems (Meier, 1962). A commonly peddled scenario is for technological advances in these areas to encourage urban decentralisation, and aggravate social inequalities, since the already privileged will gain further access to new opportunities generated by these technological developments.

Urbanisation, modernisation and social change

Just as the hallmark of urban industrialisation in the Third World is the increased economic specialisation and interdependence of productive activities so, the features of modernisation in urban areas are rapid (often institutionalised) changes in patterns of traditional behaviour. Social and economic norms change profoundly and start to resemble those of urban inhabitants of industrialised countries to the point that consumer-oriented values – similar to those in the Western world – take on a greater importance.

Myrdal (1971) summarises the ideals of modernisation as incorporating:

1 the emergence and pursuance of a new (modern) form of rationality;
2 the promotion of the concept of equity; and
3 the encouragement of effective competition, individual enterprise and social and economic mobility.

The old influences of 'Europeanisation' and 'Westernisation' are thus replaced by 'modernisation' which has become a more potent and widespread force for development. Its ideas and values are now disseminated more rapidly and efficiently (usually from urban centres), by cheaper and more comprehensive means of communication, including mass media, more widespread access to education and improved marketing techniques. The enhanced performance of the Third World city in most parts of the globe as a receiver, synthesiser and disseminator of international information and ideas (of the kind the very survival of the city often depends on), has as a result increasingly made modernisation a key force in the development of Third World cities.

Urbanisation, land-use and transport interaction

The city has been depicted by many urban analysts, such as Mitchell and Rapkin (1954), Meier (1962), Webber (1969), and Needham (1977), as a kind of dynamic interface machine of movement (transport), channels of communication (including information) links, serving activities accommodated by the settlement. Such links provide for the needs of industrialisation and commerce, encourage further economic and urban growth, and generally increase the pace of modernisation.

The rapid growth phenomena associated with Third World urbanisation, i.e., population increases, rising vehicle ownership and traffic volumes, increasing land-use densities and expanding areas, have together had the effect of 'speeding-up' urban land-use and transport interaction (see Figure 5.3). This has been experienced to the point that in many cases, traffic 'overload' on transport and communication links result.

Such rapid growth phenomena have also made the management of the Third World city complex, difficult and expensive, as the demand for additional urban space for new activities (and the traffic they generate) introduces severe competition for the use of land. Typically such cities have a total land area of below 10 per cent, and rarely above 15 per cent, allocated to roads. By comparison, in cities in industrialised countries, land allocated to roads is generally 15 to 25 per cent of total land areas; and even up to 30 per cent in newer lower density North American cities (World Bank, 1975).

Traffic problems are often aggravated by newly constructed transport infrastructure intended to improve accessibility but which leads to the displacement to the periphery of traditional means of transport, and economic and commercial activities (especially of the informal sector). In this way, many of the everyday requirements of low-income urban inhabitants are pushed out of the central areas. Within a short period of time, the 'speed-up' of the interaction of land-use and transport/communication brought about by the implementation of such projects has drastically altered the proportions of land-use types within central areas, so that housing land has been reduced, and land for purposes of new

Figure 5.3 The urban land-use transport system

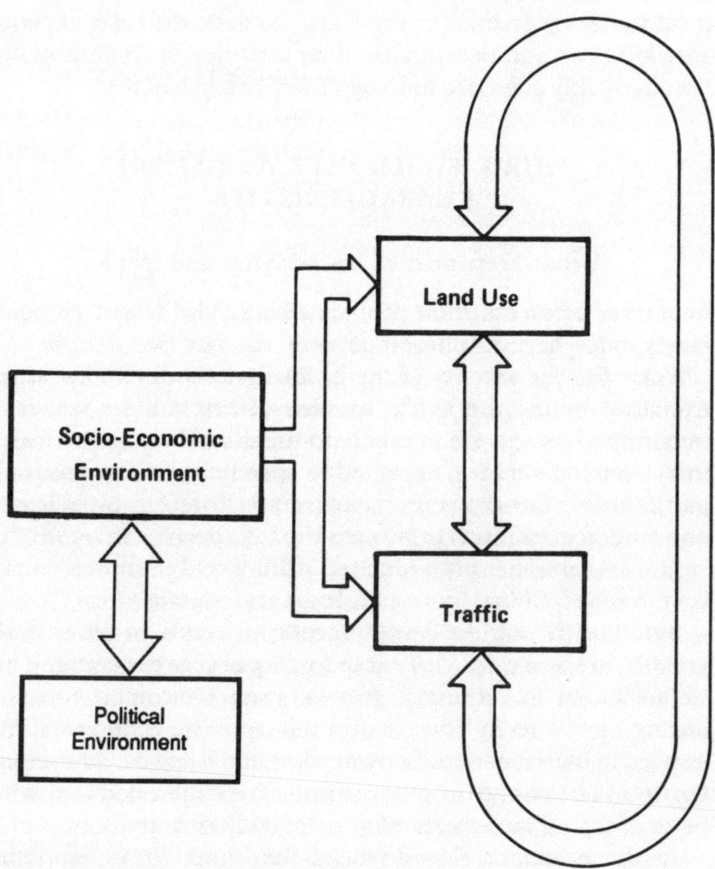

Source: Figure 1.3, Dimitriou, 1990

transport infrastructure, commerce and industry has been increased.

Such developments have been associated with the dramatic increase in cost of land and rents in central areas and the construction of high-rise buildings epitomised by developments in Hong Kong. These buildings in turn, both generate and attract high-density traffic into urban roads with inadequate capacity. They furthermore generate, far more intra-urban travel as people and institutions are unable (or unwilling) to meet the costs of central area locations and decentralise their activities. Such decentralisation inevitably gives rise to longer average trip lengths.

THIRD WORLD CITY TRANSPORT CHARACTERISTICS

Urban transport characteristics and trends

Reports of urban transport problems from Third World (especially large) cities have mushroomed over the last two decades (see Chapter 6). The severity of the problems encountered is in part explained by the rise in the number of automobiles which has outstripped the growth in urban population. These problems are, in the coming decades, expected to become even more serious – particularly in fast-growing cities currently hovering just below the one million mark. Such trends are already apparent in some of the largest and most heavily populated Third World countries, particularly in Brazil, China, Indonesia, India and Nigeria.

Many of the earlier developments in trends of urban traffic growth (in some cases well exceeding 5 per cent per annum), may be attributed to economic growth. Higher incomes, especially during the 1970s in Third World oil-exporting economies, have also led to increased vehicle ownership, the rising consumption of transport goods, and the construction of new infrastructure, which in turn, encouraged the generation of additional traffic.

As the economic slow-down of the Third World economies spread in the late 1980s and into the 1990s, however, urban transport problems in this part of the globe are forecast to become increasingly identified with declining economic growth and even stagnation in the coming decades – particularly so in Africa and Latin America. In such circumstances, the initial transport problems generated by increased vehicle ownership and the construction of new transport facilities are expected, in the face of further urbanisation, to be superseded by issues related to the inadequacy of resources to provide for the maintenance and management of transport services and infrastructure. These problems, already prevalent in low-income cities, are expected to become particularly common in the cities of oil-exporting Third World countries, whose economies have experienced a dramatic decline due to the international fall in oil prices. The difference between the more affluent and poorer Third World countries is thus that in the former, the burden of urban transport maintenance has been considerably increased by investments in urban infrastructure of earlier more prosperous years.

While the economic performance of a country obviously influences city development, the demand for urban transport is also affected by city size and population density (Linn, 1983). Large settlements with lower peripheral population densities tend to increase trip lengths and encourage efforts to raise travel speeds; transport fuel costs are thus increased. Poorly enforced (or non-existent) land-use control regulations have furthermore permitted 'unplanned' development in areas with inadequate urban transport facilities, thereby causing locational traffic congestion.

The provision and pricing of urban public transport services also plays an important role in urban development. The level of government subsidy, the capacity of the public transport system *vis-à-vis* the demand for its services, and the role of the informal transport sector, all have a great bearing on the performance of a city's overall transport system. The level of motorisation and cost of its accommodation are directly correlated with trends in per capita income. Thus, rising incomes share a positive correlation with other features, such as increases in fuel consumption, additional pollution, more road accidents and further environmental disruption (see Newman and Kenworthy, 1989). Conversely, low incomes are related to larger proportions of non-motorised movement, increased pressures for public transport facilities, and a greater likelihood of a reduction of motorisation costs.

Urban transport related costs

Needless to say, the cost of urban movement varies according to the mode of transport used, each of which has its own associated capital, operating, maintenance and foreign exchange costs. All costs are rising, and in some cases considerably (Linn, 1983).

Low-income urban communities throughout the Third World inevitably rely most heavily on the cheapest form of transport, namely, non-motorised movement and particularly walking (Rao and Sharma, 1990). Since such communities are expected to grow, so non-motorised travel – especially walking (and cycle-driven modes particularly in Asia) – will increase in importance for the urban poor. This is inevitable if alternative cheaper motorised public transport is not provided, and despite efforts to restrict the movements of rickshaws in cities such as Jakarta and Calcutta, as well as the actions of more affluent Third World settlements such as Singapore and Hong Kong which have already, for all intents and purposes, cleared rickshaws from the road.

After the cycle rickshaw, motor-cycle/scooter-driven para-transit modes, such as the *bajaj* in Indonesia, are the cheapest mode of transport in terms of operating costs. According to World Bank estimates the next most economic mode is the bus. Minibuses are somewhat more costly than buses, but the reverse often prevails where efficiently run private minibuses run side by side with inefficiently operated public bus companies. Taxis are even more costly. With cars there appears to be a quantum leap to almost four times the cost of a taxi, some eight times the cost of a bus, and 57 times the cost of a bicycle trip (Linn, 1983). Research conducted by Soegijoko (1986) in Indonesia indicates that revenue per passenger kilometre is lowest for the bus and highest for the *bajaj*. Comparing revenue to costs, rickshaws give the highest ratio followed by the bus and the minibus. The lowest ratio of revenue to cost is offered by the *bajaj*.

Statistics on private vehicle operational costs not only show that it is by far the most expensive means of transport, but that it is expected to become more so in the future. The private car, furthermore, consumes approximately nine times more road space per passenger than does a bus (Linn, 1983) and requires proportionately much heavier investment in the maintenance of roads than do buses. The considerable flexibility provided by the mode to its user is thus furnished at a very high premium and at considerable opportunity cost, particularly if one includes associated foreign exchange costs.

Urban rail transport systems, of which there are various kinds, are usually confined to main traffic corridors and are not suitable for distributing passengers throughout secondary and tertiary transport networks. At one extreme there are the light rail transit systems, such as trams, which share the roadway with other users, and at the other extreme are the highest capacity exclusive right of way urban rail and metro systems. Exclusive right of way light rail systems can, according to the World Bank (1986) cope with peak hour volumes of 36,000 passengers per hour, while metro systems have been reported to achieve 60,000 passengers an hour in each direction. According to the same source, light rail systems with exclusive rights of way cost in the region of US$ 0.10 to US$ 0.15 million per passenger kilometre to operate, and between US$ 6 million and US$ 10 million per kilometre to construct for ground level systems. Elevated systems cost between US$ 25 million and US$ 40 million and underground networks can cost up to US$ 40 million per kilometre. This compares to between US$ 30 million and US$ 40 million per kilometre for underground or elevated urban rail and metro structures; and even US$ 65 million to US$ 100 million per kilometre where 'cut and cover' methods of construction are required.

Clearly, the above costs (especially their foreign exchange costs) can only be warranted along high density corridors and in cities of particular sizes with significant proportions of populations who find the services offered affordable. Rapid transit proposals for Madras and Calcutta have both been questioned on this basis. The ongoing debate between planners and rail transit hardware manufacturers as to the minimum settlement size for different rail systems has also raised issues of contention. This was perhaps most graphically illustrated by the case of the rapid transit system proposal for Penang which has a population of 720,000. There was a clear conflict of views between the consultants proposing the system and city planners who maintained that the population size did not warrant it.

Urban transport systems

To talk of urban transport 'systems' in many Third World cities may seem to imply a greater degree of integration and co-ordination of transport modes than in reality exists. Nevertheless, co-ordination among traditional and modern, as well as informal and formal transport operations, does take place, although with varying degrees of efficiency. The structure, mix and organisation of such working relationships are, however, more a product of the evolution of the city in question, and less an outcome of the city's management and investment programmes. They generally reflect the transport needs (over time) of those who extensively use the systems.

In any urban transport system different modes often complement and compete with each other. They have different associated costs and benefits for the user and non-user, and are often associated with a variety of operators. The complementary characteristics are those which facilitate the interchange of modes, so that a combination of transport means provides coverage of a given area and accommodates the needs of different markets. Competition exhibits the contest between modes for patronage of the same routes and/or geographical area.

Many Third World cities contain a rich mixture of traditional and modern modes of transport (see White, 1990; and Rao and Sharma, 1990). In some places, they share the same routes and, although competing for road space, cater for different market segments of the public. However, where the market can stand it, there is keen competition among most motorised modes of transport, especially between formally and informally operated systems. This commonly occurs where the capacity of the former is unable to meet the demands made upon it, or where it is too costly for the majority of would-be passengers to patronise. One might conclude from this that the wider the range of transport modes offered and the greater the spectrum of income brackets accommodated, the more effective the transport system; and that diversity reflects the response to changing transport demands of different urban areas and groups. Many Third World city officials, however, do not consider diversity an asset. Instead, given a city's limited capacity to accommodate growing motorised traffic volumes, traditional and informal transport modes are often considered 'obstacles' to the modernisation (read 'motorisation') of the transport system.

In an increasing number of cities such as Mexico City, Cairo and Hong Kong, the range of transport systems has been enhanced relatively recently by the construction of metro schemes to relieve the traffic pressure on city road systems. Solutions of this kind are, however, far beyond the available resources of many other urban areas of the Third World.

Functions of urban transport systems

The significance of urban transport systems lies in their provision of linkages between points of residence and employment, their contribution to the economies of scale and specialisation of urban-based activities (particularly industrial and commercial activities), the employment opportunities they offer to the inhabitants of settlements, and their impact on geographical growth and urban form. Acknowledgement of the importance of urban transport to development has been a relatively recent affair. It was not until 1972, for example, that the World Bank became involved in urban transport projects. However, with rising levels of urbanisation in the Third World and with cities performing an increasingly recognised productive function in the development of this part of the globe, the influential role of urban transport has grown and is expected to grow further.

This expectation is reflected in the recent international development agency lending programme for urban transport. In the case of the World Bank, for example, from 1972 to 1985, 17 urban transport projects were approved, and another 32 urban projects had significant transport components. The total investment in the first set of projects amounted to US$ 1,900 million (of which the Bank financed US$ 800 million). Transport components in the second type of project cost US$ 520 million (of which US$ 240 million was financed by the Bank). Together, approval for the total financial participation of the agency over the 13 year period amounted to US$ 1,040 million (World Bank, 1986), with an average annual investment of US$ 148.6 million per annum. This compares with earlier calculated average annual investments of US$ 29.6 million between 1970 and 1974.

With World Bank estimates of rates of return on such projects having substantially increased over the years, and with urban areas of Third World countries contributing between 50 and 70 per cent of gross national product (GNP) to the economies of these nations, the agency has been encouraged to invest further in urban transport. The World Bank has thus embarked upon numerous additional projects.

Because the growing priority assigned to urban transport has been accompanied (in real terms) by declining available funds – aspects of transport systems operations, management, finance (especially cost recovery) and improvement now receive more attention than new road construction. These circumstances call for a clearer appreciation of the diverse tasks of urban transport (and their relative costs) before decisions are taken concerning the allocation of scarce resources to the sector. Two particular aspects of urban transport systems development need to be considered. One is the relative importance of current urban development activities serviced by transport, the other is the compatibility of urban development goals and policies with those assigned to the transport system.

TRANSPORT AND URBAN DEVELOPMENT GOALS

Urban transport efficiency

Urban activities serviced by transport systems are those of internal importance to the settlement, as well as those of significance to the city's function as a national and/or regional transport/communication centre. While this particular chapter focuses more on the latter, it must be appreciated that the two functions are closely interrelated and often inseparable.

Given these dual functions, an obligation of urban transport planning is to enhance the efficiency of urban transport systems, not only to respond to locally generated movement requirements, but also to relate to the country's national urban development strategy (where one exists). Such a strategy should indicate: the phasing of transport investments in relation to other aspects of national urban policy, the preferred transport inter-modal mix, the use of transport as a tool of spatial development policy, and the role of urban transport in national urban policy-making (Gakenheimer, 1986). In so doing, it would offer guidelines as to how better to ensure that urban transport investments are 'developmentally effective', economically and 'operationally efficient', and justified in relation to opportunity costs to other sector investments.

The evolution of urban transport systems can be said both to respond to, as well as to (belatedly) adapt to, changing basic needs (and aspirations) of urban activities – namely households, firms and institutions – as they attempt to maximise their accessibility to other dependent activities. The operation and development of a city's transport systems are also influenced by the organisational structure and geographical distribution of a settlement's major activities, and institutionalised and cultural norms and routines associated with their development. It is these latter considerations especially which make Third World city transport characteristics so different from those of the industrialised world.

The provision of urban transport facilities to meet the most basic of needs, however, is a major problem in many Third World cities – especially in the low-income countries (see Chapter 6). This is particularly so, as the same transport system has other tasks to perform which are often considered to be of greater economic importance. It is obliged, for example, to provide commerce and industry with opportunities for transporting raw materials to points of urban production. It must also distribute the services and goods of commerce and industry to markets within and outside the city, as well as to points of transport interchange for locations further afield.

In seeking to provide for these varied needs, Third World cities are faced with a conflict between catering for increased productivity of the urban economy (with the rising costs of expanding urban transport sufficiently to ensure continued economic growth), and catering for the under-privileged who depend on cheap means of travel to expand their opportunities. Additional influential factors which have a detrimental effect on the efficient use of transport systems include:

1 the rapid geographical spread of urban areas which encourages both longer trip-making and the generation of additional demands for ill affordable peripheral transport facilities;
2 inadequate traffic restraint and management efforts pursued by governments which fail to contain trends of the increased indiscriminate use of motorised (especially private car) transport in urban areas; and
3 the employment of ineffective development control measures and urban transport planning efforts by municipal agencies which allow major traffic generators and land-use developments to take place at locations which are incompatible with transport facility provision.

It is in this context and against an economic background of limited resources that low-cost efforts at urban traffic management and transport planning become significant (see Proudlove and Turner, 1990; and Gakenheimer and Meyer, 1990). For they are attempts at managing and planning urban movement with a view to fulfilling better both the needs of inhabitants and of the city's economy.

Changing urban development policies

Any assessment of Third World city transport systems must ultimately be made against some measure of performance that can realistically be expected of it, rather than against standards taken from the industrialised world. The degree of multi-purposeness of an urban transport system, and the level of integration offered to its component parts are, for example, far more important to Third World city development than any degree of technological modernisation it may appear to offer.

In the 1970s, in response to the agenda of Third World city development problems, more enlightened approaches to urban development planning sought to (see Safier, 1981):

1 sustain per capita growth of income in real terms;
2 eradicate poverty;
3 decrease inequalities of income distributions;
4 provide additional urban capacity to absorb rural migrants; and
5 lessen inequalities in urban services provision.

In addition to the above, to ensure that basic needs were met, some later efforts at urban development planning attempted not only to utilise resources more efficiently but simultaneously to mobilise local authority resources and power.

Changes of thought on urban development planning have, according to Safier, thus (very slowly) reflected the shifting emphasis of ideas among national and regional development planners, and (some) economists. So that, whereas in the past they saw development as synonymous with economic growth, today, there is a greater awareness of the inadequacies of the economic growth concept without some consideration of equity, and the consolidation of local (especially informal sector) resources.

The emphasis by international agencies such as the International Labour Office (ILO) and other United Nations agencies on meeting basic needs (see UN Secretariat, 1977), together with the increased concern for the urban poor by the World Bank, led in the early and mid–1980s to an apparent change in direction of goals and policies to be pursued for Third World development. The extent to which urban and transport planning practioners have been able (and willing) to adopt the same spirit, however, is open to debate. For professionals in these fields have typically been obliged to be more pragmatic and come to terms more with the constraints of everyday local political trade-offs, as well as influential industrial and commercial pressures, many of which are contrary to the above espoused spirit of urban development planning. Recent moves by the World Bank and many Third World governments to introduce or improve upon project cost recovery

Figure 5.4 Changing concepts of development in urban transport planning

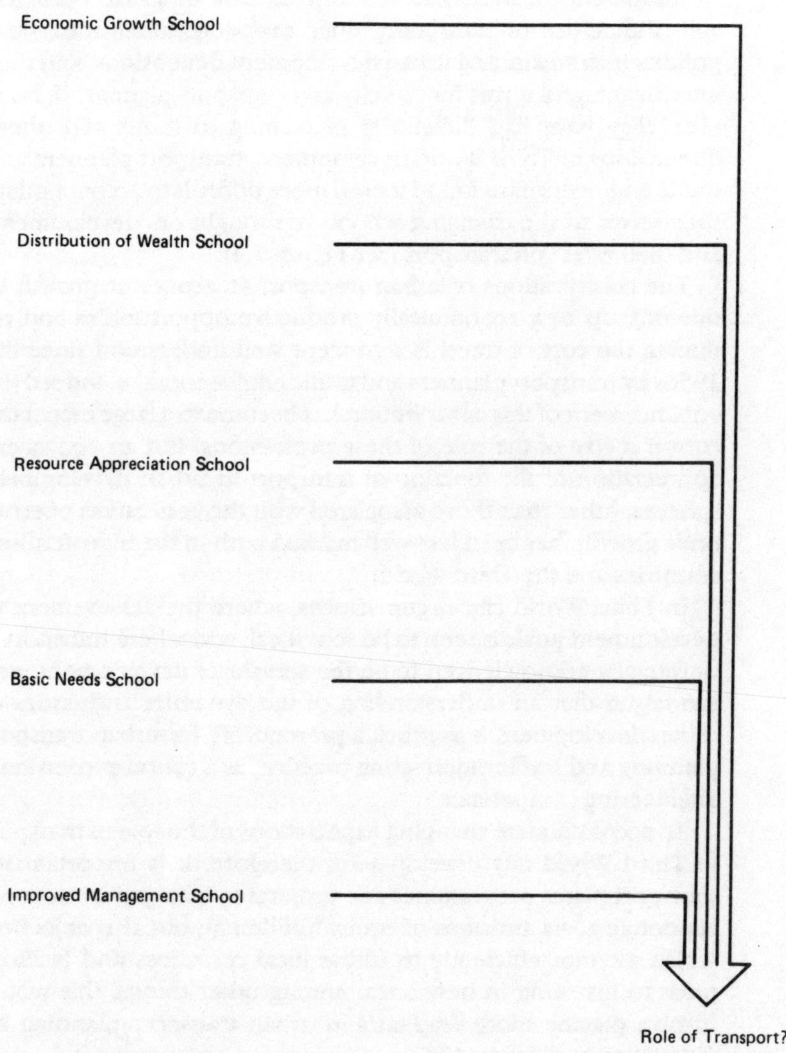

Source: Modified from Figure 1.5: Dimitriou and Safier, 1982

concepts and enhanced urban management efforts have merely added to these constraints.

Changing expectations of the role of urban transport

Development planners and economists have long had considerable difficulties in translating their macroeconomic ideas and policies into spatial and urban development dimensions, and thus into meaningful terms for the city and transport planner. If, however, *they* have had difficulties in coming to terms with these dimensions of Third World development, transport planners and traffic engineers have found it even more difficult to accommodate themselves to the changing schools of thought on 'development' and their effect on transport (see Figure 5.4).

The contributions of urban transport to economic growth in opening up new economically productive opportunities and reducing the cost of travel is a concept well understood since the 1950s by transport planners and traffic engineers alike. Indeed the enhancement of this contribution has become to a large extent the *raison d'être* of the role of these professions. But an equivalent appreciation of the function of transport in urban development spheres, other than those associated with the generation of economic growth, has been less well marked both in the industrialised countries and the Third World.

In Third World city circumstances, where the achievement of development goals is seen to be so critical, and where transport is universally acknowledged to be the servant of development, one can argue that an understanding of the dynamics and issues of urban development is as much a prerequisite for urban transport planning and traffic engineering practice, as a sound professional engineering competence.

To accommodate changing expectations of the role of transport in Third World city development, therefore, it is important for transport plans, programmes and projects to incorporate not only economic goals and aims of equity fulfillment, but also objectives which attempt efficiently to utilise local resources and facilities prior to investing in new ones. Among other things, this would involve placing more emphasis in urban transport planning on (Dimitriou and Safier, 1982):

1 the mobilisation of new resources – through, for example,

improved city staff administrative and technical manpower training efforts, and greater utilisation of private sector resources;

2 the incorporation (and thereby recognition) of the roles of the informal and traditional sectors of transport – in a manner whereby both contribute positively to an integrated and financially more viable urban transport system; and

3 the measurement and monitoring of costs and benefits of transport proposals – against cost recovery requirements and the needs of the full spectrum of income groups they are expected to serve.

In so doing, the conventional wisdom of urban transport planning may thus be reorientated toward the planning of transport specifically for Third World urban development rather than the planning of urban transport systems *per se*. The chapters that follow offer some insights and ideas on how such a reorientation may be achieved.

6

TRANSPORT PROBLEMS OF THIRD WORLD CITIES

INTRODUCTION

Although rapid motorisation growth rates have been most commonly associated with the deteriorating conditions of urban transport systems in the Third World, high rates of urbanisation and related changes to the economic base of settlements in this part of the globe are in fact the more influential contributing factors[1]. What is especially important about these trends is that they have taken place in settlements which are foci in their respective countries of forces of modernisation, industrialisation and technology-transfer, and thus constitute very important centres of local, national and regional development.

Between 1970 and 1980, populations of Third World urban areas increased by an average of 50 per cent and are expected by the year 2000 to accommodate approximately 2.2 billion of the globe's population (World Bank, 1986). Such developments are fuelled by rising natural population growth, as well as rapid migration increases to the city, especially of persons in search of employment from rural areas. Urbanisation is further encouraged by the concentration of wealth, the enhancement of development opportunities in urban locations, and the resultant physical expansion of city land areas and infrastructure. Together, these conditions have brought about a widespread rise in urban land values and new ways of life, very different from those of the traditional indigenous cultures.

The accompanying changes in the economic base of many Third World cities – brought about by a transition of a settlement's economic base from one previously geared toward serving a colonial nation, to one increasingly integrated into today's world market – have been encouraged by more aggressive sales practices and by vastly improved international transport, telecommunication and information systems.

In this chapter two sets of Third World urban transport problems are discussed: those traditionally included on the agenda of national and city governments, such as traffic congestion and related environmental impacts, inefficient public transport operations, high road accident rates, weak institutional support, limited management and enforcement capability, etc. ; and those associated with the planning and management response to urban movement needs, involving perception issues of problem identification, differing technology-transfer priorities in problem resolution, and varied approaches to urban transport decision-making. The two sets of problems are often inseparable, particularly in the long run, when some existing traffic problems become aggravated by, or are in part attributable to, misconceived planning and management responses.

An additional method of differentiating among various kinds of urban transport problems is to distinguish between those which may be considered 'root problems' such as, rising incomes and car ownership levels, and 'manifestation problems' which include widespread traffic congestion and rising traffic accidents (see Figure 6.1). Poor planning or management responses to transport problems may in fact be regarded as a particular kind of 'root problem'; an aspect discussed in greater depth in the last part of this chapter.

TRADITIONAL AGENDA OF URBAN TRANSPORT PROBLEMS

Transport problems of Third World cities inevitably take on a variety of forms, depending upon their location, associated wealth and levels of motorisation. For most such problems are also a product of differing broader Third World national and urban development characteristics of the kind outlined in the preceding chapter. Nevertheless, it is common for Third World city governments to present a common agenda of transport problems of the kind discussed below.

Figure 6.1: Urban transport manifestation and root problems

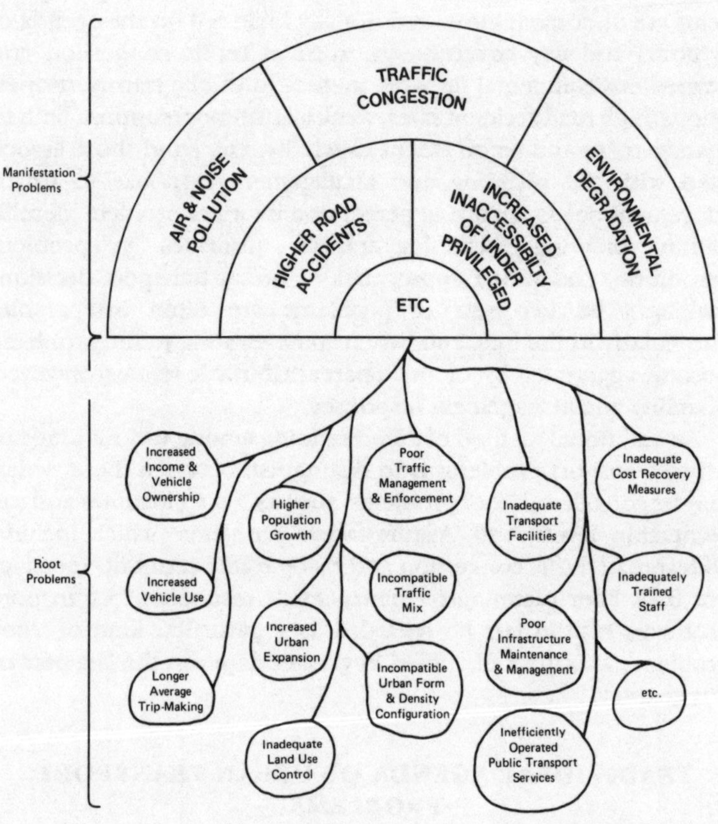

Source: Figure 2.1, Dimitriou, 1990

Rapid traffic growth

While motorisation in most Third World settlements is at relatively low levels in comparison with many cities in the industrialised world,[2] its availability has sharply increased in recent decades. The number of vehicles per 1,000 population between 1970 and 1981,

Figure 6.2 **Income and car ownership**

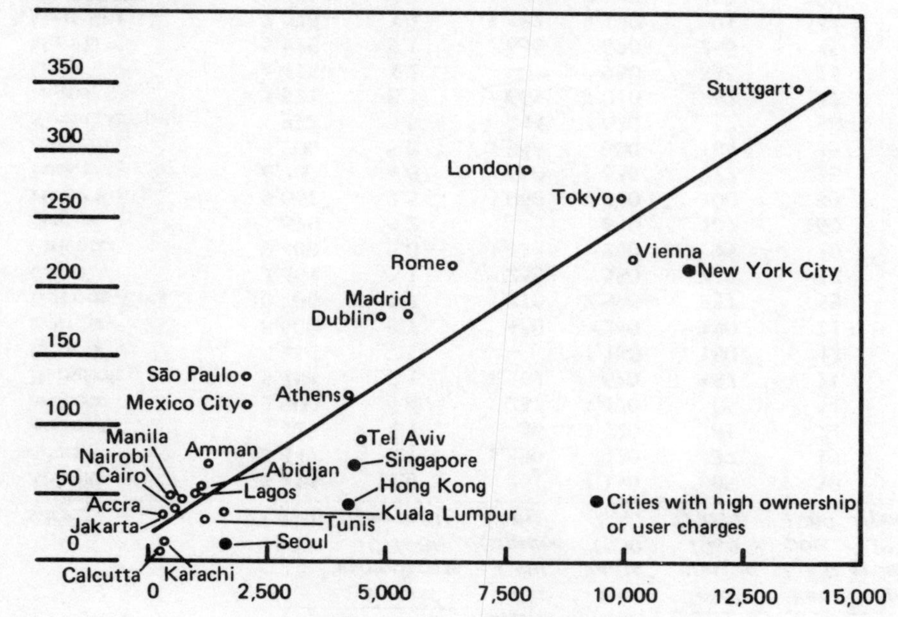

***Source*: Redrawn from Figure 4, World Bank, 1986**

Table 6.1 Urban transport data: selected cities

City	Population		Metro area 1980 (square km)	GNP per capita[a] 1980 (US$)	Cars			Buses		Commercial vehicles 1980 (number)
	1980 (1,000)	Annual growth rate 1970–80 (per cent)			Total number 1980 (1,000)	Per 1,000 pop. 1980	Annual growth rate 1970–80 (per cent)	Total number 1980	Per 1,000 pop 1980[c]	
Abidjan	1,175	11.0	261	1,150	85	50	10.0	2,410	1.41	–
Accra	1,447	6.7	1,390	420	27	19	–	709	0.49*	7,411
Amman	1,125	4.1	36	1,420	81	72	–	433	0.38*	32,000
Ankara	1,900	4.4	237	1,470	65	34	14.2	781	0.41*	–
Bangkok	5,154	9.1	1,569	670	367	71	7.9	6,300	1.22	34,155
Bogota	4,254	7.1	–	1,180	180	42	7.8	9,081	2.13	–
Bombay	8,500	3.7	438	240	180	21	6.1	3,066	0.36*	38,447
Buenos Aires	10,100	1.7	210	2,390	537	53	10.0	12,089	1.20	97,245
Cairo	7,464	3.1	233	580	239	32	17.0	8,177	1.10	42,000
Calcutta	9,400	3.0	1,414	240	95	10	5.6	3,160	0.33*	28,500
Harare	670	5.2	–	630	107	160	3.0	504	0.75	5,300
Hong Kong	5,067	2.5	1,060	4,240	200	39	7.4	9,278	1.83	58,801
Jakarta	6,700	4.0	650	430	222	33	9.8	4,798	0.72	77,781
Karachi	5,200	5.2	1,346	300	184	35	8.4	12,064	2.32	17,628
Kuala Lumpur	977	3.5	244	1,620	37	38	–	1,148	1.18	7,923
Lagos	1,321	8.1	665	1,010	62	47	–	–	–	58,857
Lima	4,415	4.2	–	930	333	75	7.2	8,853	2.01	1,060
Manila	5,925	5.1	636	690	266	45	8.0	31,403	5.30	100,725
Medellin	2,078	3.2	1,152	1,180	91	44	–	4,800	2.31	10,800
Mexico City	15,056	5.0	1,479	2,090	1,577	105	–	18,500	1.23	155,500
Nairobi	1,275	8.8	690	420	60	47	–	1,100	0.86	–
Rio de Janeiro	9,200	2.4	6,464	2,050	957	104	12.1	11,000	1.20	95,945

Table 6.1 Continued

City	Population 1980 (1,000)	Population Annual growth rate 1970–80 (per cent)	Metro area 1980 (square km)	GNP per capita[a] 1980 (US$)	Cars Total number 1980 (1,000)	Cars Per 1,000 pop. 1980	Cars Annual growth rate 1970–80 (per cent)	Buses Total number 1980	Buses Per 1,000 pop 1980[c]	Commercial vehicles 1980 (number)
San Jose, C.R.	637	3.5	180	1,730	–	–	–	500	0.78	–
Sao Paulo	12,800	4.5	1,493	2,050	1,935	151	7.8	16,400	1.28	240,000
Seoul	8,366	5.0	627	1,520	127	15	11.7	13,000	1.55	63,222
Singapore	2,413	1.5	618	4,430	164	68	6.8	6,512	2.70	78,038
Tunis	1,230	6.4	115	1,310	38	31	–	642	0.52	–

Source: Modified from Table A.1, World Bank, 1986

Notes:
– Not available
a. National data.
b. Some cities have a substantial proportion of pedestrian trips not reflected in the motorised data.
c. Figures with asterisk indicate levels of bus provision considered by the World Bank to be below satisfactory levels.

for example, increased twofold in Brazil, threefold in Indonesia, fivefold in Nigeria and seven to tenfold in Korea (World Bank, 1986). These trends received a particular impetus in the early 1980s during the downturn of the motor industry in the industrialised world, when international vehicle manufacturers marketed their products more aggressively and entered into many more agreements to build motor vehicle assembly plants in the Third World.

The most notable growth in traffic in many Third World cities has been of motorcycle vehicles. Statistics in Southeast Asia, for example, show that in 1980 more than 60 per cent of the registered vehicles in Jakarta and Kuala Lumpur were motorcycles. Between 1980 and 1982 alone, Bangkok and Jakarta had their motorcycle modal split share increased by 29 and 15 per cent respectively, to 62 and 81 per cent. Comparable 1983 estimates for Kuala Lumpur indicate a 7 per cent rise since 1980 and a 1987 modal split share of 73 per cent (Spencer, 1988). Other aspects of traffic growth and congestion in Asia are discussed in some depth in a recent editorial for *Asia Magazine* (1990).

Rapid traffic growth in the Third World (especially of motorised movement) is concentrated primarily in the larger cities (see Table 6.1). It has been largely stimulated both by increased incomes (see Figure 6.2) and an overall expansion in related urban economic activities. Many Third World settlements have, furthermore, generated additional use of transport by virtue of their physical growth which has encouraged longer trip distances, rising in the case of Bogota by an average of 13 per cent between 1972 and 1978 (World Bank, 1986). Interesting work on this aspect of transport development has been conducted by Zahavi (1976 and 1980).

As a result of their population increase, Third World cities have also generated a growth in transport demand which is roughly proportional to their urban population increase (see Figure 6.3). Additional transport demand has in some cities been further created by improved transport infrastructure and service provision.

Shortage of adequately maintained transport facilities

The traffic growth described above has taken place at a pace far in excess of the rate of investment in suitably constructed and maintained urban transport infrastructure. This in turn has contributed to both widespread and location-specific congestion problems.

Figure 6.3 **Population and total daily trips**

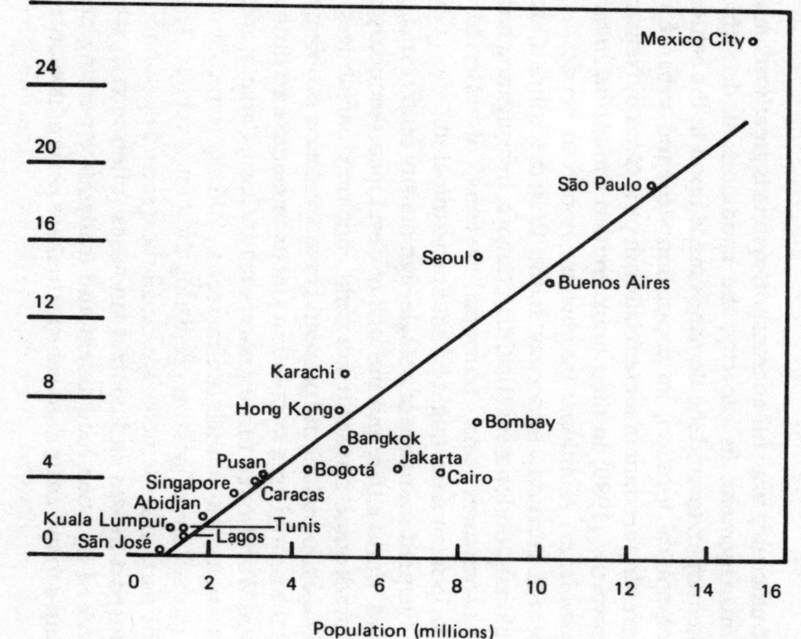

***Source*: Redrawn from Figure 2, World Bank, 1986**

Circumstances of this kind are typically a result of insufficient funds allocated to the urban transport sector and the absence of appropriate fund-raising mechanisms by which public authorities are able to raise adequate finance from those who benefit most from the transport facilities. In Indonesia, the issue of cost recovery and public sector income generation to service urban transport became a major issue during the formulation of its Fifth Five Year National Plan (1989–94).

It is not uncommon for urban public authorities to spend between 15 and 20 per cent of their annual budgets on transport related investments and operations. In some instances, the proportion is even higher, as in Calcutta, where it is reported that between 1972 and 1978, the equivalent of 48 per cent of the city's total planned investment was spent on transport (World Bank 1986).[3]

Transport systems efficiency and settlement structures

The efficiency of an urban transport system is greatly influenced by its management, its capacity, the conditions under which the system operates and the demands made upon it, the settlements' geographical location, its population size, and urban form. An interesting account of these relationships is given by Newman and Kenworthy (1989) in their book entitled *Cities and Automobile Dependency*. Additional insights are hoped to be derived from research currently underway at the United Nations Centre for Regional Development (UNCRD), Nagoya, investigating how land-use structures and transport systems of selected Asian metropolitan areas might be better co-ordinated.

The predominance of a single high-density central area in most Third World cities, and the lack of developed secondary centres with adequate transport networks, not only encourages longer average trip-making but presents grave circulation problems – both for the central area in question and its immediate environs. Many Third World cities, furthermore, such as Cairo, Caracas, and Delhi, encompass within their central area an 'old city', typically made up of narrow street systems pre-dating the motor vehicle. These historic parts of settlements are usually best served by non-motorised transport modes and contain land-uses (often mixed) which are serviced by poor road access and inadequate parking areas. Attempts to use motorised vehicles in these parts of the city not only create localised traffic congestion but often also affect the overall traffic circulation of the settlement.

Equally and increasingly important are considerations of the environmental impact of traffic movement, particularly in areas of significant architectural heritage (often these same 'old city areas') and where residential populations are adversely affected by traffic (air and noise) pollution, visual intrusion, structural vibration and community disruption. Unfortunately, these negative environmental impacts of transport in Third World cities typically receive little attention, as may be observed in Lagos, Jakarta and Mexico City. However, newly established environmental protection agencies in more affluent Third World settlements, such as Hong Kong and Singapore, are now beginning to play a more active role.

Urban transport technology mix and misuse

The mix of (especially old and new) transport technologies, highlighted by the sharing of road space by fast-moving motorised vehicles with slow-moving human-powered and animal-drawn vehicles (such as rickshaws, hand-drawn carts and animal-drawn vehicles), typifies many street scenes in the Third World (see Rao and Sharma, 1990; Proudlove and Turner, 1990; and Urban Edge, 1990a). In addition to the traffic conflict, road congestion and road safety problems commonly ascribed to these conditions, there is evidence of widespread technological abuse of transport modes. For some vehicles (particularly the motorcar) are used for trip distances and purposes for which they are not operationally the most efficient.

Research into the operational efficiency of various transport modes carried out by the Battelle Institute in Geneva (Bouladon, 1967a and 1967b) presented the misuse of transport technology as a significant contributor to transport problems in cities in industrialised countries. The research identified two 'transport gaps', one associated with the misuse of the car for inappropriate distances, the other to do with the shortage of suitable transport modes to service trip distances of between 0.3 and three miles.

A similar abuse of the motorcar, but in the Third World, was observed in a study of the use of different transport modes in various Indonesian cities (TDC SA, 1988). The study recommended policy and design guidelines (also adopted in the approach to urban transport planning advocated in Chapters 8 and 9) to encourage the most appropriate and efficient use of transport technologies in accordance with (among other things), trip distance, trip purpose and city size considerations. Unlike the Battelle Institute research, the Indonesian study noted a considerable choice of local transport modes efficiently serving trip distances of between 0.3 and three miles. However, many such modes are increasingly in danger of being marginalised by traffic enforcement efforts on the one hand, and by the sheer growth of motorised traffic on the other.

Ineffective traffic management and enforcement

Given the rapid growth rates of urban traffic and problems caused by such factors as: widespread poor driver behaviour, inadequately maintained vehicles and infrastructure, the lack of regard for traffic regulations, the common absence of adequate road signs and markings, and a growth of uncontrolled street hawker activities, more is expected from traffic enforcement in Third World cities today than ever before. The resultant need to make city transport systems more efficient through selected traffic management and control measures, including: the installation and maintenance of traffic control signals, the re-routeing of traffic, the designation of one-way street systems, and the banning of conflicting turns, have placed a great deal of pressure on traffic enforcement agencies, in excess of the resources at their disposal (World Bank, 1986).

The burden on such institutions has been further aggravated in some instances by the introduction of sophisticated measures and traffic control technologies for which they have been inadequately prepared. In Bangkok, for example, a computerised Area Traffic Control (ATC) scheme was introduced in the late 1970s by the City's Traffic Engineering Unit. By virtue of a whole series of pre-installation oversights in the dissemination of the function and workings of this scheme, it is claimed that the operational relationship between the Traffic Police and Municipality deteriorated, because members of the former agency felt their on-street enforcement powers had been undermined by the introduction of the scheme. As a result of this, it is said that traffic police personnel regularly override the computerised system on more occasions than necessary, thereby defeating the very purpose of the installation of the traffic control system.

Insufficient public transport services

Deficiencies of urban public transport in the Third World can be largely attributed both to the pace of urbanisation outstripping that of public sector investment in passenger transport services, and to the poor co-ordination among constituent parts of the public transport system. This in turn has contributed to the poor maintenance of vehicles, insufficient supply of buses, and inadequate provision of public transport service frequencies and routes. Table 6.1 shows transport data for selected cities of the Third World and highlights those which in accordance with World Bank guidelines (Armstrong-Wright, 1986) are deemed to have inadequate public transport facilities. The cities were chosen on the basis that they have fewer than one bus per 2000 persons and include Accra, Ankara, Amman, Bombay, and Calcutta.

Another indicator of the adequacy/inadequacy of urban public transport systems is the proportion of the vehicle fleet available for service. It has been suggested (Armstrong-Wright, 1986) that anything less than 70 per cent during peak periods is unsatisfactory (see Table 6.2). In reality, however, the availability of buses can range from as low as 24 per cent of the total fleet (as in Accra), to a more usual 63 per cent (as in Jakarta), and even as high as 95 per cent (as in Guatemala City).

Transport problems of the urban poor

Access to transport facilities in Third World cities is particularly important for the poor. The poor are those whose income is typically less than US$ 275–370 per annum, depending upon the country in question (see World Bank, 1990), and which is insufficient to provide them with basic shelter and nutrition. They are thus at the margin of subsistence which as Linn (1983) points out, makes them very sensitive to disruptions in earnings brought about by inadequate transport policies. Transport-related problems among urban low-income groups are exacerbated by rising transport costs and the subsequent growing need for the poor to travel longer distances in search of employment (often due to their residential displacement to the periphery). Such circumstances hamper their opportunities to engage in and contribute to economic activities of the city.

Issues of social justice in the provision of urban transport are

Table 6.2 Bus services: city comparisons, 1983 (covering principal corporation or group of private operators in each city does not include paratransit.)

	City	*Ownership*	*Number of buses (1)*	*Availability (%) (2)*	*km per operating bus per day*	*Staff per operating bus*	*Passengers per operating bus per day*	*Annual operating cost (US $ mill) (3)*	*Total cost per passenger kilometre (4)*	*Annual operating revenue (US $ mill) (5)*	*Fare (typical, 5 km) (US $)*	*Ratio operating revenue/ total costs (6)*
1	Abidjan	Mixed	1,044	85	183	7.1	829	91.29	0.07	69.40	0.26	0.67
2	Accra	Public	44	24*	292	28.1	2,092	1.03	0.03	0.63	0.13	0.51
3	Accra	Private	665	73	223	5.5	676	10.43	0.04	17.72	0.18	1.37
4	Addis Ababa	Public	164	58*	205	13.1	2,467	7.96	0.02	6.59	0.07	0.67
5	Ankara	Public	899	67*	210	5.8	1,273	25.62	0.01	15.31	0.14	0.48
6	Bombay	Public	2,325	92	216	14.0	2093	81.95	0.01	72.97	0.05	0.77
7	Cairo	Public	2,454	69*	246	14.6	2,417	60.41	0.01	36.19	0.07	0.50
8	Calcutta	Public	981	64*	133	18.0	1,641	23.05	0.01	13.09	0.04	0.45
9	Dakar	Mixed	439	70	287	9.6	1,193	22.97	0.04	20.41	0.26	0.76
10	Guatemala City	Private	1,600	95	304	–	1,037	29.00	0.02	54.60	0.10	1.55
11	Hong Kong	Private	2,392	85	243	4.7	1,610	117.96	0.03	136.10	0.13	1.00
12	Karachi	Public	646	65*	267	9.9	1,135	11.73	0.01	6.73	0.04	0.43
13	Kuala Lumpur	Private	358	80	250	4.3	753	12.03	0.02	12.38	0.17	1.00
14	Mombasa	Mixed	89	90	315	7.5	1,640	3.93	0.03	4.48	0.11	0.96
15	Nairobi	Mixed	295	84	330	9.7	1,762	16.31	0.03	17.98	0.15	1.08
16	Porto Alegre	Private	1,492	95	218	4.3	669	46.68	0.05	65.35	0.23	1.17
17	San Jose	Mixed	621	80	128	–	2,013	19.39	0.02	24.24	0.07	1.04
18	Sao Paulo	Public	2,631	83	284	7.4	795	159.51	0.03	75.64	0.26	0.41

Table 6.2 Continued

	City	Ownership	Number of buses (1)	Availability (%) (2)	km per operating bus per day	Staff per operating bus	Passengers per operating bus per day	Annual operating cost (US $ mill) (3)	Total cost per passenger kilometre (4)	Annual operating revenue (US $ mill) (5)	Fare (typical, 5 km) (US $)	Ratio operating revenue/ total costs (6)
19	Sao Paulo	Private	6,590	83	280	5.1	765	–	–	–	0.26	1.00(5)
20	Seoul	Private	8,310	95	340	3.9	1,326	398.18	0.03	443.43	0.16	1.04
21	Singapore	Private	2,859	91	269	3.9	374	110.23	0.10	147.75	0.24	1.32

Source: Modified from Table 11.2, Armstrong-Wright, 1986

Notes:

1. Number of buses belonging to the principal corporation or group of private operators covered by the survey. The total number of buses operated in the city as a whole is given in Annex I.
2. Figures with asterisk are availability percentages (at peak period) considered by the World Bank to be below satisfactory levels.
3. Operating costs excluding depreciation and interest charges.
4. Total costs including operating costs, depreciation and interest charges. For comparative purposes a uniform method to determine depreciation and interest charges has been used to obtain total costs. Passenger kilometres are imputed using an average trip length of five kilometres.
5. Operating revenue including fare box and advertising revenue but excluding subsidies.
6. Cost and revenue data for Sao Paulo private operators are not available; however, private operators receive no subsidy from the government and are known to at least break even.

not exclusive to Third World cities. They have also been highlighted in industrialised countries (see Hillman, 1975). The scale and severity of the problem in the Third World, however, is much greater and more widespread. For the urban poor in this part of the globe can constitute more than 50 per cent of a city's population, as in Calcutta and Madras. Estimates in Latin America suggest that the income of between 20 and 30 per cent of the urban population is insufficient for the adequate provision of food and shelter, and if households with fluctuating incomes on the fringes

Figure 6.4 Typology of accessibility problems

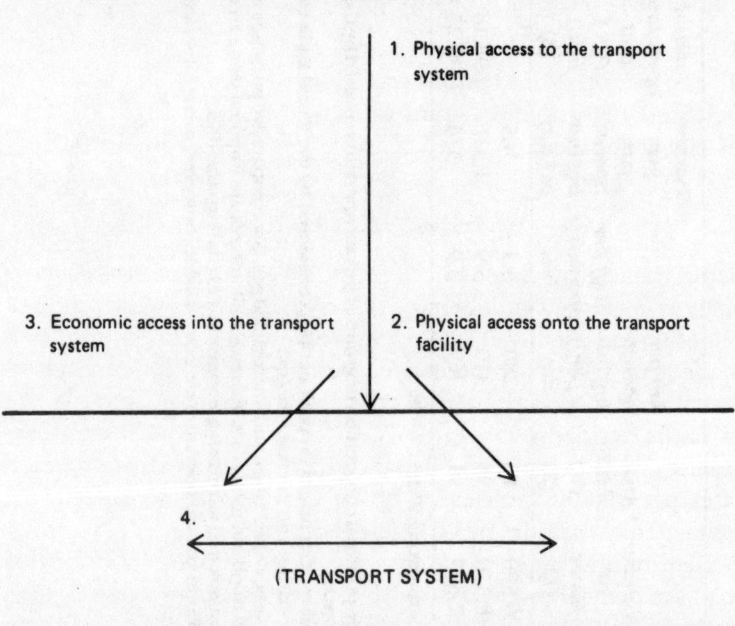

4. Citywide access provided by the transport system, this being a function of:

   i) service characteristics (including congestion encountered)

   ii) network spread

   iii) location of transport systems discharge and collection points (i.e. terminals)

Source: Figure 2, Dimitriou, 1982

of poverty are taken into account, this percentage increases to 40 per cent (Roberts, 1978).

Household expenditure surveys indicate that the urban poor tend to spend on average between 1 and 10 per cent of their income on transport (Linn, 1983). For the poorest, who often can only afford to walk, most traditional efforts at urban transport systems improvement are therefore of marginal help, unless focused on facilities such as pedestrian infrastructure and low-cost public transport facilities servicing basic needs. Four principal kinds of access problems which require a policy and management response are experienced by the poor of Third World cities (see Figure 6.4). These include problems of (Dimitriou, 1982):

1 physical proximity to transport facilities;
2 ease of access onto public transport vehicles;
3 affordability of public transport services; and
4 city-wide access provided by the transport system.

High road accident rates

Rapid traffic growth in association with a number of other factors such as increased numbers of pedestrians, widespread undisciplined road-user behaviour, mixed traffic conditions and inadequate vehicle maintenance, poor road conditions and insufficient road markings, have all contributed significantly to the rise in traffic accidents in Third World cities. Cities such as Metro Manila, Kuala Lumpur and Bangkok have reported accident death rates per 10,000 vehicles of 11.23, 22.7 and 10.3 respectively, against Tokyo's figure of 1.21 (Ichihara, 1983).

Determining which of the above factors are most responsible for road accidents, however, is, as Spencer (1988) points out, notoriously difficult. Nevertheless, there is widespread evidence to show that motorcyclists are especially accident prone. In Surabaya, for example, they have constituted 57 per cent of the vehicles involved in accidents (Jacobs and Sayer, 1977). Pedestrians who are recent arrivals from rural areas are suspected to be especially vulnerable to accidents.

Measurable costs of traffic accidents have been estimated by the World Bank at about 1 per cent of GNP for Third World countries (1986).[4] The same source indicates that road safety measures with associated education and enforcement programmes in Brazil during the first five years of its road safety agency campaign, managed to reduce traffic accident deaths from 4.5 to 1 per million vehicle-kilometres travelled. Each year approximately 500,000 persons are killed world-wide in automobile accidents. Of these, it has been reported that 350,000 are in the Third World and incur an estimated cost of US$ 1.4 to 2 billion (Urban Edge, 1990a). Given that the greatest concentration of vehicle ownership is in cities, the majority of these fatal accidents take place in urban areas. According to World Bank sources, this is particularly so along main roads and in commercial centres, where for example in Accra, 46 per cent of accidents occur and 41 per cent of fatal accidents take place (Urban Edge, 1990b).

For further information on this aspect the reader is recommended to read Ross and Mwiraria (1990), Carlsson and Hedman (1990) as well as a recent TRRL publication written by the Ross Silcock Partnership (1990).

Weak institutional support

The considerable burden placed on Third World city transport institutions as a result of the above agenda of problems (see Barrett, 1983) is exacerbated by inadequate co-ordination among the various authorities involved and insufficient trained manpower resources. There is furthermore, widespread evidence in Third World cities of the duplication of responsibilities in urban transport planning and traffic management which has led to a general lack of clarity as to who does what. Such circumstances are often aggravated by an absence at the national level of a single overall co-ordinating policy unit ready to provide guidelines for urban transport. Among public transport operators, this has proven especially problematic where it concerns co-ordinating the services of the informal sector[5] with those of the formal. These problems have led to the increasing incorporation of institutional studies into urban traffic and transport projects.

The absence of adequately trained staff constitutes a root cause of many urban transport problems in the Third World. This critically handicaps efforts at most levels – from policy investment decisions, to management and construction matters. In Indonesia, the shortage of experienced technical and management staff in urban transport was found by a World Bank study to endanger the success and viability of a proposed US$ 83 million urban transport project (Dimitriou, 1988). There have, however, been many problems in explaining the importance of manpower development training programmes to government organisations and some international development agencies. As Dickey and Miller (1984) point out, many such programmes are sponsored out of a sense of duty rather than commitment; partially because training is often viewed by management as detracting from the work programme. This attitude is, however, increasingly giving way to more enlightened views on training as more and more governments and international development agencies are now actively investing in training.

From 1972 to 1985, US$ 13.1 million of World Bank funds were made available to Third World governments for training in the urban transport field (see Table 6.3). This represented 0.6 per cent of the total sector loan for the same period (World Bank, 1986) and is expected to increase significantly over the next few years. Many Third World governments, including those of Nigeria, Egypt, Tunisia, Indonesia and China, have recently embarked (or are about to embark) upon significant manpower development and training programmes in urban transport. This is despite the fact that problems of measuring the benefits of training still remain a difficulty in project appraisal.

PROBLEMS OF PLANNING RESPONSE: PERCEPTION ISSUES

Perceptions employed

In any kind of problem-solving exercise, the choice of method employed is greatly influenced by how the problem is perceived and defined at the outset, for this determines both the scope and character of analysis which follow. In the field of urban transport, it is common knowledge that problems are perceived and presented in a variety of ways by different people and agencies (see Figure 6.5).

Such perceptions vary with, among other things, the analysts' interests, institutional allegiances, political ideologies, and educational and training backgrounds. The lack of compatibility and agreement among many of these perceptions, as well as the partial coverage of the field that some of them provide, have contributed considerably to problems of urban transport planning and trans-

Table 6.3 World Bank urban transport lending for technical assistance and training, 1972–85 (investment costs in US$ millions)

Country and project name	*Technical assistance*		*Training*	
	Cost	*Per cent*	*Cost*	*Per cent*
Malaysia: Kuala Lumpur Urban Transport	2.9	9.2	–	–
Turkey: Istanbul Urban Program	0.6	100.0	–	–
Iran: Teheran Urban Transport	10.2	15.5	–	–
Tunisia: Tunis Urban Transport	2.9	10.1	–	–
India: Calcutta Urban Dev.	–	–	–	–
Korea: Secondary Cities	–	–	–	–
Malaysia: Second Kuala Lumpur Urban Transport	6.9	11.1	–	–
Philippines: Manila Urban Dev.	5.9	21.7	–	–
India: Bombay Urban Transport	1.0[e]	2.0	–	–
Ivory Coast: Urban Dev.	1.0	1.9	–	–
India: Madras Urban Dev.	–	–	–	–
Costa Rica: San Jose Urban Transport	1.3	4.0	1.0	3.2
India: Second Calcutta Urban Dev.	–	–	–	–
Kenya: Second Urban	0.3	100.0	–	–
Brazil: Urban Transport	4.3	1.7	0.3	0.1
Thailand: Bangkok Urban Transport	3.2	9.4	0.3	0.9
Tunisia: Second Urban Dev.	0.1	10.0	–	–
Korea: Second Gwangji	–	–	–	–
Philippines: Urban Dev.	–	–	–	–
Brazil: Second Urban Transport (Porto Alegre)	3.9	1.2	–	–
India: Calcutta Urban Transport	10.6	8.8	0.6	0.5
Mauritius: Urban Rehab. and Dev.	0.5	20.8	–	–
India: Second Madras Urban Dev.	0.1	0.5	–	–
Brazil: Third Urban Transport	21.9	8.5	–	–
Ivory Coast: Second Urban	11.3	13.1	–	–
India: Kanpur Urban Dev.	0.1	4.8	–	–
Philippines: Urban Engineering	–	–	0.7	100.0
Brazil: Recife Metro Region Dev.	–	–	–	–
Egypt: Greater Cairo Urban Dev.	–	–	2.2	2.4
Mexico: Mexico City Deconcentration	2.0	100.0	–	–
Ethiopia: Urban Dev.	0.4	19.0	0.7	35.1
Tunisia: Third Urban	1.8	100.0	–	–
Cameroon: Urban Dev.	0.8	100.0	–	–
Philippines: Regional Dev.	2.6	8.6	–	–
Brazil: Parana Market Towns	–	–	–	–
India: Third Calcutta Urban Dev.	0.7	1.6	–	–
Dominican Republic: Technical Assistance	0.1	16.3	–	–
Jordan: Amman Urban Transport	1.1	2.0	–	–

Table 6.3 Continued

Country and project name	*Technical assistance*		*Training*	
	Cost	*Per cent*	*Cost*	*Per cent*
India: Madhya Pradesh Urban Dev.	–	–	–	–
Korea: Jeonju Regional Dev.	–	–	–	–
Jamaica: Kingston Urban Transport	4.3	14.4	1.1	3.7
Zimbabwe: Urban Dev.	0.7	46.7	0.8	53.3
Tunisia: Urban Transport II	2.4	2.9	4.5	5.5
Peru: Lima Urban Transport	4.7	6.0	0.8	1.0
Madagascar: Urban Dev.	0.3	42.9	–	–
Senegal: Technical Assistance	0.8	53.3	–	–
Thailand: Regional Cities	–	–	–	–
Paraguay: Asuncion Municipal Dev.	0.1	1.1	0.03	0.3
Korea: Seoul Urban Transport	1.3	0.6	–	–
Total	113.1	4.9	13.1	0.6

Source: Adapted from Table A.7, World Bank, 1986

port facility provision (see earlier discussion in this chapter and in Chapter 4).

In the case of Third World city transport problems, the differences of perception in their identification and analysis seem to be particularly marked. For while there are common characteristics of the sector widely recognised to present important obstacles to urban development, there are numerous interpretations as to which of these are the most critical. In some cases, there is no agreement as to whether certain characteristics are problematic at all. Given these circumstances, it is important that the 'problem-solver' (or 'problem-alleviator' – for one could argue that many urban transport problems are 'insoluble') possesses a clear conceptual understanding of what constitutes a problem in the first place.[6]

Perceptions of the engineer

Of all professionals involved in urban transport the most numerous are engineers, mainly civil engineers. The large majority of these adopt, in their professional practice, aims which emphasise the operational aspects of transport systems rather than the system's contribution to wider urban development goals. Urban

Figure 6.5 Multiple perceptions and dimensions of the urban transport problem

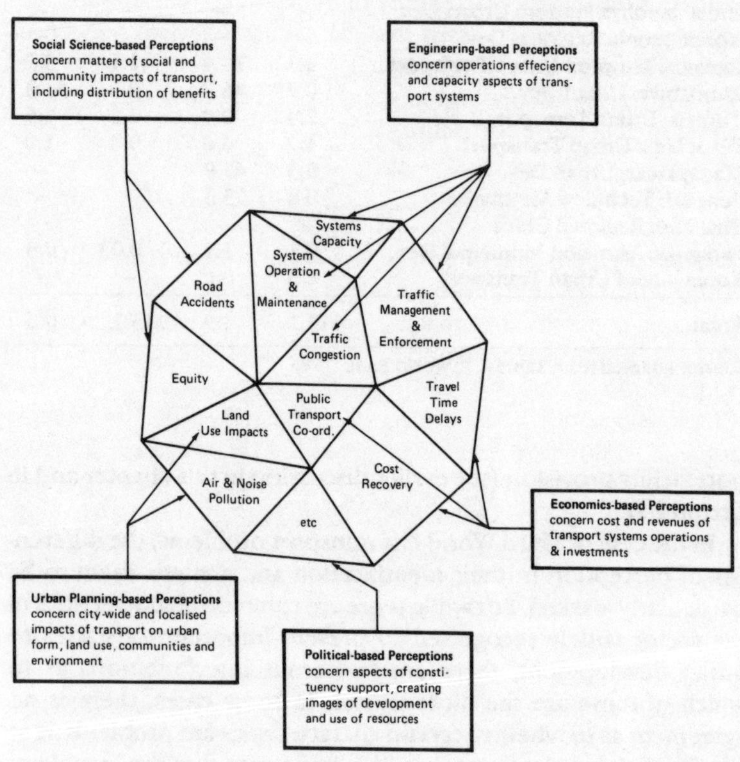

Source: Figure 2.5, Dimitriou, 1990

transport problems are thus commonly seen by them as sub-optimisation difficulties associated with the performance of transport systems.

The evolution of this perception has its origins in the highway and traffic engineering professions – the two most influential groups in the road transport sector. Their influence is especially strong in Third World countries where engineers constitute an elitist, influential and scarce group of trained technocrats, without whom governments are unable to plan, design, implement or maintain transport and other infrastructure projects. The preoccupation of many highway and traffic engineers with issues of road space optimisation has led to problems of traffic congestion being seen as a main obstacle to efforts at reducing travel time and cost, and thus the overall efficient use of transport systems capacity (see *Economist*, 1989). To assist the engineer to alleviate these problems, he relies extensively on theories and techniques of road capacity optimisation, and measures of traffic flow efficiency first developed in the industrialised world.

Perceptions of the economist

Another influential group of technocrats extensively involved in Third World urban transport matters are economists. One of their principal concerns is to match transport supply with demand. In these terms, urban transport problems are usually perceived as shortfalls in the supply and demand of transport facilities (see Chapters 3 and 4). Economists involved in the transport sector, some of whom have specialised in the field (i.e., transport economists), concentrate on efforts simultaneously to minimise the costs of the sector and maximise its benefits. This is done in the belief that some kind of economic optimisation of transport resources can be achieved. It is thought that this can best be measured by comparing transport user costs against benefits.

Perceptions and views of economists are important to the transport sector, since their advice is frequently sought by governments and international development agencies to help assess the basis upon which to invest in, and price, transport improvements and proposals. Unlike engineers, who by and large possess standardised criteria to assist them in making judgements and recommendations about the efficient use of transport systems, economists differ considerably among themselves as to the optimum use of urban road systems and associated transport services. For although they are concerned with the need to match transport supply and demand in the most economically efficient manner – differences of interpretation can arise in deciding what constitutes costs and benefits. Even where agreement is reached, differences of professional opinion also emerge as to the relative importance (i.e., weighting) assigned to these costs and benefits, and in the significance of equity in their distribution. So that while economists share a common use of monetary values in the methods and tools of analysis they employ, the advice they offer can vary a great deal. Their underlying assumption is, however, to presume most transport costs and benefits are somehow convertible and measurable in monetary terms.

Perceptions of other social scientists

Those who often do not share the perceptions and views of economists (especially the more orthodox) in urban transport problem resolution are other social scientists, including sociologists, political scientists, anthropologists and development planners. Many of these take issue with traditional economic thought (particularly in a Third World context), on the grounds that it often conflicts with concepts of equity, political reality and appropriate development. Formalised concepts of optimisation, standardised assumptions and set evaluation criteria, akin to those used by the engineer and economist, do not feature strongly in the problem analysis of these social scientists.

Social science disciplines by their very nature tend to view problems of urban transport from a much wider standpoint than either the economist or engineer. They are, for example, more likely to be concerned with social and community impacts of transport on the poor and other underprivileged groups, the use of transport in serving basic needs, and the impact of transport as an agent of urban development. In institutional areas of concern, the attention of social scientists in urban transport is increasingly directed towards the role of government and other organisations in guiding and encouraging change, and in the extent of decentralisation in the decision-making that is generated. Their interest would extend to investigating and proposing the institutional response to urban transport problems with special concern, for instance, for the lack of effective government agency co-ordination.

Perceptions of the physical planner

Architect-planners, city planners and transport planners (collectively referred to here as physical planners) tend to view urban transport problems more in spatial and physical terms than social scientists, and on a more macroscale than engineers. Physical planners pride themselves on their multi-disciplinary approach to the areas they plan, and believe that not only are physical structural developments of the city addressed by their profession but also the welfare of the community.

This broad-brush approach almost inevitably places the planner in a position of conflict with those economists and engineers who tackle local urban transport problems outside any pre-agreed city-wide planning framework or set of policies. Given the physical planner's broader perspective, he views many of the urban transport problems, particularly problems of traffic congestion, as mere symptoms of wider urban developments warranting a more comprehensive approach to problem resolution than conventionally advocated by the engineer. Physical planners have, however, been criticised by many in the development field for adopting a deterministic approach to resolving urban problems. It is widely argued, for example, that too many city and transport planning approaches assume physical plans can improve the quality of life and provide better opportunities for urban development ultimately through the mere reorganisation of space and its infrastructure, and by creating a new physical order over time.

Such an approach has been particularly evident in the planning and building of new towns, where different road patterns and transport policies have been employed, each assumed to provide specific community, environmental, economic and development advantages (see Potter, 1976). Physical determinism may also be detected in the assumptions adopted by the conventional wisdom of the UTP process and its derivatives, used in the preparation of many urban land-use/transport plans as discussed at great length in Chapters 2, 3, 4 and 7.

Perceptions of the politician

One of the principal problems of the interface of professionals with politicians in the business of resource allocation in urban development is the difference in their time scales and priorities (also see Chapters 4 and 7). This is well displayed in the transport sector of Third World cities where ribbon-cutting of highly visible infrastructure projects, especially prior to elections, is often more important to the politician than policy measures advocated by the professional. This is particularly true where longer gestation periods are required before benefits (often less tangible) emerge.

Associated with this phenomenon is the strong preference of many politicians for projects which present an image of 'modern development' through the construction of sophisticated transport systems, such as elevated high capacity urban freeways (as in Lagos and Delhi) and urban rapid transit systems (as proposed for Bangkok and already constructed in Calcutta). This is not to say that Third World cities do not require high capacity road and/or rapid transport systems. The rapid transit system in Mexico City, for example, has proved essential to its development, if not its survival. What is more in question is the affordability of such projects, and their opportunity costs. Too often the nature and scale of urban transport investments have been a product of political influence, rather than fiscal and professional judgement.

An additional facet of the often difficult relationship between the politician and the professional (especially the planner), concerns the latter's common inability to articulate in politically acceptable terms the justification of comprehensive and integrated planning efforts, and the uncertainties such an approach includes (see Chapter 4). This has reinforced the political importance of projects over plans.[7]

Multiple dimensions of the urban transport problem

In spite of the differing perceptions discussed above, since urban transport problems are a joint product of the dynamics of their component parts and their complex interaction, they cannot be effectively tackled by any one profession or interest group. What is required instead is the use of several perspectives, simultaneously considered and weighted in accordance with (ideally) a pre-set framework of priorities and resource constraints. A framework of this kind, however, needs to be capable of accommodating prevailing economic and political considerations for it not to be too easily discarded for more pragmatic and less directed decision-making.

The interdependent nature and multiple dimensions of what is commonly called 'the urban transport problem' (see Figure 6.5) is most apparent when actions taken to tackle one of its aspects aggravates another, or even creates new problems. In the traffic management field, for example, while traffic re-routeing may improve flows and reduce travel times, it has frequently led to increased trip lengths, higher energy consumption, and more widespread adverse environmental impacts. Similarly, although the construction of major transport projects such as rapid transit systems and urban toll roads may offer higher capacity line-haul routes for city-wide travel, when planned with little regard for their environments, they dramatically alter adjacent land-uses and values, as well as related traffic patterns, in a manner that does not always benefit local needs (see discussion on externalities in Chapter 4).

PROBLEMS OF PLANNING RESPONSE: TECHNOLOGY-TRANSFER ISSUES

Questions of technology-transfer

Planning and management responses to transport problems of Third World cities employing one or more of the perceptions discussed above almost inevitably involve some aspect of cross-culural technology-transfer. [8] This is particularly the case where consultants are involved in project work in countries other than their own, even though the full impact of the transfer is not always clear to them (see Chapters 6 and 7). An analysis of issues of technology-transfer is especially important for urban transport planning practice because many of the dominant professional perceptions used in the Third World have their origins in the industrialised countries (see Chapters 2, 3 and 4). Some issues that warrant examination are discussed below.

Urban development goals and traditional transport planning practices

Traditional urban transport planning practices need to be further investigated (see Chapter 7) to establish whether they are compatible with Third World city conditions. Such an investigation raises questions regarding, for example, the fundamental difference between the development objectives of capitalist-governed New York and those of Hong Kong's newly industrialising society, and how different are the development goals of communist-administered Calcutta to those of former communist-administered Moscow. Following on from this is the question of what implications do these differences have for the planning and management of urban transport systems.

The UTP process and free market land-use forces

The principal issue requiring clarification here is whether the North American heritage of transport planning practice predetermines the treatment of the relationship between transport and urban land-use (see Chapter 3), and if so, what are the implications for various kinds of cities in the Third World (see Chapter 7). This matter is particularly important for those settlements which aspire to strong land-use development controls. It raises furthermore, specific questions as to how well North American consultancy firms adapt their urban transport proposals in the Third World, to local development policies and land-use plans. It would be interesting, for example, to investigate how this was tackled by the Canadian consultants who drew up transport proposals for Dadoma, the capital of socialist Tanzania.

The influence of urban planning approaches and transport planning

The fundamental issue warranting enquiry here is whether urban transport planning practice ought significantly to vary according to the different concepts of urban planning pursued. If, for example, 'an integrated urban development programming' (IUIDP) approach is adopted, as employed for Dacca and selected cities in Indonesia, does this warrant a particular kind of urban transport planning approach which significantly differs from conventional transport planning (see Chapter 8). If so, what then are the implications for transport planning of other urban development planning efforts.

Issues of technology-transfer

An excellent analysis of various aspects of technology-transfer in Third World development of relevance to the above questions has been conducted by Streeten (1974). In this work he levels seven main charges against those involved in this kind of transfer, all of which may be applied to the field of urban transport planning. These are charges of:

1 'academic imperialism' (which for the purpose of this discussion may be said to also include 'professional imperialism');
2 'irrelevance';

3 'inappropriateness';
4 'bias of transferred concepts, models and theories';
5 'research in the service of exploitation';
6 'domination through superior and self-reinforcing exploitation'; and
7 'illegitimacy' of standpoints employed.

Each are discussed below as they relate to transport planning for Third World cities.

Academic and professional imperialism

Evidence of the first of Streeten's charges in the urban transport field may be found in the nature of the one-way communication of planning expertise that commonly takes place between some international consulting firms and their Third World clients. The latter are often made to feel excessively dependent upon consultants (through the use of specialist techniques, jargon, sophisticated software, modelling exercises, technical standards and technological hardware) in their efforts to resolve transport problems.

Similar dependency relationships (unintentional or otherwise) are created through the training and education of Third World government personnel in transport courses offered by universities and other educational establishments in the industrialised world. Many such programmes until relatively recently, have almost exclusively focused upon industrialised country situations and made little effort to address problems of Third World conditions; except where they are treated as special kinds of more general urban transport problems found world-wide.

Irrelevance and inappropriateness

Streeten's view that adopted Western concepts, models, and paradigms are frequently inappropriate, is particularly relevant to the field of transport planning for Third World cities. This concern has been the theme of several publications since the mid 1970s (see Kumar and Rao, 1975; Viola, 1976; McNeill, 1977; Dimitriou, 1977; Ziv, 1977; Banjo and Dimitriou, 1983; Dimitriou, 1990; and Newman and Kenworthy, 1990). What is of special interest is that not only are some conventional transport planning concepts, paradigms and techniques now more readily considered to be of questionable value for Third World cities, but their validity in cities in the industrialised world is also open to question (see Chapters 3 and 4). A more detailed discussion of this aspect as it relates to the Third World is presented in Chapter 7.

Research in the service of exploitation

Particular international research consultancies, foreign investment interests, aid donors and universities in the industrialised world have (wittingly or unwittingly), with the enlisted support of a small class of privileged (often Western-educated) persons in the Third World, successfully pushed research and development projects in urban transport, in a manner that reflects the interests of the industrialised nations more than the countries they are intended to serve. This kind of technology-transfer is described by Streeten as 'opportunistic' and sometimes 'irrelevant'. It is perhaps most evident in the encouragement of the indiscriminate use of the motorcar (see Chapters 3, 4 and 7). What is very important about the success of this kind of technology-transfer is its tendency to reinforce the dominant position and perceptions of professionals of the industrialised countries in a way that encourages the further reliance on their views and know-how.

Streeten argues that some presumptions made by governments of industrialised countries in assessments of foreign aid needs provide further examples of technology-transfer in the service of Third World exploitation. This is especially true where the donor's perception of what is needed coincides with the economic interests of the donor countries, whether it be air-conditioned rear-engine double-decker buses, monorails or urban rapid transit systems.[9]

Self-reinforcing exploitation

Streeten's further charge that the Third World is exploited by virtue of the industrialised countries' privileged position *vis-à-vis* its location to international funds and accumulated skills, is also pertinent to the urban transport field. For the concentration of financial and technical manpower resources in the industrialised world are such that they provide an inevitable superiority of Western expertise and interests over those in the Third World in major urban transport project developments. This was so until the entrance of Arab oil-producing countries into the business of international banking. Because so much of the resources made available to the Third World are both financially and politically supported by international institutions with attitudes and personnel derived from the same source, some observers claim that as in the examples of 'research in the service of exploitation', these developments have tended to reinforce conventional views and dampen innovative research.

Illegitimacy of stand

Streeten's final charge of technology-transfer, 'illegitimacy', refers to situations when research and consultancy studies conducted by persons and organisations from the industrialised world (the costs of which are borne by people from a different country to the consultants) make recommendations which advocate drastic, painful and often politically unacceptable measures. Streeten sees many such recommendations as 'illegitimate and distasteful'. For example, persons far removed from the scene, such as in overseas universities and professional consultancy firms, are able to recommend actions which are not only sometimes impossible to implement, but in some instances have been rejected in the consultants' own country. The responsibility to supervise the implementation of such proposals generally lies with others rather than the professionals who conducted the study. This criticism could apply especially to the advocates of road-pricing schemes in Third World cities proposed (and rejected) for Kuala Lumpur and Hong Kong.

The new generation of urban transport problems

An article entitled 'Urban Transport Problems of Third World Cities: The Third Generation' published by the author with G. A. Banjo (1983) makes reference to several of the above technology-transfer issues. The principal argument in this paper was one that partly attributed the unresolved (and more complex) nature of many current Third World city movement problems to an excessive reliance upon inappropriate transport planning approaches (also see Chapter 7). More specifically, the argument depicts transport problems of post-colonial Third World cities (typically in Africa and the Indian sub-continent) as evolving not only from the charac-

Figure 6.6 The genesis of urban transport problems in ex-colonial cities

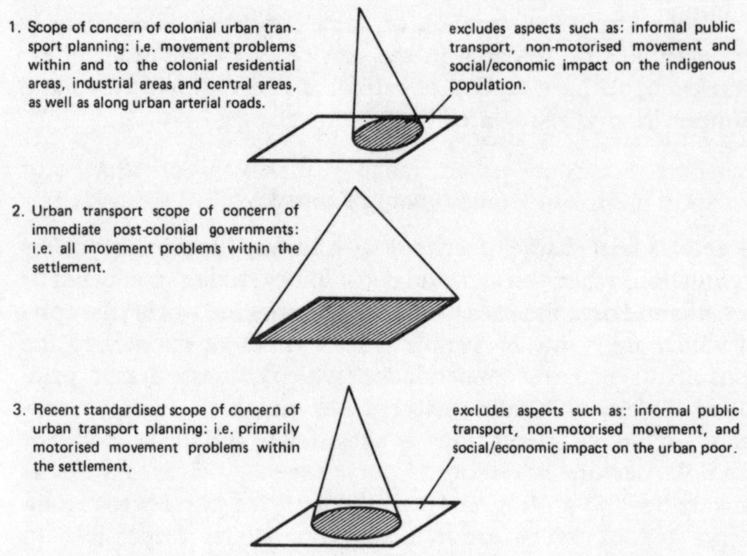

Source: Redrawn from Figure 4, Dimitriou, 1983

teristics of the settlements themselves, and their inhabitants' travel demands, but also from the planning responses to which they have been subjected.

The new generation of transport problems of these cities was presented as an historical culmination (see Figure 6.6) of:

1 the inheritance of an urban transport system predominantly designed to service colonial economic, administrative and residential needs, developed and operated separately from the local transport system predominantly utilised by indigenous populations;
2 the subsequent abandonment of separate development after independence, thus making the whole city more accessible to the indigenous population, in turn dramatically changing demands made upon the city's transport systems overnight; and

3 the reliance upon foreign technical assistance to tackle the resultant transport problems, involving too restrictive a scope of analyses and often a poor understanding of local conditions.

Although the particular characteristics of the new generation of urban transport problems differ from city to city, features most closely associated with it include the destruction of existing (especially old) urban form structures; the penalising of the non-motorised community; a failure to incorporate the informal transport sector into urban transport plans; the dominance of transport user considerations; and the use of past trends as a basis for 'blueprint' planning.

Problems of goal setting

What much of the preceding discussion implies is that one of the most common sources of transport problems has been unclear and unrealistic goal-setting in urban transport planning, both during plan-making and in project implementation.[10] For transport planning goals not only formalise the direction(s) and purpose(s) towards which transport investments may be orientated, but also help to reveal more clearly over time (with the assistance of monitoring), the degree to which these investments are compatible with grass-root needs. Good goal-setting, furthermore, offers a sounder basis for making judgements concerning the desirability of different kinds of technology-transfer on offer.

The often observed mismatch between adopted urban transport planning goals and Third World city grass-root needs is most notably reflected in the preoccupation of many urban transport studies with meeting private motorised transport demand and tackling related problems of traffic congestion, rather than addressing wider issues affecting a larger proportion of society. As a result, there has been an under-emphasis of the importance of pedestrian, cycle and animal movement; matters of social justice; and on the productive role of the informal transport sector (see Chapter 7).

Although, in Sao Paulo and Mexico City, which have more motorised vehicles than Philadelphia or Dallas respectively, the emphasis on motorised traffic is understandable (though not laudable), in other cities, this approach blatantly ignores the needs of the majority of trip-makers. These cities include: Dacca, with a population of 3.45 million in 1981 and 50,000 motorised vehicles

(Bangladesh Bureau of Statistics, 1989) which represents a mere 35 per cent of on-street traffic; Madras, with 44 per cent of all daily trips undertaken by non-motorised means (Madras Metropolitan Development Authority, 1977); and Calcutta, where in 1980 fewer than 0.1 per cent of the inhabitants possessed a private car (World Bank, 1986). In this approach, problems of urban transport, particularly those associated with the poor, have not only been perpetuated but accentuated, for public participation is uncommon in these cities.

Goals and availability of resources

Many aspects of incompatability between urban transport planning goals and the resources available to meet them may be traced to an underlying presumption that there is some kind of 'obligation' to accommodate traffic growth (see Chapters 3, 4 and 7). Associated with this view is the inherent belief that increased traffic speeds are desirable, even though related overall costs and benefits are often less clear than presented. However, levels of resource scarcity in many Third World cities are in reality so considerable that to accommodate the traffic and motorisation growth rates experienced (often higher than those in the industrialised countries), is to expect more (from less resources) than has been feasible in the industrialised world.

Another aspect that requires scrutiny with regard to resource implications is the premise that it is better to plan for a wide choice of 'modern transport modes', even where this leads to the displacement of traditional vehicles performing important functions. This has led to the erosion of a previous rich spectrum of local transport modes in many Southeast Asian cities and its replacement by newer (often less flexible) modes, unable to meet travel needs previously served.

A final matter warranting consideration is the fact that many urban highway and traffic engineering schemes associated with transport planning efforts seem to rely on the misconception that problems of traffic congestion and car parking can be successfully tackled by engineering measures, independent of meaningful land-use control. The prevalence of this in a Third World context may reflect in part the weak enforcement capability of planning agencies. In more general terms, however, it is also indicative of the unrealistic expectations frequently associated with much of urban highway and traffic engineering practice.

This raises two final issues. The first has to do with the appreciation of the level of complexity of the problem at hand. For if the complexity of a transport problem is not reflected in the approach employed to resolve it, there is the danger that the very simplicity of the approach will ultimately lead to more costly solutions, after several failed attempts at 'getting it right'. The other issue concerns the resources needed to implement projects. Many central highway and traffic engineering agency schemes tend to arrive at higher cost solutions beyond the means of many local municipalities. Whilst this in part may be explained by the kind of analysis adopted, it is also attributable to the reliance upon international (often inappropriate) standards and the lack of adequately formulated indigenous standards, an aspect addressed in greater depth in Chapters 8 and 9.

7

A CRITICAL REVIEW OF THE APPLICATION OF THE UTP PROCESS AND ITS DERIVATIVES TO THIRD WORLD CITIES

INTRODUCTION

This chapter pursues many of the more theoretical issues raised in Chapters 3 and 4 and places them in the context of the Third World. In so doing, it reflects much of the rationale of the analysis employed in these earlier chapters, in addition to relating to several of the issues raised in Chapter 5.

The ensuing discussion draws extensively from the scripts of interviews conducted by the author with numerous academics, consultants and representatives of international development agencies concerned with urban transport in the Third World (see Appendix 3). The author's questions (also see Appendix 4), were asked with a view to helping ascertain the value of the UTP approach and its derivatives to Third World cities, and arriving at parameters of a more appropriate urban transport planning methodology for such settlements (see Chapters 8 and 9).

The reader should note that the undated references in this chapter are to the interviews conducted by the author, as in Chapters 3 and 4.

FUNCTIONS, ASSUMPTIONS AND ADAPTATIONS

Functions

The response from those interviewed indicated that the principal function of the UTP process in the Third World is much the same as in industrialised nations – i.e., to justify investment decisions regarding additions to be made to the urban transport network. However, according to Ingram of the World Bank, there is much evidence to suggest that the decision to proceed with a particular urban transport project often has very little to do with the analyses. He explains:

> I have a feeling that we had a highway solution and we generalised a technique to go with that. Later we had a transit solution and we adapted our technique to go with that. These (UTP) models cannot help you make decisions. I have the sense that the relationship between (investment) decisions and the analysis is a lot less clear and may run in the reverse direction to that most people see.

In contrast to Ingram's views, Watson, of the World Bank, argues that there is in fact significant scope for the potential adaptation of many of the UTP models to Third World conditions. He makes the case as follows:

> I see some very simple virtues in these models, in terms of getting your sums right. To the extent that the planning process is going to be improved by that particular virtue, there is some reason to do it. The thing that complicates life with these models is that they cannot handle very sophisticated differentiations among (transport) modes... and when you move to a LDC (less developed country), one of the striking things is that there is a significant menu of modes.... If you start introducing a richness to the representation of modes then the models are going to continue to work.

Assumptions

What are the main foundation assumptions of the UTP process as applied to Third World contexts?

A primary assumption of the UTP process, irrespective of context, is that there is a land-use system with an employment base from which trips are generated, and that this relationship (between land-use and travel) is basically stable (see Chapter 2). It is believed one can measure this relationship in any given situation. While cultural differences need to be taken into account, if motorised vehicles alone are considered, then the overall transport picture of Third World cities is incomplete. As a result, the immediate transfer of the West's preoccupation with motorised transport to the Third World, which by and large ignores walk trips, is quite misplaced as indicated in Chapter 6.

Another key assumption warranting further attention is the aggregation assumption – i.e., that a group of people can be treated in the same way if reference is made to their mean characteristics. In view of the greater diversity of income and ethnic composition of the inhabitants of many Third World cities, Watson claims:

> to take a piece of land, which you call a traffic zone, and believe that people within it would behave in much the same way, is questionable.... There is a fair amount of evidence which suggests that you are often getting as much, if not more variation within the traffic zone, than you get between the traffic zones. It would, therefore, be far better to try and get the basic relationships calibrated on a much more detailed set of information bases that establishes that these relationships are fairly stable and that they hold up through time and across cities.

Such reservations regarding the use of aggregated data did much to encourage the development in industrialised countries of more accurate calibrations using disaggregated information and modelling techniques (see Chapter 2). However, few of these models have been successfully applied to Third World contexts. This is despite the fact that it is increasingly recognised that one does not necessarily have to employ a vast amount of data to use such models. One can obtain the basic relationship established early on in the analysis and subsequently use disaggregated data for making predictions and/or improving upon predictions.

Another problem concerning the assumption employed by the UTP process is its deterministic character. Watson explains:

> What you are basically saying (by using the UTP approach and its derivatives) is that if people behaved in 'X way' previously, then by inserting a new set of circumstances, they will continue to respond according to the same criteria, in the same way....

In Dean's opinion, yet another problem is that in constrained Third World situations, any kind of forecasting of transport demand shows that the facilities will be super-saturated. This, he argues, needs to be fed back into the process. In reality, however, it is an aspect that is not very well taken care of. Gakenheimer (1990) strongly concurs with this view. He claims that so long as Third World transport systems are inevitably going to be overcrowded, why take such pains in estimating the level of future transport demand.

Adaptations

> *Have all the major adjustments of the UTP process and its derivatives been incorporated within most Third World applications?*

Commentators on the application of the UTP approach and its derivatives to Third World cities fall into two broad categories. Some argue that the use of methodologies developed in the industrialised countries has little or no relevance there, on account of the totally different development contexts. Others see such techniques as of even greater relevance than in the industrialised countries. This is argued on the grounds that Third World cities exhibit rapid growth trends akin to those experienced in the past by cities in the industrialised world. Persons holding the latter view claim, furthermore, that the amount of consensus in the Third World to accommodate this growth of demand is not dissimilar to the position of many previous Western governments.

Both positions are, however, a gross over-simplification of two valid points. Firstly, discussions in Chapters 5 and 6 indicate that the source and type of urban and traffic growth in the Third World is very different from that experienced in industrialised countries. The argument that the developments in the UTP process and its derivatives are not appropriately transferable to Third World locations requires more specific examination of the kind offered here.

Levinson believes that if the same kind of transport investment strategy is developed for a Third World city as in the USA, then the adaptations to the UTP process, particularly those that involve factors of capacity, supply and restraint, become meaningful. However, the critical issue is not the techniques but whether it is appropriate for a Third World city to duplicate the same kind of strategy as pursued in the USA. The evidence is (see Chapters 5 and 6) that it is not, if only because in most instances, Third World cities cannot. Despite this, many early studies, such as those conducted by Kain and Fauth for Teheran, adopted as their premise that it *was* reasonable to try to answer the same kind of questions that the UTP models addressed in the USA. Levinson comments:

> I am not certain whether or not the process is relevant to Third World cities. In part it is relevant, because some of the exercise tries to find what factors influence mobility and what levels of mobility are necessary to sustain economic development – and from this see that the transportation system serves the various parts of the population. However, how well the process can estimate demand... and how well the recommendations from the process can relate to the demand that comes out of the estimates, remains to be seen.

Expanding upon Levinson's doubts, Watson suggests that a change in direction of the UTP process is both critical and long overdue for Third World countries. He argues:

> Resources are seen to be much scarcer now, especially after the (mid 1970s) energy crisis.... Much of the balance of payment problems (of non-oil producing countries) arise from an over-reliance on gasoline, petroleum-powered transportation, so that simply building more roads and encouraging people to use more and more cars is not a good solution for a Third World country – for many of them it is totally disastrous.

This stance is supported by numerous other planners on the assumption that many Third World cities have now had sufficient experience of building urban freeways to appreciate the futility of road-based transport solutions. In addition, what the energy crisis, as well as the growing awareness of environmental issues, has shown is that the UTP approach and many of its derivatives have become too cumbersome to be able to respond to such questions (see Chapter 3).

Models of the UTP process and their derivatives have furthermore not kept up with the change of direction of urban transport planning towards the resolution of specific problems. Nor have they adequately addressed the need to make more efficient use of vehicles (thereby favouring public transport) and infrastructure – both of which are very difficult to deal with in models. Policy measures to discourage the use of motorcars, such as traffic restraint and increases in parking fees, are difficult to include in the models, as skilful and thoughtful analysts are scarce anywhere in the world!

Notwithstanding his earlier reservations, Watson argues:

> the models themselves – within limitations – work... but what has happened is that the people who use them no longer have the skills to use them correctly.... In general, people are not being very innovative in the use of the models. They are not modifying the models sufficiently nor are they coming up with enough new models.

Perhaps an exception to this are the models developed over the last twenty years by Echenique which Dean maintains are among the earliest and most useful responses to the UTP process in its application to the Third World. While these do not constitute an adaptation of the process, Echenique's work is in the same mould. Indeed, Echenique's work was so widely acclaimed in the late 1970s that efforts were subsequently made to encourage the US Department of Transportation to incorporate some of his techniques in the UTP package it promoted overseas.

Despite the extensive dissemination of the US DOT package to both industrialised and Third World countries (see Chapter 2), and the agency's active dialogue with numerous Third World governments, Hillegass claims that there have been no efforts by the DOT to work on a more sensitive package consistent with Third World policy issues. This is in marked contrast to the World Bank which has hired staff to investigate this field (see Thomson, 1983) and unlike the US DOT, has many ongoing urban-transport projects throughout the world with staff adapting and making modifications to the process and its derivatives in their everyday work.

Though the dissemination of the UTP package overseas by the US DOT has been fairly extensive,[1] Stopher believes that some of its major USA adjustments have not been incorporated into the process's application to countries of the Third World. Echoing this point and drawing from his working experience in Central and South America, Sudra claims that there is much evidence to suggest that many consultants are in fact giving governments of these countries advice that is years out of date. He cites the decision to build an intermediate inner city super-highway ring-road in Mexico City in 1973, when in 1970 the Boston Transportation Planning Review marked the moratorium on highway building as a result of opposition to the Boston inner ring road.

The above discussion makes it clear that the main means by which technology-transfer takes place in urban transport planning is through international consultancy firms working on World Bank and/or other international development agency projects (see later discussions on technical assistance). These consultants have been operating for a long time, especially in the principal cities of Latin America. During their assignments they typically receive requests from their clients to look out for the latest adaptations to the UTP process (in the form of UTP computer model programmes) in order for them to update their clients' software. In so far as they do this, it suggests that there is no significant time lag in acquiring new adaptations to the UTP process by those who wish to do so in the Third World. There are, however, many Third World settlements, particularly provincial and intermediate sized cities, where there is no direct contact with the consultants. As a result, the professionals in these settlements rely on second-hand access to these developments via contacts with professional colleagues in their own capital cities.

Regarding the consultants' role in the dissemination of the UTP package and its derivatives, Gomez-Ibanez explains:

> My impression is that a pretty well developed set of international consultants spread this kind of technology rapidly.... They cart the same people to each job and only know one set of techniques. So in one sense, there is a great deal of homogeneity in the techniques used. The difference may be less in the techniques actually applied in the Third World and the transport planning projects in US and the UK, than in the difference between what those in universities are saying, and the practitioners are doing.

According to Watson, one of the major problems regarding the application of the UTP process and its derivatives to the Third World, is that one can still find many decision-makers who are indifferent to whether or not the poor benefit from urban transport projects. Such persons do not seem to care, he claims, if public transport deteriorates as car users become better off, nor are they concerned about the environment. There are, on the other hand, others who have quite strong beliefs in a totally different direction. There have been several occasions, for example, when the World Bank has focused upon more of the social aspects of the UTP package, by trying to induce governments and consultants alike to address the needs of the poor in addition to those areas more traditionally addressed. In this regard, the World Bank in some way substitutes for the 'public'.

Public debate as a source of adaptation

Some major amendments to the UTP process were made in the industrialised countries as a result of issues which surfaced from public debate. Given the relative absence of this kind of debate in the Third World, does this mean that urban transport planning in this part of the globe is likely to be 'less socially orientated' and thus less well developed?

Public participation, Manheim argues, is largely an Anglo-Saxon phenomenon, or at least a phenomenon of modest affluence and a commitment to democracy. On this basis, he explains:

> The transportation planner operating in a developing country faces a real ethical dilemma. My own position is to strike a balance between maintaining leverage in the process and seeing that the issues which should be raised from a broader perspective do get raised. Where participation can be encouraged and can exist, it can then add pressures to issues that are important. I think we have a professional responsibility to surface these issues, but the trade-off is how much influence you can have over the long-term process... and taking a confrontation position in the short term.

Addressing the same issue, Gomez-Ibanez points out that although in the USA some groups participate politically more than others, there is a reasonable level of overall participation that is not matched in most Third World countries. In the latter, therefore, one needs actively to solicit participation in order to get more socially responsible urban transport planning. It is only to be expected, Ibanez-Gomez claims, that transport planning efforts in the Third World will thus be less socially-orientated and less developed.

On this point, Ingram is of the view that it will take the public in most Third World countries at least as long as it has taken in the USA to appreciate that the analysis and the solution of urban transport planning exercises are inseparable, and that what the consultants are really doing is making a case for investment. In the

USA, the Freedom of Information Acts have facilitated public interest groups participating in the process, whereas in Third World countries, such legislation is a long way off. Furthermore, Ingram claims, the public of these countries is unlikely to be willing to embarrass a government's highway construction programme when road communications are typically so bad. It is even less likely to be able to embarrass a subway construction programme it cannot afford, as witnessed in Calcutta.

On the other hand, as Dean explains, events and perceptions can change almost overnight. He recounts that he was told, in a country ruled by generals where there were problems of human rights and censorship of the press, and many other characteristics associated with a lack in participatory government, that it was unpatriotic to include the environment in the evaluation of transport investments, as it would constitute an obstacle to rapid development and greater productivity. However, within five years, the pendulum had swung radically in the other direction, whereby the mayor of a major city in the same country subsequently took environmental issues on-board in urban transport planning exercises. Levinson argues that such unexpected changes mean that planning in the Third World has to be conducted within a different frame of reference to that employed in industrialised countries. This alternative set of ground rules needs to be more introspective and much less mechanistic.

Because of their influential automobile and construction industries (see *South*, 1989), Brazil, Mexico, South Korea and Taiwan are more prone to adopt highway-oriented solutions, and thus override the interests of the majority of their people, than other Third World countries such as Colombia and Indonesia, where the motorcar industry is less well developed. There is thus much less at stake if the public were to become more vocal and active in determining the future of the urban transport sub-sector in these latter nations.

Stopher believes that some major amendments to the UTP process would not have taken place without the public debate and social response/opposition which took place in the industrialised countries – notably the USA and the UK. He argues that the extent to which these amendments are adopted in the Third World depends very much on how much the transport planning profession has learnt from lessons of public participation in the West. In South Africa, where Stopher encouraged public participation in the transport sector, he encountered two diametrically opposed reactions to the introduction of public participation. These had more to do with differing professional values (see Chapter 6), than with differing development contexts. The engineers regarded planning as a technical exercise, wherever one worked, while the town planners wanted to encourage public participation. The eventual dialogue led to a commitment to public participation 'of sorts', for which the South African Department of Transport subsequently later developed procedures whereby it could involve the public in the UTP process.

ISSUES OF THE PROCESS

Travel demand

What are the major parameters that control urban travel and efforts at meeting travel demand in Third World cities?

The overwhelming evidence is that cost is the key factor in travel demand, with some consideration of time costs incorporated within this assessment (see Chapter 3). However, the value of money is so high for most of the population in the Third World, that the relative value of time is low. As Watson explains:

> If by Thursday the poor cannot afford the bus, there is no use asking them on Wednesday if they would like to pay a little bit more to get there a little bit faster, or for more convenience, or for more comfort, or for a cleaner bus, or even for a less crowded bus.
>
> They are trying to get there with any mode they can. The transport decisions for them are 'do I scrape up the 30 cents for a bus today or do I walk the 8 miles'? Do I walk 12 miles and eat an extra bowl of rice or take a bus? All these fancy parameters that some transport planners are trying to model are absolutely irrelevant to these people.

In order to identify the major parameters of travel demand in Third World cities that differ from those in the industrialised countries, there are a number of aspects on which to focus on. For instance, in many such settlements the trip home for lunch and subsequent return to work have a marked impact on traffic movement patterns throughout the day (see Chapter 6). A second consideration is the widespread ownership of refrigerators in the industrialised countries, the absence of which in most Third World households has an obvious impact on urban trip-making. This situation has a consequent impact on the location of stores and on the working capital of business.

Dean has found that overall trip rates are much lower in Third World cities than in those of the industrialised nations. These differences are for the most part explainable in terms of incomes, family sizes, motorisation rates, etc. (see Zahavi 1979). The transport mode mix and emphasis also differs, with a much heavier use of public transport in Third World cities.

Travel needs

What constitutes the difference between 'travel needs' and 'travel aspirations' in a Third World context?

The economist's standard answer to the above question is that if someone is prepared to pay for the trip, then there is a 'need' for it. Conversely, if he/she is not willing to pay for it, or not able to pay for it, then there is no need for the trip. This position is well illustrated by Ingram's response to the above question, as follows:

> I am not sure what the meaning of those words are. I can certainly understand what the points on the demand curve are – which is that if you tell me the price I will tell you the demand.... My sense is, as long as they pay for them (i.e., transport services), I do not have any problem (about the use of these terms).

Dean argues that a trip-maker will only be prepared to pay for a trip if the benefits gained exceed all associated costs to himself and (it is to be hoped) society. He maintains that the reason conventional thinking in the field of urban transport planning is unable to distinguish between a 'travel need' and a 'travel desire' (aspiration), is because urban transport facilities, particularly in the Third World, are priced in such an obscure way that no one can tell what it is really costing.

Watson claims that this limited perception of the economist represents a position they back into because of the difficulties of planning for needs that are not evident in the market. The realities of Third World city life, however, are that there are people who cannot afford public transport to get to work but who clearly 'need' to be mobile (see Chapter 6). This 'basic needs' position has also been argued by Altshuler (see Chapter 4) who claims that a 'travel need' is related to survival and that it is irrational to assume that when people cannot pay for transport facilities they do not need them. Watson is against subsidising public transport services, particularly if it is cheaper to give more money directly to people who need it for travel. Watson argues that the relative importance of basic needs should be investigated to establish where the greater demand is – i.e., for shelter, food or whatever. Treatment of the problem in this way avoids the danger of allowing professional or disciplinary prejudices to determine the definition of 'needs'. He claims:

> The World Bank has in the past been willing to consider something like food stamps but for transport i.e., 'transport stamps'. So instead of subsidising the bus company to give cheaper trips to everybody, including those that do not need it, you take the 10 per cent that, say, need it, and then allow them to buy bus tickets at half price or a quarter of the price.

Ingram points out that a 'travel need' in a Third World context is quite different from a 'travel desire' – the technical term usually used in urban transport studies. The appropriate perception instead is of a 'minimum standard' to be supplied regardless of costs. He refers to this as an 'entitlement'-i.e., the minimum amount of services that people have an inherent right to for survival, such as housing/shelter, clothing, food, etc. – which is not the meaning of the term as it is used in the UTP process (see Chapter 4). This issue, however, is often side-stepped, as the following quotation from Ingram suggests:

> defining a basic entitlement is in fact a political issue. LDCs generally have to pay for providing those entitlements themselves in which case, they then presumably have a lot to say about what these are. If they can get other people to pay for them (the entitlements) that is terrific!

Whether or not the entitlement argument is valid, it is clear that urban transport needs can also represent opportunities for better living standards, jobs, healthcare and education (see Chapter 5) for which employment is the prerequisite.

Land-use control and transport

To what extent is the ability of government to control urban land-use a significant factor in determining the success of an urban transport planning approach for a Third World city?

Watson is of the view that a failure to control land-use is a distinct disadvantage in the use of the UTP package in Third World settlements (also see Chapter 4). He claims that what typically transpires is that a land-use planner's idea of what would benefit a city twenty years hence is identified, and then used as a basis for which to find the best transport option. However, he points out:

> in developing countries, plans are frequently already out of date – i.e., green space has buildings on it, an area not supposed to have industry on it has industry, etc.... I do not think this is inherently a drawback – it just makes life a lot more difficult because if you do not have development control, then you have to basically test the transportation solution you have devised against failures for the land-use pattern you have employed.

The real issue in these circumstances then is whether one can design and build a transport system that is robust enough to work under different urban land-use options?

Watson argues that this is rarely possible, partly because the land-use/transport models employed are blunt instruments for achieving this. It is also because urban transport planning studies take so long to complete that there is typically very little time left for testing all the alternatives. Thus, a great deal of effort goes into building the UTP model and relatively little into testing the alternatives generated – which is something else the model should be used for. Adding another year for testing could cut down the development of the programme and would make it much more useful. However, politicians look toward shortening the duration of transport studies, not lengthening them.

Doebele points out that any strong government which has firm policies is likely to have a strong set of transport policies. It can, for example, impose greater restrictions on travel or on direct capital investments more easily than a weaker government which has a lot of restraints imposed upon on it. Apart from the socialist countries (or rather, those once described as socialist countries), where a great deal of development is undertaken directly by the government, Doebele claims that many Third World governments notionally have that kind of control. However, apart from Hong Kong and China (for very different reasons), it is hard to think of a Third World country which in reality has such control over land-use, and is thus able to have a different strategy for transport planning.

Henrickson and Tummarallo of the United States Agency for International Development (USAID) address the same issue from another angle. They argue that the influence of development control legislation greatly depends on the capabilities of the staff of central and local government. Many South American countries have sufficient numbers of capable staff, as do Taiwan and South Korea, to tackle this aspect. However, numerous African countries, particularly Zaire and other French-speaking African ex-colonies, lack both the capability and the legislation to the enforce the required laws.

Transport consumerism and the motorcar lobby

Is there a significant element of 'transport consumerism' within the UTP process and if so, does this encourage the indiscriminate abandonment of old transport technologies for new in Third World cities?

Watson claims there is a widespread belief held among planners, especially in the Third World, that:

> high technology is better than no technology, that super expressways are much better than widening your road and fixing up the intersections, that a subway and/or a rail solution is automatically better than a bus solution.

This attitude, he argues, also permeates the consultants. While working in Recife (Brazil) for a World Bank project, he was told by a consultant that with traffic volumes of over 10,000 people an hour, a rail system was essential, since buses could run no closer than 30 seconds apart. After much discussion and numerous calculations, it was estimated that buses could in fact carry up to 12,000 persons per hour and that, therefore, a rail solution was not needed.

Unfortunately such technical debates regarding capacity capabilities often take place independently of the more important question of affordability. The separation of interrelated aspects occurs because the underlying real issue is often of acquiring 'an image of development' (see Chapter 6). In Singapore for example, Watson recounts, many people in government thought that the construction of the subway, would make Singapore a high technology country, like Japan. While the UTP process cannot be tied directly to promoting this notion, it certainly does nothing to prevent it.

Taking a different position, Dean concurs that in its early development the UTP process did not respond very well to public transit investment. But he points out, it was not then an aspect of interest. He claims, that the then financial policy not to provide funds for public transit determined the scope of the study, so that it was useless to answer that kind of question.

There is no real evidence from the experiences of those interviewed that the motorcar industry has influenced the application of the UTP process and its derivatives in the Third World. Dean, for example, recounts that the commissioning of transport planning consultants in the Philippines by General Motors did not have any significant impact on the field. The lack of major involvement of the motorcar manufacturers is confirmed by Watson who claims that they are not interested in comparative time and cost studies but are far more concerned with attitudinal measures of aspects such as visual amenity, comfort and safety, as a basis for improving the marketing of their vehicles.

Sudra (now working for UNCHs) notes that there is in the Third World a potentially very risky fascination with new technological gadgets which has spread into the transport field. This is despite the fact that there are numerous good reasons for supporting indigenous modes of transport and despite their lowly ascribed status by government (see Chapters 6, 8 and 9). Such modest status he claims, is a result of the commercialism of other competing modern transport modes. The appropriate use of traditional means of transport is therefore very important, and in this sense Sudra believes there is a vested social interest in certain quarters to maintain the existing modes of transport and not substitute them with newer more modern modes.

Role of models

Have UTP models been developed to answer design rather than strategy or policy questions, and if so what are the implications of this for Third World cities?

Dean is of the view that urban transport models were *not* designed in response to policy issues but initially to answer transport planning questions within a given policy framework from which questions of design are then addressed (also see Chapter 4). The implication for Third World countries, Stopher argues, is that it:

> prevents one concentrating upon the development of more normative aspects – i.e., looking at what it is one would like to have, rather than how to get it. Being rather design orientated, the UTP process and many of its derivatives do not tend to ask such questions. The designer (instead) asks what it is he has to cater for and then designs on that basis, so you end up doing something that is fairly remote from planning.

The World Bank, according to Watson, uses models to design and justify the value of projects. Models are also employed by the agency to test the economic justification of proposals; project evaluation is carried out on the presupposition that a decision has been made to make funds available. The position of the Bank is that governments ought to be able to evaluate the projects they finance and where they cannot, technical assistance should be provided (to include training and manpower development programmes) to overcome such problems. In Watson's experience, Third World governments frequently use models to justify projects rather than legitimise policies. In such instances, the World Bank tries hard to oblige governments to use models to test alternatives rather than principally to elaborate on one project. He explains:

> If anybody comes to us (the World Bank) and says – we want to build six lanes of highway – we ask what were the (modelling) results for four? So we are very seriously trying to use the models to give us information about the relative benefits of alternatives that cost different amounts of money. We can in other words, do a marginal cost benefit, incremental cost benefit analysis of what we are trying to do.

Such exercises are valuable, since there are instances when the extra benefits for additional costs become increasingly smaller to a point when it is plain that the best alternative is often the simplest.

The preceding discussion implies that while models are important they have limitations in any context (see Chapters 3 and 4), particularly in the Third World. However, as Owen of the Bookings Institution argues, any data that can be brought to bear on a problem is important, so long as it is not the model or the data that makes decisions. At the same time, it is important not to reject the contribution of data to understanding alternative courses of action and their impacts. In making these points, Owen obliges one to return to an earlier point raised, namely that the intelligent use of models is dependent on the user. This point is eloquently articulated by Watson, as follows:

> an intelligent user can design a way to use models for policy as well as design issues.... You can interpret the results of modelling, so long as you do not get stuck in the models and it (the model) is not the gospel. Nobody should be taking modelling results as the absolute answer. If your assumptions change within reasonable limits, what you want to know is whether you come out in the right 'ball park'....
>
> If your assumption of population growth is about 20 per cent (which it could easily be), you need to check if you have, for example, put a bus system where you really should have put a railway system. What you want to know is whether you are making any big blunders? What you have got to make sure is a reasonable change in your assumptions will not push you over a margin into a different type of solution – and that is just a question of running the different assumptions (and variables) through the models and seeing what the implications are.

Echoing the above position, Manheim argues that urban transport models for Third World use should be:

> employed to basically clarify judgment, and not to produce 'the answer'. Models are never (totally) rational or objective tools, they are constructs which help us to explore the logical implications of a whole set of alternative premises. We try to make models mirror reality but we are always uncertain as to the extent to which they achieve that.... Our role as staff advisors should be to help gain an insight into issues which we then try to communicate to the political process. This is

> distinct from the style (of approach) in which we recommend the answer because it came out of the computer and we encourage the decision maker to accept it simply because he is impressed by the 'magic' of the tool.

One of the biggest design issues associated with the UTP process in general, and some of its sub-models in particular, is whether it systematically over-designs urban transport systems. As Ingram explains:

> One argument would be that (as in the USA) you get a reasonably capital intensive facility because there is a trade-off between capital intensity and future maintenance. Another argument would be that their future maintenance would be cheaper, particularly in an LDC, if you have a less capital intensive facility. My general sense of that is that the people who have looked at this question as carefully as they can, find it very hard to come down on one side or the other.

Many involved in the US urban transport field, including Heanue (1989) of the US DOT, have, as already indicated (see Chapter 4), argued that a huge amount of the country's urban transport capital investments have been built as a result of the UTP process. They claim that while some notable failures may be observed in the application of the process, these errors have been compensated by the hundreds of thousands of miles of roads that were constructed, and the investment in billion dollar facilities which are today working perfectly well. The Third World, however, does not, as Dean points out, have the option of tearing down its cities to build its roads in this way. He argues:

> They (particularly the poorer Third World cities) do not have the money to do that, i.e., to build up the facilities as we did (in USA) and try and meet all these demands – so it is not going to happen. They are rather going to be bogged down by the question of what is worth building and what is not worth building for the next generation? These questions are going to continue to arise and we must respond to them.

An important question that needs to be addressed in the context of this discussion is whether one can plan for Third World urban transport without models (also see Chapter 4). Watson believes it is possible, since the Paris metro and the London underground were both built without a model of the kind discussed above. Dean similarly indicates that there is scope for such an approach, in that an experienced transport planner will always make some reasonable judgments without the models. The probability, however, of successfully doing this on a continued basis, is, in Watson's view, low. He describes the case of a transport planning approach employed for a city in Brazil, prepared by a local consultant without a model. It proved highly successful in his own city but when transferred to another city less familiar to him in the same country, it produced disastrous results. This experience suggests close familiarity with the city in question is essential to plan successfully without models.

Planning style and politics

> ***Do sustained systematic efforts at clarifying major urban transport planning goals meet with resistance in Third World nations?***

Much confusion in the pursuance of goals associated with the transport sub-sector of Third World cities has to do with the lack of co-ordination between ministerial and municipal responsibilities (see Chapter 6). The aim of the housing ministry, for example, may be to build houses where the land is cheap. Where people are housed is often far from their work and the fact that the vast majority of Third World city inhabitants heavily rely on public transport is seen as a Ministry of Transport problem. If travel demand is to be reduced by creating housing and job opportunities close together, then the Housing Ministry must be made to rethink its actions.

If an inadequate budget is the reason for building housing on the cheapest available land, bringing this problem out into the open might, according to Watson, be the only way that it can be solved. In his dealings with Third World governments in the urban transport field, Watson claims that:

> In general, I found people quite reasonable in setting out what their objectives are. They like to do that especially in the more politicised areas – strangely enough because they then have goals.

At first sight this observation is contrary to the expectation of many political scientists. They claim that the non-clarification of goals very often masks a hidden agenda, and that by exposing the agenda or by having people come from the outside to make goals more explicit, exposes the secret agreement which gives planning the protection needed for its implementation. These observations can, however, in part be explained by the fact that although policy changes take place frequently, if the politician wants to get ahead politically, he must show some achievement. The best way to do this is to start off with a firm programme of projects which he focuses on wholeheartedly. The politician then sets out in the first year to obtain government finance. In the second year, he gets the funds, and builds the projects in the third and fourth years. What this sequence implies is that to obtain government funds and to get anything built, the politician must know clearly what he wants and take the initiative to get it.

Another interpretation of these same developments is that these persons are not articulating goals, but merely stating what they will do. The politician's statement that he will build 'X kilometres of roads' plus 'Y number of houses' is not a goal but a target. The target does not represent, for example, a statement of one's stand concerning the equity question of transport facility provision among different income groups. In this way, this alternative interpretation argues that politicians can be clear on targets (which are politically useful) and yet remain secretive about those goals which they leave unchallenged, by making vague platitudinous statements about, for example, the enhancement of the environment.

Henrickson and Tummarallo argue that in any government organisation anywhere, an outside consultant brought in to help the government identify its own goals is going to meet a certain amount of resistance. For as Gakenheimer (1990) points out, there are public goals and personal goals. Even some of the former cannot be divulged for fear of betraying allegiances that should be kept hidden. Furthermore, much of political survival depends on reacting to events without even considering goals.

In these circumstances, the World Bank, but especially the UN agencies and USAID, have in the past often tried to encourage the government to set up some kind of planning commission – a kind of planning ministry – so the government and its constituent ministries can identify their own goals. This is sometimes seen as a prerequisite for the identification of programmes and stipulation of their goals.

On the other hand, there are many who have expressed their disenchantment with the uncomfortable relationship between planning and implementation. This is very apparent in local project implementation and urban transport planning, in the lack of attention given to the transaction costs and expense of implementing, for example, cost revenue measures. The costs of putting a system in place and the losses associated with doing this can, according to Ingram, be so large that one may be better off with a system that does not work so well but is easier to introduce and is much more acceptable. On this basis, Dean argues that the implementation of transport plans needs to be an integral part of transport planning. This is especially because in the Third World many of the issues do not really surface until the implementation phase is reached.

ISSUES OF TECHNOLOGY-TRANSFER

Cross-cultural differences

> *What are the most significant issues of cross-cultural intervention that international development agencies and consultants should consider when preparing urban transport planning projects?* [2]

Stopher believes that one of the most important prerequisites for transport planners working in another culture is that they should try to understand the background and values of the culture they are working in. By illustration he explains:

> You find in the basic tribal structure of black Africa for example, that there is no conception of the sort of model of economic man on which we base a great deal of the transportation work we do – i.e., the 'John Kain man'. If you, however, go ahead and simply transfer the model to that culture, you could waste quite a lot of investment by proposing things which may not be appropriate or useful to that culture.

In response, Dean claims that planners can be broadly classified, whether they belong to international development agencies or are employed by consultants, into two categories. Namely, those who stress cultural differences and those who focus on common factors. Dean belongs to the latter category. He argues that in Third World countries, just as in the USA, if one conducts a public transit study in order try to make decisions about how much subsidy and public assistance a scheme should receive, one would get an enormous range of different responses. However, in both parts of the world, as soon as one becomes involved in these exercises, it becomes apparent that there is a need to interface with the decision-makers to get feedback. Only then can one pose the right alternatives that are responsive to preconceived notions, and adjust them as one goes along. Without that feedback failure is certain.

In contrast to Dean, Watson's focus is on the cultural and development differences. Watson argues that in those Third World cities, such as in Brazil, where the infant mortality rate is very high (61/1000 live births [World Bank, 1990]) and where 75 per cent of all families live with incomes below the World Bank poverty level; where housing provision is, by and large, a disaster and where disease and medical problems are epidemic or endemic; where the urban poor have no clean water, and virtually no access to sanitation facilities; where they are either unemployed or (at best) under-employed, or even scrounging a living, where illiteracy is widespread; and where children have negligible opportunities – then by comparison the city's transport problems appear rather less serious. He explains:

> One has to bear in mind constantly that every dollar you take for urban transport is a dollar taken away from housing, from medical facilities or from educational facilities. It puts inter-sectoral comparisons into a much stronger focus. Despite this, one still has to do something about transport. For if people can't get to work then there is no hope of breaking out of this (poverty) trap. In Brazil we (the World Bank) have put into our studies an examination of the relationship between urban transport and unemployment, to see how sure it is that people do not work because they cannot get to places (where the employment is).

Another difference, already alluded to, is the problem of how to support public transport much more, given that the proportion of motorcar owners in Third World cities is so low. In many cities there is probably 20 per cent of the population who cannot even afford public transport and who are walking perhaps ten kilometres each way to work and back (see Chapters 5 and 6). In these conditions, issues of fare structures, choice of mode, etc., need to be put into a totally different perspective than that usually associated with industrialised countries. Watson again explains:

> For the people who ride the bus from Monday to Wednesday, and who walk Thursday and Friday, because their funds do not last for their bus fares all through the week – when one starts to talk about financial liability of services, and bus company subsidies – it is a totally different focus one is presented with. Because you would (conventionally) say raise the fares and remove the subsidy, but in so doing, you may then take 15 per cent off your market by just forcing them (this patronage) out.

Gakenheimer suggests that, among the most important cross-cultural considerations to be taken into account by an international consultant working in transport in a Third World city, are differences in the sub-markets of urban transport in which the demand for transport facilities are located, and the forms to which transport planners from the industrialised countries are accustomed to organising these sub-markets into. In the Middle East, for example, the sex of the trip-maker is an important factor determining trip-making. Many Western planners, Kain claims, have not taken this into account in the changing relationship between household structure and size in many Third World cities experiencing rapid urbanisation. Yet, projecting changes in household size and composition is critical in travel behaviour forecasts.

Other cultural issues have to do with political systems. In Britain and America, for instance, transport planners are more concerned with car ownership and this is more or less incorporated within the institution's planning constraints. In Third World countries, however, Gakenheimer believes, there may be considerable leverage in the hands of the government to affect car ownership by adjusting import regulations and devising policy about the domestic assembly of manufactured automobiles. Substantial cultural adjustment on the part of expatriate consultants working in Third World countries is also required, regarding government confusion about the desired relationship between the formal urban public transport sector and its informal equivalent (see Chapters 5 and 6). It is common, Gakenheimer explains, that there is:

> a poor management relationship. The government is likely not to favour informal public transit very much. An effort is often made to suppress it. Informal transport is made up of numerous small-scale ownerships that in aggregate are politically influential, but have no corporate organization with which government can bargain.

In these circumstances, it is essential that the expatriate consultant is both clear about the role of such transport systems and the implications of various options under consideration affecting them.

Technical assistance

> *Under what circumstances should non-nationals be involved in Third World urban transport projects? Are foreign planning consultants able to perceive their clients' needs as the clients see their needs?*

Henrickson and Tummarallo suggest that concern about this issue was most vocal in the late 1960s. At that time, donors were subject to much criticism for having preconceived ideas about what was good for the client country, and about the most suitable technology, and how the donors could provide it. In the late 1970s and into the 1980s, this criticism is more commonly levelled at private consultancy firms and especially the transport hardware industry.

Stopher sees it as quite a bold decision for a non-national to decide to become involved in foreign urban transport projects. He views such participation as legitimate where certain countries lack the necessary resources to help themselves. The assumption here, however, is that the 'know-how' and skills of the foreign consultant *are* of some value. Stopher, like Gakenheimer, warns that particular care is needed when an outside expert is expected to transfer his/her skills to a different country without any local knowledge. One of the key questions which is continuously raised in this context is whose standards one adopts and whether this should be purely a matter of the consultant's personal conscience.

Gakenheimer believes that foreign consultants should become involved in Third World planning:

> When they may be associated with a planning project using relatively sophisticated techniques that only the foreign

> consultants are able to adapt adequately, for example the needs for adaptation of the Lowry series models. Lowry created his model for Pittsburgh, where the primary section of the economy is very important, so it was appropriate to use forecasts of it to estimate consequences on spatial structure at many levels. When borrowing this model for use in the developing world, that unmentioned assumption is seldom valid.

Pointing to another example of the care needed in the technology-transfer of ideas and values embedded in the UTP process and its derivatives, Gakenheimer cites the interesting cases of land-use zoning. Zoning, he explains, originated in Germany in the first quarter of the nineteenth century. It subsequently became an aesthetic feature of town planning in Britain and Germany. By the time it was imported to the USA, Gakenheimer claims it was primarily used as a means of maintaining income level homogeneity among residential areas and creating areas of social exclusiveness. The concept was, he explains, exported, 'lock, stock and barrel' to Third World countries, where generally they do not use spatial isolation as a way of accommodating social prejudice. A radical critique of the damage that zoning has done to the social fabric of the Third World cities through the application of conventional wisdom planning is thus, according to Gakenheimer, long overdue.

When asked to provide finance for a specific urban transport project to a particular country, agencies such as the World Bank, must be sure that it is a viable and 'developmentally effective' project. To ascertain this, an analysis and an appraisal need to be conducted. Therefore, either the agency has to undertake such studies or it must employ another party to do it on its behalf. Watson explains:

> In some cases, we (the World Bank) find that there is quite a lot of analysis already done. In other cases, we find we have to start from scratch. In certain instances, we can't say anything until a transport study is conducted, which itself might require financing. In which case, people are asking for external funding, either from an agency like the World Bank or from government. To make an efficient use of resources, and ensure an efficient transfer of funds, that agency or government has then to get involved in transport planning.

The World Bank claims that it does not get involved in issues when it is not asked, whereas field observations suggest that in fact it does. The Bank often sets conditions. Prior to offering loans to buy more buses, for example, a government may be asked by the Bank to commit itself to raising bus fares, or to changing a certain policy to do with the operation of bus companies. Ingram confesses that in these negotiations:

> there is a tremendous amount of trading that goes on, where you are essentially trying to extract some surplus by changing policies in a way that it seems to be appealing to the people who are making the model.

Commenting on this negotiation process, Berry claims that international agencies say all the right things, about multi-skilled, multi-racial and multi-national co-operation, simply because in order to progress they are obliged to communicate with people from different backgrounds and with different expectations. Much of what goes on in these agencies, however, he argues, involves:

> defining the mode and range of acceptable social behaviour and interchange. That being so, much time is spent designing the way that things get put together in particular 'boxes' that there is very little energy left in putting anything into them.

Apart from special assignments or project identification missions, when the World Bank and comparable agencies involved in urban transport in the Third World generally utilise their own staff, they hire external consultants to conduct feasibility and preparatory studies, since they do not usually have the in-house capacity to do the studies themselves. As Watson explains:

> We have no alternative but to use external consultants... it would be nice if there were better consultants... I would, however, much rather see for example, Brazilian consultants going to Ecuador than American consultants. They (the former) are culturally closer. In certain countries, like Brazil, one would not use foreign consultants, except extremely specialised ones, for very specialised jobs. I would be quite happy if the situation arose whereby the industrialised country consultants all go 'bust' because there was not enough work for them. At the moment, however, they fulfill a valuable role.

> The only problem is how to try and control them – which is what we try to do but not very successfully.

Dean argues that the foreign consultants' role is far more effective in an assistance capacity, with a local consultant or government agency taking the lead. The most attractive working arrangements in this context, he argues, is for the external consultants to come in and help increase the local capacity on the basis of some kind of flexible contract. In this way, the foreign consultant can be called upon for short-or long-term visits, as the need arises, in order to execute specific tasks. At any rate, Dean explains, the consultants must acquire an insight into the environment in which expatriate advisors are to advise. They must appreciate the mix of technical and public policy pressures that prevail, as well as the public attitudes that might be important.

In general, two kinds of consultants involved in the Third World urban transport field can be identified. They are the salesmen, who come come to sell a particular technology and who do a study to prove the excellence of a particular piece of hardware (such as a light rail system). This sort of salesmanship in Third World countries was in the past considered despicable. The other sort of consultants have been described by Watson as not very receptive to local situations. This is because they are sent out from the UK or the USA, do not speak the local language at all or very well, and are not so sensitive to the local political situation. Their response to what they encounter in the field is typified by Watson's illustration:

> The Governor says, for example, – you have got to build roads – and they (the consultants) say – all right. They orient themselves therefore to the road solution. Whereas, the Governor in fact has not really thought about it, rather it seems to him that in his administration it would be good to build a series of roads. If he was presented with the real cost of that option against other alternatives, and shown that he could politically sell himself by cutting travel times all over the city instead of building roads, he could again win political points. What he (the Governor) cares about, is looking good.

Berry concurs with this analysis. He believes that most foreign consulting businesses will ultimately see the client's need and deliver a report incorporating what the client wants, without seriously investigating other options. Expanding upon this practice, he claims:

> what you will find is that they (the foreign consultants) pull volume 13 off the shelf – this being the standard formula – and just change the name (of the place) and statistics (of the problem).... This is not to say that there are not some consultants who are genuinely concerned, responsible and perceptive about their role, with the necessary empathy and who consider that leaving behind something that is valuable is important. There are some – but a few.... It paints a pretty nasty picture of what is going on but it represents the real situation out there.

Given that the role of the World Bank and other international development agencies is usually for it to come in and supervise a government employed consultant, and subsequently use his work to help do the appraisal, the visiting representatives of the international agency in effect build a bridge between the consultants and the client. Henrickson and Tummarallo explain that under similar circumstances, USAID typically seeks to link up a team of US consultants to a matching local team and tries to survey exactly what they perceive is needed, and is the most economical way to take action. It is this part of the exercise, Henrickson and Tummarallo point out, with which the agency's team of consultants usually have the most difficulties, because there are different priorities in the different ministries involved in urban transport. Henrickson and Tummarallo explain:

> We are government agents but at the same time, somewhat independent. USAID retains a consultant, we set out what the problem is and what the goals are. Then we undertake to finance and conduct the study... we really know what the goals are before we go out and the government pre-agree that these are the goals... we will develop a project, take in local needs and try to design what their tradition is, and not endanger and affect their environment.

The guidance given to consultants in the field by USAID is derived from the US Congress. There is an annual programme of USAID development projects which acts as a mandate that is submitted to Congress for approval and includes every proposed project.

The role of USAID since 1973 has, according to Henrickson and

Tummarallo, dramatically changed. In the mid to late 1960s, if the client government wanted to build a steel mill, USAID would finance a steel mill. Since the late 1970s, however, the agency changed its emphasis to assisting the very poor, and promoting rural development projects. Much more recently, the agency has turned also to aspects of management, institution-strengthening and training of Third World government agencies involved in both infrastructure provision and maintenance. Henrickson and Tummarallo, however, point out:

> There is an inherent resistance to maintenance... everyone likes to cut ribbons. Maintenance has never been popular in these (Third World) countries anywhere. The fact that the government assigns US$ 300,000 annually to maintain this or that road attracts no attention. Whereas, if US$ 300,000, whatever, is spent on a new section of road, there is a big splash in the newspapers – you are showing 'progress'. It is costly to have to deal with that problem. I think you will find that the World Bank goes through this same problem.

Development models

How important is it to appreciate the role of cities in Third World development before deciding what the contribution of transport is to these cities?

One response to the above question is a very pragmatic one, namely to see it as a 'red herring' – i.e., in Watson's words:

> if you have got transport problems – you have to sort out transport problems. If we are dealing with countries that do not have vast amounts of skilled manpower to go around preparing all kinds of policies and plans and do not have a national urban policy – but the nation's capital city transport situation is deteriorating – then I would view our (the World Bank's) job as helping them solve their transport problem. The Bank may suggest, as an aside, that they hire a team of consultants to do a national urbanisation study to see to what extent the problems are being caused by migration but the agency normally operates outside this scope.

A directional change in policy for the World Bank has for some time now involved an attempt to focus increasingly on medium sized cities with populations of 500,000 and above. This has been done with a view to helping create basic infrastructure and employment in those settlements, so as to act as a buffer to the further growth of major metropolitan regions, as well as to stimulate the medium sized cities themselves. However, while some see it as a challenge to be able to work within the framework of the whole development system of a country, Watson claims that it is not a prerequisite for urban transport planning.

Henrickson and Tummarallo take a somewhat different position to Watson. They point out that urban areas are the principal commercial and industrial production centres of a country, as well as the seats of regional and national governments. They further claim that the germane development of urban areas will reflect on the overall national economy (see Chapter 5). They furthermore argue that the reason for the kind of urban development that takes place in major Third World cities like Lagos, Rio de Janireo and Sao Paulo, is because the national policies of the countries in which these cities are located stress the need for urban development. They stress certain factors of overall development that encourage the massing of great numbers of people in cities without any consideration of the ability of the urban infrastructure to cope with what is happening.

One of the mandates given to USAID by the US Congress is that if a Third World country has not identified its national development priorities and has not set up a Planning Commission to oversee its proposed projects and put them in context, it can de-sponsor any of the projects that USAID is involved in. As a result, particularly during the late 1970s and early 1980s, the agency became actively involved in setting up national planning commissions and helping them with the formulation of their goals.

Following the establishment of such national guidelines, certain countries such as Indonesia, aided by the setting up of proper legislation, are inviting and successfully attracting foreign capital to actively participate in their national development on their own initiative. Others, particularly socialist countries, have wanted first to develop their own industrial base. In the closing years of the 1980s, however, this resolve has not only weakened but in many cases has been reversed.

Henrickson and Tummarallo go on to argue:

It seems to me logical that if you have a centrally planned

> economy, centrally planned prices and centrally planned allocation of resources, then you clearly cannot go out and expect a market oriented planning process to take care of the system for you.... As a result, your transport planning approach must affect your physical planning approach.

Sudra points out that increasing centralisation resulting from the function of capital concentration and the introduction of new technologies that maximise profits of centralised enterprises, contributes to the need for more sophisticated means of transport. Substituting capital intensive for labour intensive employment, and substituting production in the larger metropolitan areas, and then exporting the goods to the hinterland (rather than vice versa), leads to a type of spatial structure which suffocates the city centre. This situation, he claims, contributes to an undesirable urban transport planning approach. To counter these trends, Sudra argues:

> Policies should instead be introduced to maximise local reliance and regional resources, and thereby minimise the substitution of local modes of production. This is more likely to achieve an even distribution of population. Transportation (if one is not careful), can therefore be used as an agent of destruction of local productivity in the interest of improving centralised economic activities.

Motorcar dependency

Are those Third World cities which as yet have not committed themselves to the motorcar at an inherent advantage?

Third World cities not committed to the motorcar have an inherent advantage on three counts. Firstly, such settlements have more options and more freedom among options to tackle their movement problems (see Newman and Kenworthy, 1989). Secondly, particularly in the case of more affluent cities, the authorities can actively prevent public transport services from deteriorating in the face of rising motorcar ownership and usage. Finally, given that public transport is the principal transport mode for Third World city movement (see Chapters 5 and 6), it is important on equity grounds to protect the investment already sunk into these systems against its marginalisation by the affluent few. Regarding the equity issue, Watson comments:

> If you are to feel comfortable with what you are doing to benefit a very large number of people, you cannot orientate all trips towards the motorcar. If you (as a transport planner/traffic engineer) take a lane away from private car use and give it to buses – whatever the car drivers do, however much they yell and scream, you can feel confident that you have done something valuable.

Of the above three advantages, the key is to give Third World cities a chance to salvage public transport, as many have already started to do. For as long as public transport does not enter into the spiral situation whereby increased motorcar usage makes it necessary to cut public transport services, and increase fares (thereby further encouraging motorcar ownership), there is a real chance of maintaining viable public transport services. More to the point, as Kain suggests, such cities can probably achieve the same level of accessibility and mobility at much lower resource costs. While Gakenheimer supports this view, he also warns that many Third World cities are rapidly losing these inherent advantages by not adopting appropriate policies to protect themselves against the misuse of the motorcar.

Sudra claims that the degree to which a Third World city has any of the above inherent advantages, is directly proportional to the extent that planning and planned intervention have taken place there. He argues:

> wherever you have planners to influence the way a city is to grow, then they do it with the motorcar in mind. They always seem to have some kind of image of how many cars exist for so many people and therefore make a plan which is motorcar orientated. Actually, I do not know of an urban planning process (in the Third World) which was not orientated towards the motorcar.... When you think of cities which do not have the motorcar as an important determinant of their plans... you are thinking of cities in their pre-planning phase.

Expanding the same point, Levinson claims:

> What is needed in Third World cities is to find out how much mobility they require and stop at that point, and not over-de-

> sign the roads. If you look at what alternative measures exist, whether it is traffic restraint, traffic management, the promulgation of *jitneys*, the introduction of extensive bus priority schemes, cycle paths and/or walking facilities – these cities are at some advantage. But the advantage exists only if you intelligently relate the plans of change to the plans of transport that you want.

Ingram, however, does not see such cities having any inherent advantage. He argues that in any situation where one requires a greater highway capacity, whether for taxis, buses or whatever, it is an expensive exercise to provide this for compact and high density cities, wherever they are. This is because there is a great deal of durable capital investment that has to be removed in order to build the additional infrastructure. It is a great deal cheaper, Ingram claims, to do this in a growing city, where the highway system can be laid out as the city grows.

John Harris, of Boston University, believes that some Third World cities, particularly (but not exclusively) the more affluent, do not in fact have any options left, since they have already committed themselves to the motorcar. He explains:

> The majority of people (in such cities) have no choice because they just cannot afford the choice. So whilst on one hand you have a government commitment to a specific (motorcar-orientated) transportation system, the people themselves have no commitment to it.

Planning commitment in this context, Harris argues, is not a function of a technical rationale but of the ideological predisposition of the planner and the type of development model he is pursuing. Dean claims that many of the governments that have not committed themselves to the motorcar have not done so because they do not have the resources and the time to do. He argues:

> Given the limitations in the resources, I would say there are advantages in this because they cannot do what we did. The real question you are asking is – what is the success and failure of our own policy? Have we made the mistake of committing ourselves fully to the automobile....? Well I guess my views on that – which you have not asked but I will give anyway – is that we made mistakes by putting such a huge over-emphasis on the highway.

Interestingly enough, as an aside, Dean also argues another, more unusual line of thought, namely that if city governments in the industrialised countries had not taken the path they chose, while the current transport situation would have remained by and large much the same, the exceptions would have fared much better.

8

ELEMENTS AND FRAMEWORK OF A DEVELOPMENTAL APPROACH TO TRANSPORT PLANNING FOR THIRD WORLD CITIES

INTRODUCTION

This, the penultimate chapter of the book, describes the characteristics and elements of a 'developmental approach' to urban transport planning.[1] It also outlines a methodology for a sketch-planning to be employed within this that is consistent with development planning principles.

While the chapter expounds on an approach based on the experience of Indonesia (see TDC S. A., 1988), it is generally applicable to other Third World contexts, particularly low-income and lower-middle-income countries that occupy large land masses and contain a wide spectrum of urban settlement types and sizes, such as Brazil, India and China.

Much of the fundamental thinking outlined here is especially reflective of the reservations discussed in Chapter 7 concerning the limitations of conventional wisdom transport planning practice in Third World cities.

The main elements of a 'development approach' to urban transport planning (see Figure 8.1) have regard to the translation of the principles of urban development planning into the urban transport sub-sector. Within this, the approach employs the concept of Integrated Urban Infrastructure Development Programming (IUIDP) as a policy, planning and management framework for urban transport.[2] The approach also relies on matching settlement and community size considerations with development policy contexts and the use of appropriate transport technology.

Figure 8.1 Elements of the developmental approach to planning the urban transport sub-sector

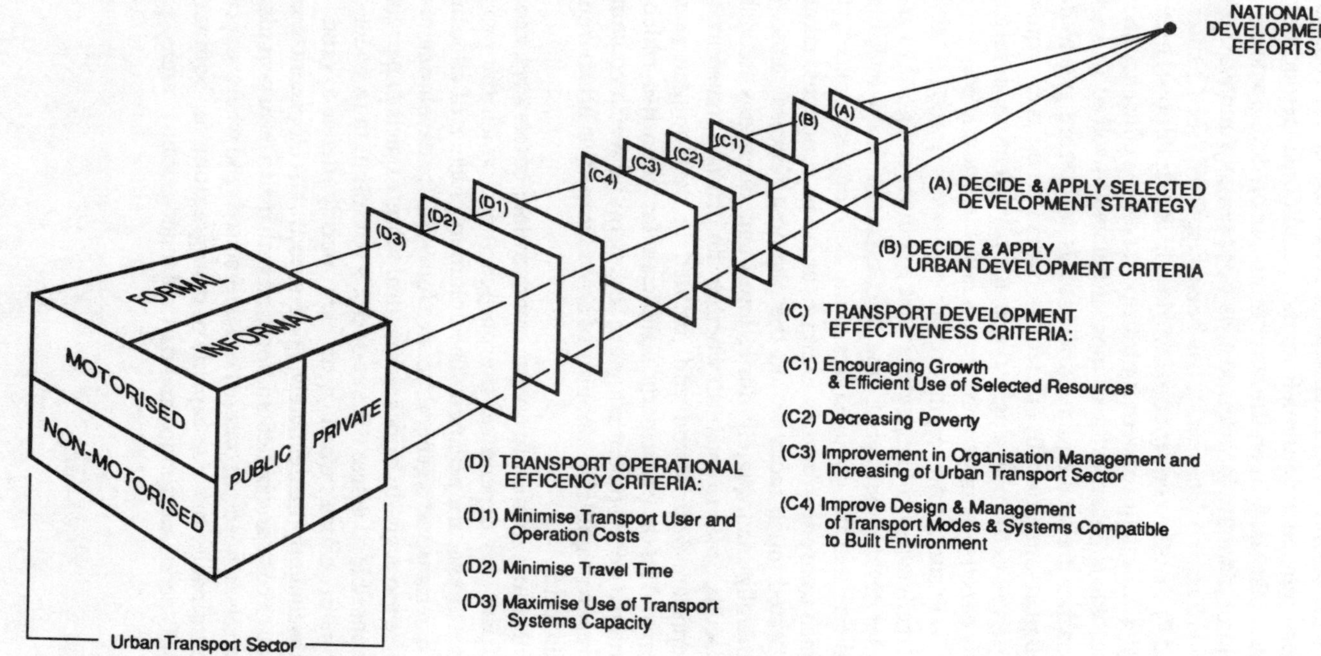

What essentially differentiates the 'developmental approach' to urban transport planning from more traditional methodologies is that unlike the former, the latter rely more on developments in the field of planning for transport, as opposed to planning transport *for urban development*. It has been suggested (see Chapters 3, 4 and 7) that the conventional wisdom bias in traditional methodologies with their concern for transport systems efficiency above all else, exists because those most intimately involved in such approaches are well equipped with tools and techniques to design and plan 'operationally efficient' networks, whereas the equivalent expertise in the planning and management of more 'developmentally effective' transport systems is much less advanced.

To ensure, however, that urban transport planning is 'developmentally effective' i.e., subservient to efforts designed to achieve wider development goals, the discussions in Chapters 5, 6 and 7 indicate that the complexities of the development context within which transport planning exercises are to be conducted should be reflected much more within the planning process. Since this is generally inadequately done, important questions need to be raised in order to establish whether the planned transport investments are *both* sound and justified in development planning terms. This is particularly significant for countries which take national development planning seriously and which contemplate investing significant amounts of capital into their urban transport sub-sector.

Realistic answers to investment questions of this kind, however, in part also depend on the purpose(s) to which the proposed investments are assigned. The common practice of allocating to urban transport a general 'service function' for development tends to be too vague to be of any practical value, especially because it is impossible to assess the sub-sector's contribution to wider development efforts when goals are poorly defined (and often subsequently inadequately understood). Development goals, as well as costs and benefits associated with urban transport planning exercises, need not only to be clearly stated (and wherever possible quantifiable) but also capable of disaggregation for both targeted socio-economic groups and particular geographical areas.

PRINCIPLES OF URBAN DEVELOPMENT PLANNING

Principles

The tradition of urban development planning from which the 'developmental approach' to urban transport planning is partly derived,[3] has been described as (see Dimitriou and Safier, 1982):

> an approach founded upon the systematic application of evaluation criteria, derived from the diagnosis of urban development as a process of social, economic, technological and physical change that has been managed (or mismanaged) by government operations and interventions.
>
> It is based upon offering selected and organised guidance in the planning of urban development and the managing of public sector action with the intention of providing planning advice and assistance to government and public and private sector agencies involved in the accommodation of basic material, environmental, social and cultural needs of urban populations.

The implementation of this approach requires the adoption of measures aimed at improving the productive potentials of cities, the distribution of urban opportunities, and the improvement of social life and the physical environment.

Urban development planning adopts as its unit of operation, individual cities and towns which it regards as 'public enterprises' – each with its own contribution to national development. It takes into account four principal considerations:

1 the role of urban areas in achieving national development strategies;
2 the role of urban areas in contributing to rural and regional development policies;
3 the capacity of urban areas to provide for the 'basic needs' of its own population; and
4 the capacity of the urban area to provide for the absorption of migrants.

The principles and practice of urban development planning are not expected to replace the already operational traditions of urban planning, town and country planning, or urban traffic and transport planning. Rather, it is intended to support a continuing dialogue with other types of planning, whether they be based on scale, subject, or sector. The model and format of this dialogue should, however, be open and continuous so that the subject matter is better understood and relationships become clearer. What follows is a presentation of one such model for the treatment of the relationship of transport to urban development, in which the former is subservient to the latter.

An examination of past experiences of planning urban areas and their transport in both industrialised and Third World countries has attracted considerable criticism (see Chapters 3, 4 and 7). The failures of these planning experiences and the consequent attempt in certain quarters to improve on the concepts of 'development' employed (see Chapter 5) has led to the introduction of a series of interrelated development planning performance criteria which are applicable to various elements of the urban economy, society and environment. These may be grouped into four sets of objectives, namely:

1 the maintenance and creation of growth of real resources per capita;
2 the decrease of poverty and deprivation;
3 the promotion of increased accessibility to, and responsiveness of, public sector administration in urban affairs; and
4 the promotion of adaptable urban physical and spatial arrangements accommodating needs, as well as cultural and social identity.

Maintenance and creation of economic growth

The pursuit of the goal of maintaining existing economic growth performances, as well as of simultaneously creating additional growth, implies that urban transport systems need to be planned, provided and operated in a manner whereby they both maintain or increase the efficient use of current real resources, and avoid the use of transport technologies which are inconsistent with prevailing development constraints and objectives. Transport systems, therefore, need to be used to increase the mobilisation of presently idle resources, before additional facilities are provided. An approach of this kind would be resource sensitive, in that it would both maximise energy conservation and minimise negative ecological and environmental impacts.

Decrease of poverty

Planning and managing urban transport in support of decreasing poverty, requires at the 'grass roots', a focus on issues of inequality of access to transport services and inequality of provision of transport infrastructure (see Chapter 6). City transport systems, for example, which link the major residential areas of the less privileged with work, educational, recreational and other important locations, would contribute to the decrease of poverty. The use of urban transport systems in a manner which would also accommodate the basic needs of the great majority of city inhabitants would do likewise. This would inject an element of equity into the development equation and also help bridge the growing gap in many Third World cities between the increasingly mobile affluent and the immobilised poor.

Increase in responsiveness of urban administration

To make progress, urban transport systems need to be planned, provided and operated in a manner whereby more active participation is encouraged in government by members of the urban community. Government support in these circumstances should be given to local groups involved in providing and maintaining their own transport facilities. Such support may be pursued in a number of ways – from reducing excessive enforcement measures on local initiatives at providing transport operations, to involving some form of public representation in the management of city-wide public transport services. Measures of this kind would not only raise the performance of the overall public transport network by making it more answerable to its users and more self-sufficient but also provide additional employment opportunities for those on the margin.

Promotion of adaptable spatial urban formations

To avoid transport systems and services detracting from efforts to accommodate the cultural and social identity of cities, the transport systems need to contribute to urban form patterns, city structures and development densities that are consistent with both the evolution of the settlement in question, and its resource constraints. In this way, new transport technologies which dramatically and indiscriminately alter the social life styles of an urban society, and impose new unwanted urban form patterns (see Brotchie *et al.*, 1985), can be better monitored and avoided.

Policy priorities

The above four objectives principally operate at the level of policy priorities. Together they offer an overall 'guiding concept' of urban development planning as they relate to urban transport. However, at the different stages of planning, design, programming and operations, more specific technical and organisational criteria will be required if these objectives are to be translated into more useful guidelines to assist the formulation and implementation of urban transport plans and schemes. The ensuing discussion (in this and the following chapter) concerning the use of IUIDP *and* the matching of transport technologies to settlements of different sizes and development contexts is intended to provide the required level of detail within an overall 'developmental planning' approach to urban transport.

CONCEPTS AND PRINCIPLES OF IUIDP PROGRAMMING

General concepts and issues

The IUIDP approach

IUIDP represents a particular kind of 'development planning' approach for the (integrated) planning and programming of infrastructure for urban development which has been applied to a number of countries in Asia, including Bangladesh, India and Indonesia (see Dimitriou, 1991).[4] IUIDP in particular, seeks to respond to critical problems of urban expansion in a context of limited public sector resources.

The general features of IUIDP include making the optimum use of existing resources, co-ordinating potential development resources, enhancing the effective integration and decentralisation of sectoral urban development programmes, and taking measures to increase locally generated revenues to recover costs of urban infrastructure (so as to contribute to new investments). Ideally, the approach should be applied to the full range of urban infrastructure and services within both the public and private sectors. Prevailing constraints, particularly with regard to the institutional complexity of agencies associated with urban development have, however, meant that IUIDP has often had to be introduced on a gradual and limited cross-sectoral basis, as is the case in Indonesia.

The Indonesian experience in IUIDP initially addressed housing and water supply. The approach was later extended to inter-sectoral areas of concern regarding transport and waste disposal, focusing on:

1 the stimulation of efforts to increase locally generated revenues, especially to cover the maintenance and operation costs of existing infrastructure, as well as contributing toward the financing of new urban infrastructure investments;
2 the expansion of low-cost urban infrastructure investments and maintenance in a planned and co-ordinated manner;
3 the decentralisation of planning and implementation responsibilities of urban development projects to local government; and
4 the strengthening of provincial and municipal capacities in the fields of project preparation, appraisal and evaluation.

As implied above, in addition to encouraging the better use of existing resources, the major underlying development objectives implicit in IUIDP are to increase the economic productivity of cities and help to fulfil the basic needs of their inhabitants. This involves the very difficult task of balancing competing demands for resources, while simultaneously improving the management, use and generation of resources. A careful strategy is needed to do this for it not only calls for infrastructure improvements but the development or modifications of public sector financial support mechanisms.

IUIDP warrants both an overall awareness of urban development issues and opportunities at various levels, and in different sub-sectors. This in turn calls for the employment of technical and procedural guidelines, together with associated standards for the execution of programmes and projects. Such guidelines would typically include:

1 a statement of the IUIDP approach;
2 details of IUIDP procedures;
3 information regarding the relationship of the IUIDP programme with forthcoming development plans;

4 operational guidelines for preparing IUIDP programmes; and
5 technical guidelines for the implementation of IUIDP projects.

An additional important prerequisite of an IUIDP approach is the clear understanding of concepts and terminology associated with its application, particularly with regard to efforts at achieving:

1 sustained economic productivity;
2 basic needs fulfillment;
3 integration; and
4 decentralisation.

It has been argued (see TDC S. A., 1988) that an appreciation of these concepts needs to go hand in hand with the task of clearly identifying linkages between the physical and financial aspects of urban development, and among the sub-sectors themselves. This is particularly important for urban transport, as it services both other sectors and sub-sectors.

Investment in an IUIDP approach requires careful identification being given to the costs and benefits involved in its application, as well as details of their distribution. Guidance must therefore be provided on who should benefit and who should pay for the initiated efforts. To be consistent with urban development planning principles articulated earlier, IUIDP must encourage city agencies to initiate new projects within a framework of nationally acceptable guidelines and related technical standards. This emphasises the need for guidelines and central government involvement to remain in urban development (and thus in urban transport), at least in its initial phases of IUIDP. Such involvement is best provided in a supervisory capacity, whereby over time, central government agencies gradually devolve their technical involvement to provincial and municipal levels of government.

IUIDP principles and urban transport

Applying IUIDP principles to the sub-sector implies the optimisation of the use of existing transport infrastructure and services before providing additional facilities. The approach also entails the co-ordination and synchronisation of transport facility provision with the programming of other facilities, and the integration of the planning and programming of transport facilities with other urban development programmes. Finally, the approach seeks to increase efforts locally to generate revenues from road transport for both the sub-sector itself, and for wider urban development purposes.

An IUIDP emphasis on urban transport is thus likely to focus on selected low-cost traffic management and road maintenance schemes in preference to new infrastructure provision, as well as the rehabilitation of surfaced and unsurfaced local roads and footpaths considered essential to the development of local communities. The approach would also be expected to strengthen the technical and management capabilities of provincial and municipal agency staff concerned with urban transport. It would, furthermore, introduce measures to increase revenues from (and for) the urban transport sector through, for example, the better enforcement of parking revenue collection, the encouragement of financially viable and locally taxed (formal and informal) transport services, as well as the collection of public transport route franchise revenues.

The main planks of an IUIDP approach to urban transport planning involve efforts of: sustaining economic productivity; servicing basic needs fulfilment; integrating sectoral efforts; and decentralising the responsibility for project planning, programming and appraisal. All these are discussed in greater depth below.

Focus on strategic self-sustaining economic growth

The long-term objective

The ultimate intention of IUIDP is to reach a level of urban infrastructure and service provision at the provincial and local level that can sustain economic, physical and cultural development in an accelerated and equitable manner. This point can be said to be reached when settlements, through improved economic productivity, become capable of financing further infrastructure developments without significant assistance from central government.

Many Third World countries whose economies are overly dependent on one or two primary resources and/or commodities, are successfully moving away from relying on revenues from a narrow resource/commodity base toward the introduction of a broad tax base. Such changes portend to introduce a more balanced and sustainable national revenue base which simultaneously helps to maintain economic stability, while striving for growth. The move also reflects the now widely held view among several Third World governments that they can no longer act as the primary engine of economic growth and that there is, therefore, a critical need for a harmonised approach to economic development in cities at the national and local level, both in the private and public sectors.

The IUIDP strategy is one whereby growth is to be especially promoted by central government through the development of infrastructure projects, education programmes and public utility schemes, etc. – i.e., through public sector investments designed to spur further development within the private sector – guiding it towards its national development plan and programme objectives.

The basis for the attraction of economic activities to cities is, as discussed earlier (see Chapter 5), of course, tied to numerous advantages such as those offered by economies of scale, scope for specialisation, opportunities of access, etc. However, there is considerable evidence to show that these advantages have not been optimised, which suggests that levels of urban economic productivity can be further increased if infrastructure improvements are made to enhance the advantages already offered by urban locations – this being the very aim of IUIDP.

Informal sector involvement

To mobilise fully and utilise efficiently resources in urban areas, IUIDP recognises that it is not enough to focus only on the economic activities of the formal sector. The full spectrum of urban economic activities including those of the informal sector must therefore be incorporated. This consists of activities characterised by (see Moser, 1978):

1 ease of entry into the activity concerned;
2 reliance on indigenous resources;
3 family ownership of enterprises;
4 small scale of operation;
5 labour-intensive and adapted technology;
6 skills acquired outside the formal school system; and
7 unregulated and competitive markets.

Because employment in the informal sector is little organised, difficult to enumerate, and rarely covered by legal statutes, it is typically ignored by official censuses. Since, furthermore, the description of the sector is inadequate, arbitrary listings associated with it are often of those whose activities take place on the streets such as street vendors, newspaper sellers, hawkers, rickshaw drivers, etc. (Breman, 1976). These are often unskilled workers and others with a low and irregular income on the margins of the urban economy. Despite their under-privileged status, however, it has been argued by Weeks (1975) that there is significant advantage for a city having an evolving and dynamic informal sector, in that it contributes to the economy in three important ways:

1 through its provision of significant volumes of consumer goods bought particularly by the lowest income groups;
2 through its workshops as a provider of a source of indigenous capital goods; and
3 through its growth, in that it could lead towards a more labour-intensive form of urban-based industrialisation.

An integral part of the IUIDP approach is for human material needs to be satisfied *not* by transfer payments to the poor but by the provision of sufficient productive employment and of essential public services to sustain economic growth with which to finance the meeting of these needs. Also essential to this approach is central government commitment to the encouragement of innovation in and of appropriate technologies (Sandbrook, 1982).

Economic productivity

At the same time as serving the needs of the economically weaker sections of the community, an equally (some would argue more) important focus of the IUIDP approach is the servicing of the needs of urban economic activities known to be both highly productive and strategic to further self-sustaining urban economic development. Such an emphasis requires clarification and specification as to firstly, which activities are 'highly productive' and which are 'instrumental' in the generation of further development; and finally, what measures would both protect and maintain the development already achieved.

In the light of the growing recognition that central government cannot afford to act as the main engine/primer of economic development at the city level, the meeting of urban transport needs that have in the past significantly contributed to the productivity of the local economy is one of greatest significance. Such needs, however, have to date been considered of secondary importance in relation to transport requirements of national development. This is perhaps most dramatically illustrated in urban areas in instances where priority is given by central government to inter-regional road infrastructure, and too little attention to the adverse impacts they generate on the cities they traverse.

Priority action and projects

On the understanding that opportunities for local financial participation in the urban transport sub-sector will in the future be improved, and assuming that local revenue generation will increasingly help finance the sub-sector, to maximise the strategic value of investments in urban transport, sub-sector efforts need to be synchronised and co-ordinated with other urban development programmes in a mutually supportive way. On this basis, the following aspects of city transport are envisaged to warrant IUIDP attention:

1 National and regional highway links passing through cities – particularly major junctions with sections of the urban network and requirements of freight traffic needs (e.g. lorry parks and routes, laybys, etc.).
2 National and regional public transport services and related infrastructure transversing, terminating and/or commencing in cities – with particular attention given to public transport terminal provision, public transport routeing requirements, as well as their service needs by local public transport facilities.
3 Selected strategic city-wide major and minor road links – particularly those servicing industrial, commercial and retailing areas, that are absent from the designated urban road hierarchy, providing access to principal traffic generators, and connecting with economically vibrant local communities.

The use of urban transport investments as a strategic spur to further economic growth and sustainable integrated urban development, however, entails more in-depth investigation and higher risk-taking than might at first appear.

Situations believed to trigger off development opportunities include investments in:

1 Approved real estate, planned as part of a decentralised urban

development programme, where the communities in question are able to participate financially in the infrastructure provision.

2 Industrial estates, where there is either a demand for industrial land in excess of that currently available, or where phasing of the movement of industrial functions to a new geographical area is planned.
3 Carefully located off-street car parking, serviced by public transport at strategic sites within the central area on the periphery of the central area (in larger settlements), and on the urban periphery.
4 Selected viable local public transport operations (both of the formal and informal sector) serving the central area and/or linking it with high density communities on the periphery.

Investments of this kind are intended to provide more efficient public transport services, help develop the local transport industry and related employment opportunities, as well as encourage the more widespread use of appropriate transport technologies. The last is consistent with the IUIDP objective of seeking to harness more of the local economic energies of the city, and is an aspect of urban transport development that has been too often neglected.

Employment of cost recovery principles

In financial and economic terms, one of the corner-stones to future urban transport facility provision within an IUIDP approach are the dual objectives of confining central government investment at the city level to strategic infrastructure of the kind that acts as a primer to growth opportunities, subsequently expected to be taken up by the private sector. This also provides funding to economically viable sub-sector projects with the commitment at a satisfactory level of local government financial participation.

A combination of a deterioration of economic circumstances in many Third World countries and a realisation that up to now local economic resources in urban areas have been inadequately exploited, has led to the recent opening-up of a host of ideas concerning possibilities for the generation of municipal revenues from/for the urban transport sector (see Roth, 1987). Among the most commonly discussed are the receipt of municipal revenues from the enforcement of property taxes, the issuing of municipal performance bonds, and the conducting of regular municipal lotteries. Other examples of appropriate cost-recovery measures but more specifically in the urban transport sub-sector, include:

1 the issuing of franchises to operators' public transport routes;
2 the imposition of a public transport tax on registered businesses alongside public transport routes (as in France) that employ more than a certain number of people;
3 the increasing of vehicle registration taxes;
4 the introduction of a sidewalk tax in major commercial areas;
5 the imposition of a fuel tax (of which a percentage becomes a municipal revenue);
6 the stricter enforcement of parking fee collection; and
7 the creation of opportunities for the municipality to participate in the benefits of 'land value capture' by enjoying part of the land appreciation created by public sector urban transport investments.

Quite apart from these measures, efforts at making improvements to financial management and control measures in municipal-earning activities can also do much towards the creation of local resources. A prerequisite, however, is the existence of personnel capable of thrift management, the common absence of which gives rise to the need to embark on manpower development and training programmes.

Urban transport in service of basic needs

The premise of basic needs planning

This is perhaps most straightforwardly articulated by the following quotation in a United Nations document (UN Secretariat, 1977):

> given a limited amount of resources available for development, the allocation of these resources should be such that the basic needs of the population are met.

The setting of basic needs, however, requires a greater understanding and elaboration than the above quotation implies (also see Chapter 7), since the needs which should be met are often greater than those which can be met. An important aspect is thus the balancing of basic needs. This involves a balancing exercise among:

1 levels of service and investment within and between sub-sectors;
2 decisions regarding the demands of urban residents versus the sector resources;
3 available technologies versus the capabilities for system operation and maintenance;
4 equitable coverage of existing urban areas versus the special service needs for economic growth;
5 physical and non-economic investments; and
6 programmes for development and urban management capacity.

The balancing of the above must be seen as an ongoing task that differs between urban areas and changes as standards of living rise or decline. This in turn calls for a change from the reliance on fixed numerical quantifiable targets for investment programme coverage, to a more carefully analysed and defined set of basic needs.

It should be appreciated that needs are defined differently by technocrats (such as planners) and members of the local community. Basic needs in one situation and/or time-frame may, furthermore, differ radically from those in another. Two types of basic needs have been postulated by the UN Secretariat (1977), namely 'objective needs' that are defined by technical criteria, and 'subjective needs' perceived by people at large and less prone to quantifiable assessment. The two types can alternatively be differentiated in terms of:

1 Technically defined needs – i.e., international development agency defined needs, central government or provincial agency perceived needs, and municipal government perceived needs.
2 User defined needs – which may be disaggregated into community, household and individual level perceived needs.

Basic needs thinking presents the concept that for every defined population group, there is a set of needs the satisfaction of which (at definable levels) can become the minimum level of acceptability for development programmes. These, however, not only have to be disaggregated but territorially targeted – often on the minimum survival requirements of the 'economically weaker' inhabitants of communities. In so doing, however, the development emphasis shifts from a preoccupation with economic growth to a broader concern to eradicate absolute poverty, promote growth and redistribute its benefits – i.e., the very aims of urban development planning.

Economically weaker sections of the community

Efforts at identifying and more particularly, quantifying the characteristics of the 'economically weaker' communities in cities encounter problems at every stage of analysis, since data associated with this group is often scarce and unreliable. Furthermore, while identifying urban poverty in the lowest income groups usually raises few problems, there is a grey area in the middle of the income spectrum, for it is difficult to know where to place the cut-off point between 'poverty' and 'absolute poverty' (Thomson, 1984).

Conceptually, the urban poor can be said to consist of those households whose income falls below a level necessary to satisfy the basic needs of their members in housing, nutrition, clothing and access to certain essential public services, such as portable water, sanitation, transport, health and educational facilities. If then one is to characterise the urban poor in the Third World, they may be typically described as:

1 being over-represented by large families with many offspring;
2 having a large proportion of household members in search of work; and
3 being persons often forced to seek credit from a variety of means to finance their survival.

If poverty is defined on an income per capita basis then according to Thomson (1984), the income level for the lowest 40 per cent of a Third World's country's population can be crudely used to represent the baseline for measuring population movements of the poor, above or below this. Past World Bank literature presents individuals with an annual international purchasing power of under US$ 236 as constituting the 'absolute poor'.[5] More recent estimates from the same source as discussed in the overview of *World Development Report* (1990) which focuses on poverty, argues that because the global poverty line is inevitably arbitrary, an income range of US$ 275 to US$ 370 per person per annum is more appropriate. This spans the poverty line estimates for a number of Third World countries with low average incomes, including Bangladesh, Egypt, Indonesia, Kenya, Morocco and Tanzania.

However, because many of the development efforts targeted at the poor end up benefiting more than this group, Thomson argues that the broader the definition of the urban poor the less will be the anticipated resource diversions away from the targeted group. Nevertheless, information is also needed to differentiate between the 'badly-off' and the 'worst-off' – especially where the urban poor constitute the majority.

Since definitions of poverty based upon per capita or household income are widely acknowledged to be inadequate, an alternative method of poverty identification advocated by Sandbrook (1982) warrants consideration. This draws a poverty line by plotting the relationship of household income to food expenditure sufficient to purchase a nutritionally adequate diet. Making allowances for non-food items of expenditure, such as urban transport expenditure, however, is much more difficult. For although there are certain international standards set by agencies such as the World Health Organisation (WHO) to identify minimum acceptable nutritional levels of intake, no such standards can be applied in the provision of many other basic needs as in the case of basic forms of public transport.

In most Third World cities, the 'economically weaker' communities are found either in squatter settlements on the urban periphery or within the central areas and their environs at much higher densities, usually close to both transport routes and water resources. It should be appreciated, however, that while not all people who live in urban slum and squatter conditions are poor, almost all the urban poor live in such areas.

Towards a basic needs strategy for urban transport

Translating the above thinking about poverty into an IUIDP context as it applies to urban transport constitutes a 'basic needs strategy' (see Figure 8.2). This would involve the focusing of development efforts in accordance with national development priorities, with a concern for basic needs, in a manner which simultaneously addresses the needs of economic productivity, utilising appropriate technology and relying on greater local participation and decentralised modes of government. Among other things, priority in such a strategy is likely to be assigned to the mobility needs of the 'least privileged' of low income urban communities, as well as to the use of transport to enhance/promote access to community

Figure 8.2 Components of a basic needs strategy for urban transport

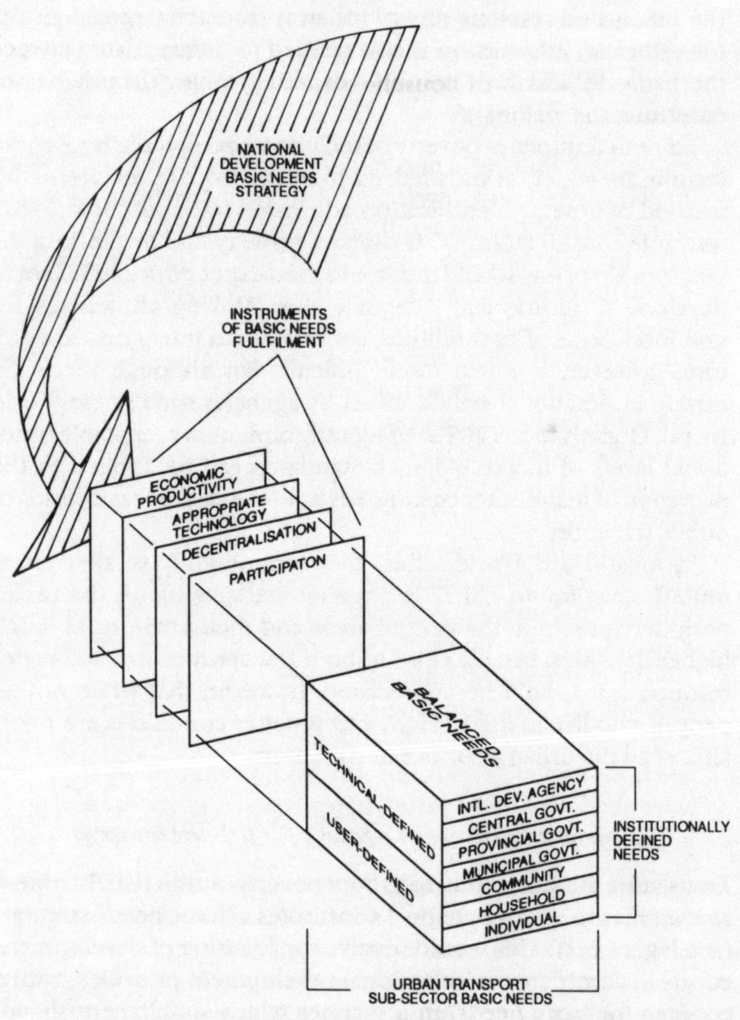

facilities which contribute to both the local economy and encourage the better distribution of wealth.

The strategy also places considerable emphasis on differentiating among the various needs urban transport is to serve. The identification of needs of this kind may be arrived at by using a 'basic needs survey' of households and/or individual city inhabitants, in order to identify:

1 Household unit basic needs – i.e., needs that are fundamental to the survival and development of the household for which transport facilities are required. They include: the need (in the case of units with no piped water) for physical access (i.e., footpaths/roads) to a free/cheap water supply; the need for access to a means of goods carriage (such as bicycle, hand cart, etc.) at an affordable price, for the transportation of food, water, building materials; as well as physical access to nearby market areas and employment opportunities.
2 Individual basic needs – these can also be identified from a 'basic needs survey' of households, or by means of footpath/roadside interviews. As in the case of household unit basic needs, individual basic needs are greatly influenced by disposable income. Some such needs perceived by individuals are outside the priority structure set by community leaders or household heads, and while they may be similar in their expression on transport demand, their formulation is more determined by individual activity patterns associated with survival, work and recreation. For those individuals not belonging to a household (e.g., street dwellers) the opportunity to convey their needs by a means other than a household survey is of great importance.

As indicated earlier, efforts at basic needs fulfillment in urban transport will inevitably encounter conflict among the varied levels of basic needs expression, both among different aspects of the sub-sector and among other sub-sectors, such as water supply, housing, industry, etc. Guidelines are thus required not only to offer guidance in the resolution of conflicting sub-sectoral demands, but also to provide a framework for cross-sectoral urban infrastructure resource allocation, meanwhile making consistent reference to wider national development objectives and planning frameworks.

Although sufficient resources are unlikely to be available to meet all urban transport needs of the 'economically weaker' sections of the community, in balancing efforts at basic needs fulfillment, as many resources as possible should be made available as a matter of priority to meet first those of the 'least privileged. Thereafter, resources should be allocated to tackling problems of resource wastage affecting the sub-sector and to investments needed in the more productive transport activities (see Figure 8.3).

To be effective, it is essential that the application of basic needs thinking to urban transport planning targets on particular communities, and the disaggregation of these targeted populations, both geographically and sociologically. Presuming, for instance, the 'economically weaker' section of the community, constitutes (on a per capita basis) the lowest 40 per cent of the population as proposed by Thomson (1984), and the least privileged are those earning less than (say) US$ 275 per annum, an initial basic needs investigation of the urban transport sector should focus on the low-income housing areas where the majority of them reside. For the best method of understanding the movement needs of the 'economically weaker' inhabitants is to gain an insight into their lifestyle, household characteristics and trip-making patterns.

Integration of sub-sector urban development efforts

Concept of integration

The objective of inter-sectoral integration within the concept of IUIDP is directed at limiting the duplication of urban development efforts and ameliorating adverse side-effects of sectoral developments, especially important to resource-constrained environments. Efforts at integration are intended in the context of urban transport to lead to an appropriate balance of investments between road development and the various other urban development sub-sectors, thus providing a useful context for urban transport investment decisions.

Success in this requires efforts at the co-ordination in the use of resources towards common ends, and the synchronisation of actions in the formulation and phasing of projects and programmes at the various tiers of government. This is to be done along inter-sectoral, interdisciplinary and inter-agency lines, so as to mobilise both existing and potential development resources at these various tiers. The approach implies the need for the develop-

Figure 8.3 **Balancing basic needs in urban transport**

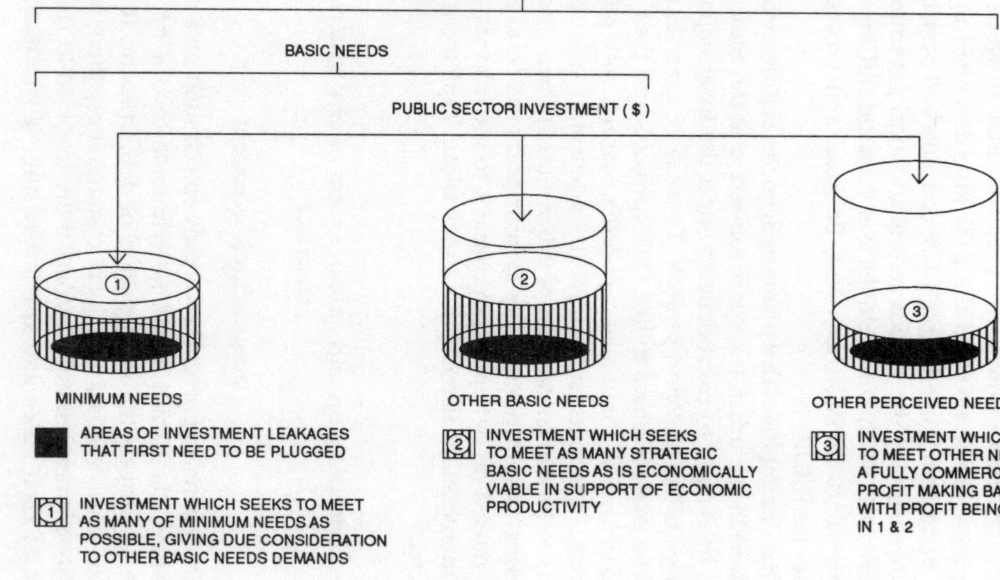

Source: **Figure 4.2, TDC SA, 1988**

ment of multi-sectoral programmes, and a more systematic co-ordination of aims to maximise the positive impacts of improving human settlements in target locations and on strategic policy areas.

Institutional requirements

In most instances, the integration component of IUIDP typically requires the establishment of an inter-agency (i.e., inter-ministerial) co-ordinating committee to act as an overall project co-ordinating unit for the monitoring and reporting of all inter-agency activities. However, to ensure that progress towards integration can be achieved along the lines described above, common agreement is needed on IUIDP concepts and principles to be employed among the various central and local government agencies involved. This in turn, emphasises the need and importance of pre-prepared common technical, financial and procedural guidelines for IUIDP.

What this implies is that planning agencies of different ministries involved in the urban transport sub-sector at the central government level need to collaborate to select the most important and strategic urban transport projects. These same agencies thereafter need to take measures to link these projects and their phases of development in a mutually supportive manner with other urban projects. To be consistent with IUIDP's decentralisation objectives, efforts at further integration of urban development projects will necessitate the responsibilities for transport projects to be increasingly passed on by central government to the relevant provincial and municipality agencies for supervision, implementation and funding.

Decentralisation and enhancement of city institutional capacities

Decentralisation concept

It is increasingly apparent, as already emphasised on a number of occasions, that Third World governments cannot be relied on alone to provide the main engine of development. It is instead widely acknowledged that local communities, their inhabitants and governments should become more involved in the management of their cities and revenue-raising. It is anticipated that measures taken to encourage this shift in responsibility will provide city municipalities with the opportunity not only of funding or contributing towards the finance of their own urban development projects, but also give them a greater say in their local development. This in turn is expected to speed up ongoing efforts at decentralisation and greater public participation.

In fact, the decentralisation of basic responsibilities for implementing IUIDP is, together with the concept of integration, the backbone of the IUIDP approach. In the context of urban transport, it encourages central government to support local government in the formulation, appraisal and programming of their own projects (within given financial and technical guidelines), as well as the operation, maintenance and management of transport facilities and services.

Enhancement of institutional capacity

One of the main problems associated with decentralisation is the question of whether local government has the capability and capacity adequately to respond to the initiatives of decentralisation. This issue is of particular importance to the urban transport sub-sector, given not only is there typically a considerable degree of institutional confusion in this sub-sector over the respective responsibilities of the various central, provincial and local agencies (see Chapter 6) but there is increasing evidence that a determining factor of the success of major projects is the institutional framework and capacity of government (at all levels) to implement project proposals. In this regard, the limited professional and management expertise identified in Indonesia (Dimitriou, 1988), and developments in Brazil (see Barat, 1990), suggest that institutional and manpower development considerations are almost as significant as the engineering and financial viability of urban transport plans and projects.

Typically, two sets of training might be required for a major project to support an IUIDP approach to urban transport planning. They are those which relate to the principles and practice of IUIDP, and those which relate to the technical aspects of the sub-sector. The former is usually best conducted as workshop training focusing on IUIDP concepts, terminologies and techniques, an aspect which is particularly important for senior/middle management personnel if there is to be an effective marriage of specialist training with that of the broader IUIDP approach to transport in urban development. The latter kind of training might typically include technical training in (see Dimitriou, 1988):

1 urban transport and land-use planning, and their interface;
2 urban transport project programming and appraisal;
3 traffic management and engineering; and
4 traffic enforcement and regulation.

Experience in Indonesia (Dimitriou, 1988) suggests that training for urban transport is best provided on an inter-agency basis for:

1 highway engineering and design;
2 project management;
3 road maintenance and rehabilitation;
4 heavy equipment use; and
5 financial management and control.

The same source (Dimitriou, 1988) suggests urgent areas of training are best offered on an agency-specific basis (depending upon the institutional arrangements) in:

1 transport project programming and appraisal;
2 traffic management and engineering;
3 traffic enforcement and regulation; and
4 project management and financial management.

The Indonesian experience indicates that consideration should also be given to the need to differentiate between 'project-related' training and institutional/agency training. An illustration of this differentiation is given in Figure 8.4.

MATCHING TRANSPORT TECHNOLOGY TO SETTLEMENT HIERARCHIES AND DEVELOPMENT CONTEXTS

The need for a theoretical framework

To encourage the use of urban transport technologies that are 'developmentally effective' and simultaneously 'operationally efficient' for the environment in which they operate, it is important to discriminate between these two types (and levels) of performance, and to highlight the subservience of the latter to the former in a 'developmental approach' to urban transport planning.

Figure 8.4 Differentiating between project-related and institutional strengthening/training

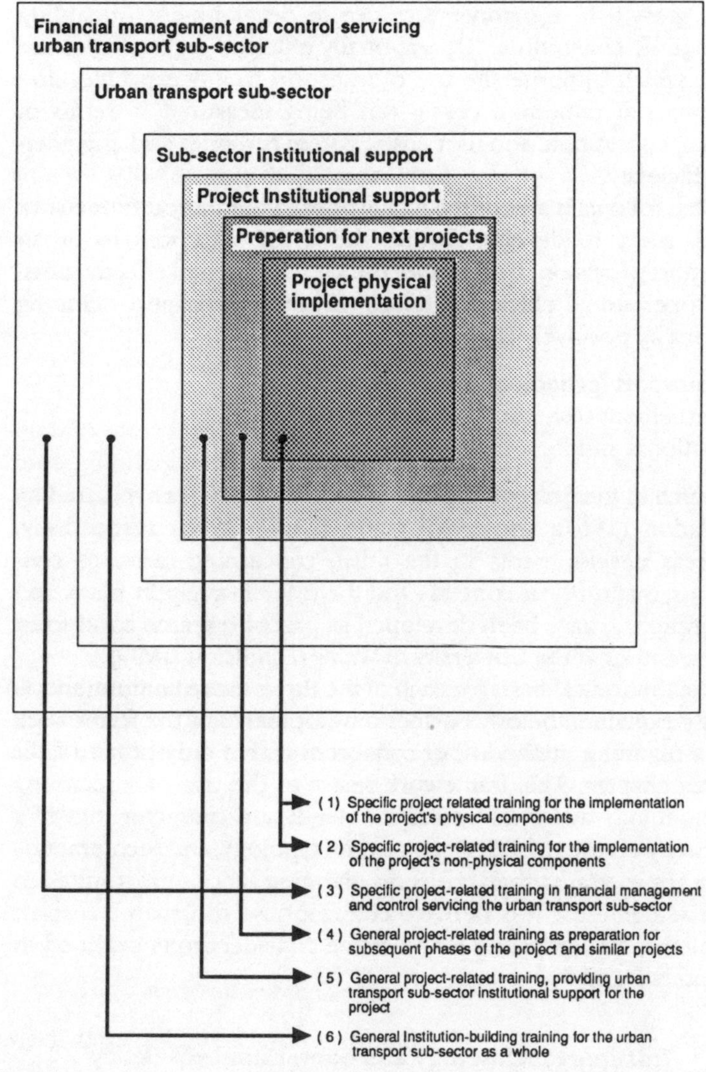

Note: Shaded areas represent project-related manpower development and training areas
Source: Figure 3, Dimitriou, 1988

'Developmentally effective' transport technologies are defined here as those that contribute to and are consistent with indigenous national and local development objectives that contribute to economic growth in a manner sensitive to development (including ecological) constraints. 'Operationally efficient' technologies are those which optimise the use of transport facility capacities and resources at minimum cost – this being measured in terms of capital, operational and user costs, system revenues and engineering efficiency.

What follows is an outline of a proposed theoretical framework which seeks to develop further the IUIDP approach to urban transport provision. It addresses the 'developmental effectiveness' and 'operational efficiency' issues of various transport planning options by positively correlating aspects of:

1 transport technology,
2 settlement size, and
3 national and local development policies.

Research in the first two aspects of the above has been initiated by Bouladon (1967a and 1967b) and Sasaki (1970) respectively, whereas developments in the third, concerning resource constraints, institutional contexts and the role of transport plans and programmes, have been developed as part of research conducted by the author at the University of Wales (Dimitriou, 1989).

The theoretical basis for each of the three above components is briefly explained below. Further developments of the framework and a planning methodology consistent with it are outlined later in this chapter. This framework refers to the use of a planning methodology which addresses the needs and characteristics of a hierarchy of cities of differing sizes and typology, and recommends more appropriate urban transport planning actions most suited to such settlements. It is derived as a response to urban transport problems, incorporating many of the considerations outlined in Chapters 5 and 7.

Transport technology and operational efficiency

Gabriel Bouladon (1967a and 1967b), in his seminal research at the Battelle Institute investigating the operational engineering efficiency of various transport systems, identified two 'transport gaps':

1 one between pedestrian and car users, and
2 the other between the conventional aeroplane and the space rocket.

It is the first of these gaps which is of significance here. However, to appreciate the importance of Bouladon's research, where he presents his Unified Theory of Transport in which each transport system is placed into its rightful role from the point of view of the engineering requirements it is to satisfy, the theory will be explained.

The 'transport gap' identified by Bouladon between the pedestrian and the motorcar user is best described by the following extract from an article of his in the *Science Journal* (1967b):

> The diagram (see Figure 8.5) emphasises that, as one might expect, the greatest demand (for travel) is for very short distance transport. The graph shown is in reality three dimensional. It forms a triangle, the top line of which represents optimum use as defined by maximum satisfaction to users. The line below represents the point at which 50 per cent of the users would declare themselves satisfied and thus marks a lower limit for reasonable use.
>
> In each of the five areas into which the figure is divided there should be an optimum means of transport. In practice this is so only in three areas, in which pedestrian, car and air transport dominate the whole hierarchy of transport. Between these three regions many other methods of transport are currently in use, but these give less satisfaction. It can be seen that there are (therefore) two significant gaps, one in the second area and the other in the fourth....

In explaining the speed/distance relationship Bouladon employed to assess the operational efficiency of vehicles in his Unified Theory of Transport, he goes on to explain in the same article:

> the time and speed scales on the abscissa of the diagram are complementary. For any journey it is possible to establish the optimum speed for a car. The greater the speed, the greater must be the separation distance maintained between successive vehicles. As the separation increases rapidly between fast cars, the flow actually decreases. Conversely, the flow is also decreased at too low a speed and the optimum speed of utilization is found by taking the tangent of the flow/speed

Figure 8.5 The transport gaps

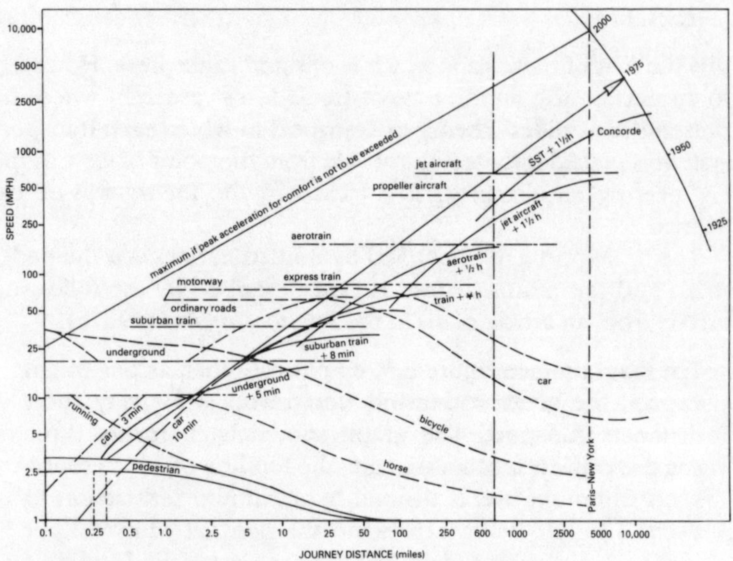

Source: Redrawn from Bouladon, 1967b
Note: DEMAND FOR SPEED is closely related to distance to be travelled: greater distances always demand greater speed. With time, all forms of transport tend to become faster, as shown by the pivot arrow. All systems falling above this pivot can be regarded as fast enough, those falling below as too slow. Dotted horizontal lines show the theoretical performance of transport systems and continuous curves show practical performance, including waiting time. When the car was not widely used, and average waiting time on a car journey was 3 minutes, it compared favourably with many other forms of transport. Now that waiting time is at least 10 minutes, the care is far less satisfactory and falls below the pivot line. Uppermost line shows limits imposed by acceleration and suggests it will never be possible to cross the Atlantic in less than one hour (assuming maximum allowable acceleration of 0.25 *g*): this limit may be reached by 1990. Figure also highlights importance of transfer systems.

> curve from zero. It is thus possible to relate optimum speed to distance.

Bouladon's work was based solely on observations made in industrialised countries. Had he extended his research to encompass Third World nations, particularly those of Southeast Asia, he would have found the first of the 'transport gaps' not so immediately apparent given the wide selection of non-motorised transport modes available. This is confirmed by Ocampo (1982) who in a review of available transport technologies of Southeast Asian cities concludes that the transport planner of this part of the world has a much broader basis upon which to plan urban movement than his counterpart in the West.

Transport technology and settlement hierarchy

The work of Yasunaga Sasaki (1970) conducted at the Athens Centre of Ekistics further developed Bouladon's theories regarding the operational efficiency of transport systems, by correlating transport technology efficiency criteria to settlement size.

Sasaki's thesis rests on the assumption that a given type and size of settlement requires a consonant type of transport mode, and that if the settlement's internal organisation follows a hierarchical pattern, it may have several types of transport, serving different functions and distances, operating at maximum efficiency. Correlating the two, he concludes that:

1 the absence of a hierarchy of transport technologies consonant with the needs of a settlement hierarchy is the fundamental cause of many urban transport problems; and
2 since settlement growth and transport development are closely interrelated, urban transport technologies must match the needs of the settlements they serve.

Sasaki substantiates his conclusions by positively relating the hierarchy of a settlement with its constituent communities, to a hierarchy of trip distribution frequencies for each type of community. From this, he concludes that different kinds of communities within the same settlement generate a demand for consonant means of transport and that settlements which vary in size and complexity necessitate different types of services and infrastructure.

Among other principal observations he made is that motorcar use is most operationally efficient for trip-making distances in cities with populations in excess of 300,000. Sasaki furthermore argues, there is often no appropriate transport mode for the kind of trip-making usually associated with communities of 300,000 and less inhabitants. The use of the motorcar in such circumstances in industrialised countries, therefore, constitutes, a 'sub-optimal use' of transport technology. His research also reveals that urban transport systems are typically mal-integrated and that this constitutes part of the urban transport problem.

Because Sasaki's work was confined to cities in the industrialised world his conclusions warrant re-examination in the light of different Third World contexts. A study of four Indonesian cities directed by the author had as part of its remit to do this and found that many of Bouladon's conclusions could in fact be substantiated in Indonesia (see TDC S. A., 1988).

Development context, transport technology and settlement hierarchy

The analysis of the preceding sections regarding the research conducted by Bouladon and Sasaki suggests that while positive correlations may be drawn to determine the most efficient use of alternative transport technologies for different speed/distance relationships and different sized settlements and communities, the conclusions relate solely to the development circumstances of industrialised nations. For the research to become pertinent to Third World cities, much more attention needs to be paid to the development contexts of the available transport technologies and settlements.

Apart from the more conventional categorisation of Third World countries based on per capita income, different development contexts may be more sensitively identified by referring to:

1 the national development policies, priorities and planning systems of a country (or region);
2 the resource constraints (and riches) of a country (or region); and
3 the institutional and political contexts of a country (or region).

Different combinations of these features generate different development contexts within which transport technologies operate and city growth takes place. This suggests that more appropriate approaches to urban transport need not only take into account the important findings of Sasaki (1970) and Bouladon (1967a and 1967b) but also the development circumstances to which transport plans are applied. It may, for example, be that while a specific transport system is considered the most appropriate for a city of a particular size in accordance with Bouladon and Sasaki's technical criteria, the unavailability of local technical expertise to manage, operate and maintain this system makes the system not developmentally practical until other actions are taken.

A similar conclusion may be arrived at for very different development-related reasons. For example, the desirability of introducing a technically superior urban transport system may be queried on development grounds, if it makes a large number of persons unemployed, in an economy where unemployment is already high. In such circumstances, the argument that improved transport systems' efficiency automatically generates increased employment opportunities will inevitably be used against those seeking to protect existing jobs in the transport sector. Hence a wider development debate will be opened up.

CHARACTERISTICS OF A SKETCH-PLAN METHODOLOGY

Scenarios, plan robustness and flexibility

In order for a 'developmental approach' to urban transport planning of the kind outlined above to become a practical reality, there is a need to employ low-cost planning methodologies that are capable of providing quick responses to complex problems that are often characterised by limited or invalid data. One such methodology proposed for Indonesia as part of its IUIDP efforts is 'sketch-planning' (TDC S. A., 1988). What follows here is a description of the characteristics of such a methodology for urban transport.

A basic characteristic of sketch-planning shared by the 'developmental approach' to urban transport planning is a recognition that it is not fruitful to convert all dimensions into quantitative and monetary terms. This is not to say that the quantification of costs, benefits and probabilities should not be attempted. Rather, that the success and failure of doing this need not be the overriding consideration.

Among other important qualities of sketch-planning is its 'robustness' and 'flexibility'. The former being defined in terms of the performance offered by the planning methodology across a range of development scenarios, while the latter involves the capability of a transport plan, once implemented, to be altered without excessive penalties in the light of changing situations.

While likely development scenarios which do not greatly affect the performance and outcome of an urban transport plan and its projects may be ignored in a sketch-planning exercise, less likely scenarios that would play havoc with reasonable urban transport planning proposals should *not* be ignored (Royce, 1978). It is also important in this context to appreciate that development scenarios of Third World countries with a strong central government are more likely to be affected by central government generated influences than local circumstances. However, local variations of national developments will feature increasingly as greater decentralisation emerges.

To decide on development scenarios which a sketch-plan for urban transport must address, one needs to take into account:

1 the scenario which looks most likely to transpire, i.e., that which has the highest probability of materialising;
2 the 'worst case' scenario, and how it might relate to the highest probable scenario; and
3 the need for the 'design plan' scenario to be capable of acceptable performance over all likely outcomes.

Sketch-planning usually employs long-term time horizons in the region of fifteen to twenty years, medium-term time-frames of five to eight years, and short-term time horizons of about two years (Patsalidis *et al.*, 1978). These may alternatively be defined, as: 'concept plans', 'guide plans' and 'action plans', respectively (see Harris, 1987).

Cost-saving characteristics

Where, as is common in many Third World situations, primary urban transport data is not available, transport sketch-plan methodologies are especially useful in that they can rely on traffic generation and production relationships derived from former studies of settlements with *similar* characteristics. They are useful where data collection costs need to be minimised and/or where it is important to expedite the execution of the planning exercise.

In instances where origin and destination (O&D) surveys have been recently conducted, transport sketch-planning methodologies can benefit from the use of low-cost methods of updating trip patterns in travel demand forecasting as advocated by Willumsen (1990). Having said this, although conventionally most planning exercises in the transport field focus on travel demand, it should be emphasised that a sketch-plan methodology servicing a 'developmental approach' to urban transport planning needs to address a wider scope of concern than this.

While sketch-planning in the Third World transport field may well entail the use of simple manual traffic forecasting techniques, there is growing evidence to suggest that current 'state of the art' personal computer software can now accommodate most tasks of the kind included in a transport sketch-plan methodology and that, therefore, the reliance on these manual methods can be reduced. This is substantiated by Harris (1987) who claims:

> steps in the transport planning process which at first glance seemed complicated to the uninitiated, can now be packaged as 'expert systems' for operation by those with only the most basic of training in urban transport planning.

To follow up on modelling opportunities pinpointed by Harris, Willumsen and others, without simultaneously falling into the pitfalls of over-simplification characterised by many earlier transport modelling exercises, additional research is needed in urban transport of the kind conducted by Kammeir (1986).

The development of computer software in support of the kind of transport sketch-planning exercises advocated here is especially timely, since more powerful and durable personal computer hardware, suitable for use in Third World conditions, has now been developed for application even in small and intermediate sized settlements.

Methodology guidelines

A 'developmental approach' to urban transport planning employing a sketch-plan methodology is summarised in diagramatic form in Figure 8.6.

The approach is intended to provide a nation-wide planning framework for a low-cost, quick-response, sketch-planning methodology for urban transport that is consistent with the development planning principles and concepts expressed earlier. It seeks not only to offer a greater degree of sensitivity in the planning of transport for urban settlements of different typologies, but also to be consistent with IUIDP policies and principles. The approach is principally designed to assist in the formulation of urban transport plans that are compatible with anticipated national development

Figure 8.6 The sketch-plan methodology and supporting guidelines/handbooks for urban transport

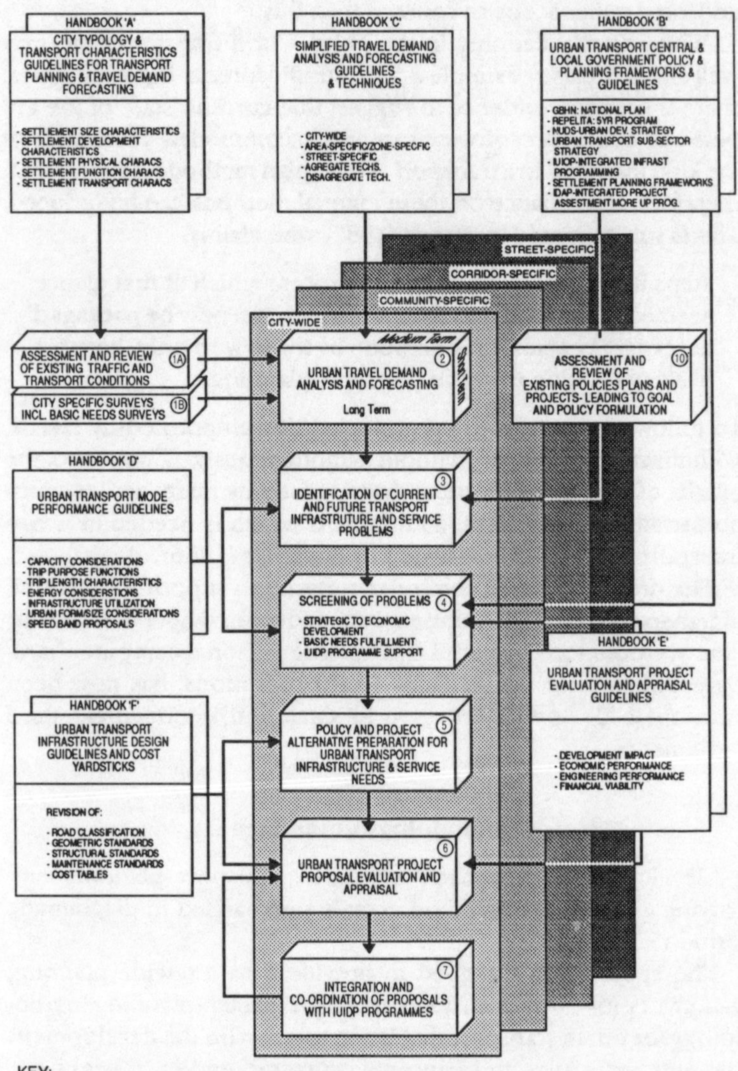

KEY:

1. STEPS 1 TO 7 INDICATES STEPS OF SKETCH-PLANNING METHODOLOGY
2. AREA SHADED ABOVE INDICATES AREA OF STUDY NOT ADDRESSED BY THIS RESEARCH

Source: Adapted from Figure 5.1, TDC SA, 1988

scenarios for the next fifteen to twenty years. These may be ascertained from:

1 the National Development Plan, where one exists;
2 Five Year Development Programmes;
3 the national urban development strategy, if one has been formulated; and
4 a national urban transport strategy and its related policies, where one has been arrived at.

The assimilation of the output of the above can be seen as part of an ongoing centralised 'shadow planning exercise' designed to provide a set of up-to-date national guidelines for urban transport planning studies conducted at the local level (preferably by municipalities). Such policy and planning guidelines are best formulated by a central government unit which is also to be responsible for their ultimate translation into related technical handbooks which would prove invaluable to the sketch-planning exercise at the city level.

Guidelines that would suit an urban transport sketch-planning exercise of the kind described is given below. These have been derived from proposals made for Indonesia (see TDC S. A., 1988) and address matters regarding:

1 city typologies and associated transport demand characteristics;
2 the relevance of different central, provincial and local government policy and planning frameworks affecting urban transport, plus traffic regulations and related funding arrangements;
3 simplified urban travel demand analysis and forecasting techniques;
4 methods of transport mode performance assessment;
5 priorities in urban transport plan evaluation and project appraisal; and
6 infrastructure design and cost yardsticks.

Principal steps

The core of the 'developmental approach' to urban transport planning in effect constitutes the sketch-plan methodology. This, as may be seen from Figures 8.6, can be applied:

1 city-wide;

2 on the basis of particular areas (e.g. to the CBD, to a specific community or zone, or group of communities and zones);
3 along particular transport corridors (see Gakenheimer and Meyer, 1990); and/or
4 along major streets (see Proudlove and Turner, 1990).

Addressing the three time-frames – long-, medium- and short-term – the sketch-plan process is comprised of the following seven steps (see Figures 8.7 and 8.8).

Step 1: An assessment and review of existing conditions. This concerns:

1 current national, provincial, urban and local transport policies, plans and projects affecting the study area (Step 1a);
2 the characteristics and condition of urban transport services and facilities (Step 1b); and
3 selected priority areas of concern for which critical data is needed (Step 1c).

Step 2: The undertaking of simple urban travel demand analysis and forecasting exercises. This being done by the use of tailor-made computer software based upon simplified traffic forecasting techniques, employing O&D survey information (where it exists), as well as traffic generation and production models with factors, where possible, derived from land uses from cities in the same country, of similar size and kind to those under study.

Step 3: The identification of transport infrastructure and service problems. This is made on a:

1 city-wide;
2 area-specific;
3 corridor specific; and/or
4 street specific basis,

differentiating among existing and forecast problems, including those:

1 generated by the transport sector as obstacles to the achievement of national development and IUIDP goals,
2 of unmet transport needs, and

3 obstacles to the efficient use of urban transport infrastructure and services.

Step 4: The screening of identified urban transport problems. This involves the categorisation and prioritisation of problems in terms of:

1 spatial and aspatial characteristics;
2 different professional and vested interests;
3 'root' and 'manifestation' problems; and
4 current and future problems,

impeding important development considerations, such as:

1 the strategic creation of economic growth (particularly at the local level);
2 basic needs fulfillment of the least privileged communities and households;
3 completion of the city's road and public transport hierarchies; and
4 the provision of transport facilities which link IUIDP programmes and projects.

Step 5: The preparation of policy, plan, programme and project options. This entails the preparation of responses to screened problems for city-wide, and area/corridor/street-specific situations. In project-specific terms, this must be done in a manner consistent with both IUIDP principles and the transport/community hierarchy concept as advocated in the urban development planning guidelines. This may be done in one or more of the following ways:

1 by physically expanding or improving existing transport systems capacity;
2 by constructing new systems;
3 by improving transport operations through better management and financial assistance; and
4 by influencing travel demand patterns through land-use control, management and policy measures.

Step 6: The evaluation and appraisal of urban transport proposals. These are assessed first, in terms of a proposal's contribution to development objectives and their compatibility with environmental constraints and available resources, and second, in terms of more conventional resource optimisation measures. The former involves an assessment of plans, programmes and projects at whatever level they are prepared, assessing their contribution to and impact on:

1 the achievement of national development, IUIDP and environmental and resource conservation goals, policies and targets;
2 resolving problems of un-met transport needs; and
3 overcoming obstacles to the efficient use of urban transport infrastructure and services.

Where the above evaluation yields positive results, the assessment exercise continues for the same plans, programmes and projects, at a lower tier of evaluation and appraisal, utilising more conventional techniques which appraise:

1 economic performance;
2 engineering performance;
3 financial viability; and
4 institutional viability.

On the basis of the above, infrastructure improvements and selected new construction can then proceed, using design guidelines which reflect the planning principles and transport mode preferences derived from a Bouladon and Sasaki type analysis.

Step 7: The integration and co-ordination of proposals with IUIDP programmes and projects. This is to be principally achieved through a five-year rolling programme of projects and annual budgets, in which priority is given to urban transport services and road infrastructure projects which:

1 link areas already in receipt of IUIDP programme support; and
2 are proposed for IUIDP investment in areas along corridors and/or in streets offering a viable basis for future IUIDP investments.

The above seven steps are not strictly linear in sequence, in that there is much backward and forward interaction among each of the stages. The various steps may furthermore change over time in accordance with variations in the development scenario, the sketch-plan addresses, and in accordance with alterations and modifications made to the development guidelines as new information comes to light and as their detailing is expressed in technical handbooks.

SPECIAL FEATURES, LIMITATIONS AND GENERAL APPLICABILITY

Special features and limitations

The attempt of the proposed 'developmental approach' to urban transport planning of the kind outlined above, to offer a sensitive treatment of travel requirements to cities and communities of different characteristics and sizes is an important feature, despite the use of a somewhat standardised and simplified sketch-plan methodology.

The use of an agreed settlement typology and community structure as a basis for the storage of information of factors believed to affect urban transport provides a matrix of data, the basis for the formulation of disaggregated national urban transport planning guidelines and for related travel demand forecasting exercises (see Figures 8.7 and 8.8). It also offers a critical start to the building-up of a national computerised urban data bank of essential information for settlements of different kinds for use in future similar low-cost settlements, and possibly for transport planning exercises elsewhere in the Third World.

The special emphasis of the approach on the appropriate use and performance of different urban transport technologies and the attention given to transport mode integration by adherence to a proposed nation-wide set of technical guidelines that seek to relate on a hierarchical basis of trip purposes and trip lengths traffic generated by communities of different sizes provide an important new basis for urban transport policy-making. Among other things, this allows for the development of the concept of transport 'speed-bands'[6] and the use of a road utilisation function[7] more appropriate to Third World city needs.

Of all the features of the outlined approach, the low-cost character of the sketch-plan methodology and its potential flexibility and robustness in application at various scales of urban development is one of the main operational advantages. Notwithstanding this, it should be noted that an investigation of the application of this approach to Indonesia suggests that rapid urban development changes commonly experienced by fast growing Third World

Figure 8.7 City data and inventory frameworks: settlement size, structure and area characteristics

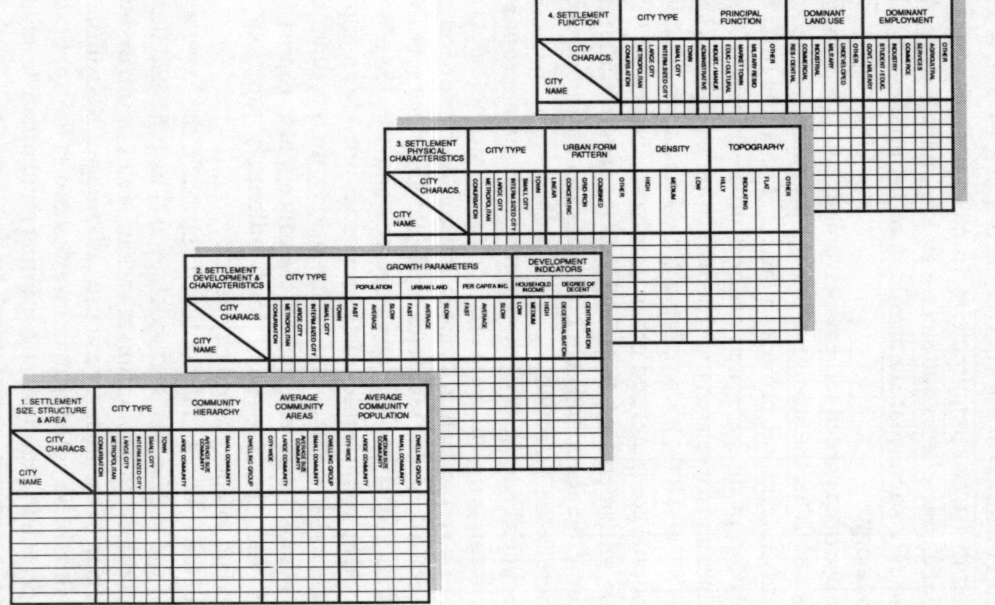

Source: Figure 3.7, TDC S.A. (1988)

Figure 8.8 City data and inventory framework: road transport and travel characteristics

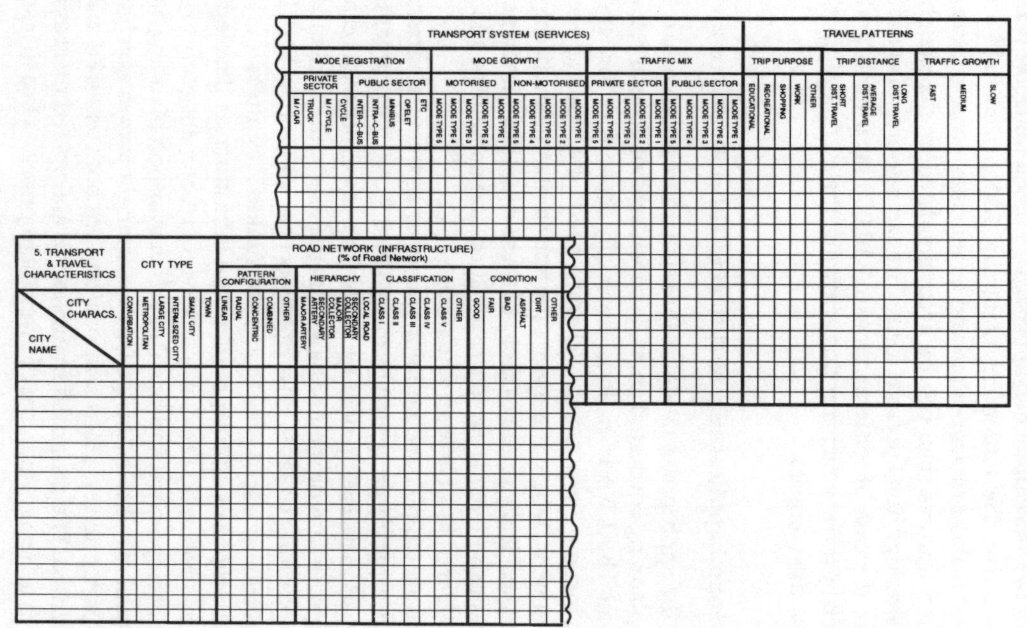

Source: Figure 3.7, TDC S.A. (1988)

settlements, together with the inherent limitations of sketch-planning, make the use of planning horizon dates of more than fifteen years impractical for the sketch-plan component. This suggests that the sketch-planning component is more useful for the formulation of five year investment programmes and medium-term planning exercises than for the preparation of long-term strategic plans.

Also apparent from the Indonesian study is that the sketch-plan methodology is best confined to settlements with populations between 150,000 and 1,000,000. For while the advocated principles of the 'developmental approach' to urban transport planning apply across the settlement hierarchy, Indonesian field studies suggest that the metropolitan and larger cities possess more complicated features than can be accommodated by the sketch-plan methodology in its present form. The same source also indicates that in the case of settlements with 150,000 inhabitants and less, especially those which are slow-growing, the methodology would appear too complex.

General applicability to differing Third World contexts

With the appropriate modifications, the approach to urban transport planning advocated above is considered of general relevance to most Third World nations, especially those with low and medium-income economies characterised by strong central government. Where it employs the sketch-plan methodology it is more specifically suited to those of these countries with large land masses experiencing rapid urbanisation and containing an identifiable hierarchy of human settlements.

The sketch-plan methodology seeks to address paradoxical requests, typically presented by many Third World governments and international development agencies, for a low-cost quick-response transport planning methodology that address both short-and long-term planning issues in environments characterised by high levels of uncertainty, rapid growth and constrained resources.

The emphasis on integrated urban infrastructure development and the approach's sensitivity to wider development goals suggests the 'developmental approach' to urban transport planning has the potential to radically change for the better, the way in which urban transport policies, plans and projects are both assessed and implemented. The proposed framework is anticipated therefore not only to generate a new set of investment priorities but to lead to a more careful choice and promotion of urban transport technologies. This in turn is expected to generate important changes in recommended infrastructure design, particularly with regard to transport infrastructure needs of communities such as local roads, footpaths and mixed use transport routes.

A great deal of the uniqueness of the 'developmental approach' to urban transport planning has to do with the emphasis it places on the importance of assessing both the development context and the policy-making environment of transport planning, *before* addressing specific problems and issues of transport operations and infrastructure design. Notwithstanding this, the approach does capitalise on past positive experiences of conventional practices of urban transport planning, where techniques and models can be made to be, or are consistent with, the constraints of Third World environments and the planning framework outlined above.

9

CONCLUSIONS

BUILDING ON THE PAST FOR THE FUTURE

The 'developmental approach' to urban transport planning outlined in the previous chapter is founded on three sets of considerations, namely:

1 experiences of urban transport planning in the industrialised countries, especially in the USA;
2 experiences of urban transport planning practice in the Third World; and
3 concepts and principles of development planning as they relate to urban transport, including consideration of urban development planning practice, concepts and principles of IUIDP, relationships established between transport technology and settlement hierarchies, and the use of sketch-planning.

The following is a summary of the first two areas of concern – the third already having been extensively discussed in Chapter 8.

Lessons from industrialised nations

Discussions of specific problems and pitfalls of technology-transfer in urban transport planning have occupied many pages of this book. Listed below are ten important lessons from the experiences of industrialised countries. They in particular relate to the USA (see Chapters 2, 3 and 4) but nevertheless, also have a bearing on Third World cities.

Lesson 1 *Urban transport planning still awaits a true multi-disciplinary approach.* The treatment of the field as essentially an engineering science is inappropriate *in any context*, and especially in Third World countries. While the use of specific 'scientific' tools is extremely helpful in tackling certain problems, it is ultimately *not* the technical rationale that determines the outcome of urban transport investment decisions, but rather a mixture of many rationales of which the political is paramount.

Lesson 2 *The institutionalisation and standardisation of urban transport planning practice is advantageous in broad terms.* It is particularly valuable as a means of ensuring consistency of approach on a national basis among states, provinces and cities. Both institutionalisation and standardisation can, however, prove to be stifling when applied to detailed planning procedures, local decision-making and infrastructure design.

Lesson 3 *More explicit planning efforts need to be introduced to cater for urban travel other than motorised movement.* Despite claims to the contrary and the increased emphasis on public transport, the UTP process and its derivatives are more supportive of private motorised transport than other modes.

Lesson 4 *A movement away from the preoccupation with the urban travel demand component of the planning exercise is needed.* The 'four stage model' of travel demand has remained the corner-stone of urban transport planning practice for too long. Not only has this model misrepresented the scope of transport planning in urban areas but it has also constrained more innovative thinking in the field.

Lesson 5 *The contextual realities and political socio-economic environments of urban transport policy-making, particularly as they affect planning and model building, need to be taken more into account.* These have for too long, with dire consequences, been underrated in the interests of the mechanics and techniques of planning and model building.

Lesson 6 *More politically ratified directives of a normative kind are required in urban transport planning.* Because trend planning has characterised most planning practices in this field, not only has the normative content of such exercises been under-emphasised, but trends (rather than policies) have formed the basis of too much policy-making.

Lesson 7 *It needs to be more widely realised that the claim that conventional approaches to urban transport planning are 'comprehensive' is a myth.* The demand for broader and more 'open planning' approaches to urban transport, involving greater consideration of environmental factors and public participation have revealed, beyond doubt, that aspects of transport systems operation have undeservedly overshadowed those of transport systems impacts.

Lesson 8 *The UTP package and its use by public sector agencies have been stretched to its limits in terms of both political and technical viability.* The focus on public projects has, as a result, increasingly given way to planning practices driven by the market approach. These are epitomised by short-term considerations, an emphasis on cost revenue schemes, a greater involvement of the private sector and the development of projects outside a coherent planning framework.

Lesson 9 *Although the UTP process has by and large disintegrated as a single comprehensive planning process in the industrialised nations, there has been in its place a proliferation of UTP derivatives that only offer 'partial' and 'disaggregated analyses'.* These however, employ principles and assumptions closely akin to some of those already discredited of the UTP process. The continued indiscriminate use of these techniques, therefore, not only perpetuates many past errors of urban transport planning practice but also draws attention and investment away from alternative, less formalised and potentially more open and useful approaches.

Lesson 10 *Greater planning attention needs to be given to the 'lowerarchy' of city transport systems.* The tendency is for urban transport planning studies typically to focus on 'line-haul' travel of major transport routes. This has led to the construction of imbalanced urban transport systems, as well as to inadequate attention being paid to the detailing of the lower levels of urban transport systems, particularly at the neighbourhood and community level.

Lessons from Third World countries

Of the numerous lessons of transport planning that can be learned from Third World city experiences (see Chapters 5, 6 and 7), while not exclusive to these settlements, the following are among the most significant for the formulation of a 'developmental approach' to urban transport planning.

Lesson 1 *It is prudent in most Third World countries for the government to remain in the decision-making 'driving seat' of all major urban development investments, and thus transport investment.* The government can then remain the pilot, initiator and protector of *overall development*. This is especially important for low and medium-income economies, despite the growing involvement of the private sector in urban transport.

Lesson 2 *Greater attention needs to be paid to issues of the management, operations and maintenance of urban transport systems.* Transport problems of Third World cities are expected to become more serious, not only in metropolitan areas, but also in the fast-growing cities with 500,000 to 1,000,000 inhabitants. In the face of further urbanisation and world-wide recession, the initial problems of increased vehicle ownership and subsequent demand for new transport facilities will ultimately be superseded by more acute problems of transport management, operations and maintenance.

Lesson 3 *More concerted efforts are needed to translate macro-development planning objectives into meaningful local and sectoral terms.* Development planners and economists have long had considerable difficulties in translating their macroeconomic ideas and policies into spatial and urban development terms. Understanding the dynamics and issues of Third World urban development, however, is as much a prerequisite for urban transport planning and traffic engineering practice in these parts of the world as is sound professional engineering competence.

Lesson 4 *Transport problems need to be perceived, and thus tackled, from different (but co-ordinated) standpoints.* The lack of compatibility and agreement among professions involved in urban transport have contributed considerably to the problems of the sub-sector in the Third World. While urban transport problems are readily presented in terms of their traditional agenda, they also need to be differentiated in terms of 'root' and 'manifestation' problems.

Lesson 5 *Unclear and unrealistic goal-setting should be avoided.* Unfortunately, this represents one of the most common sources of problems in urban transport planning during both plan-making and project implementation in the Third World. Some aspects of this particularly relate to the mismatch between adopted urban transport goals and urban grass-root level needs.

Lesson 6 *Resorting to traffic and highway engineering measures independent of land-use planning cannot resolve urban transport problems.* Many highway and traffic engineering schemes associated with urban transport planning efforts in the Third World seem to rely upon the misconception that problems of traffic congestion and parking can be successfully tackled by engineering measures, independent of meaningful land-use control. Planning approaches that do not accommodate the complexities of the problems they are asked to address are destined not only to fail but generate additional and more costly problems which Third World cities in particular can ill afford.

Lesson 7 *Critical technology-transfer questions in urban transport planning are not those which concern techniques but development strategy.* The principal issue of this kind is whether a Third World city should duplicate the same type of development and transport strategy as is typically pursued by industrialised countries. A further issue not generally appreciated about a constrained Third World situation is that a major problem of the UTP process (and many of its travel demand forecasting derivatives), in any kind of travel demand forecasting exercise, is that it will show all facilities to be super-saturated. This is a fact that needs to be fed back into both the development and transport planning strategies, and its impacts duly assessed.

Lesson 8 *There are severe limitations to the use of the economic rationale in urban transport planning.* Conventional urban transport planning practice does not distinguish between 'travel needs' and 'travel preferences'. This is in part because transport facilities in Third World cities are often priced in an obscure way. However, it is principally because the deterministic role of the economic rationale in the UTP process makes it very difficult to plan for basic needs or 'entitlements' that are not evident in the marketplace. It is, though, irrational to presume that when people cannot afford to pay for transport needs, they do not need them – particularly in those parts of the world where the poor predominate.

Lesson 9 *The value of money is so high in Third World countries that paradoxically the relative value of time for most of the population is low.* While the overwhelming evidence is that cost is the key factor in urban travel demand, the relative value of time, especially among the less privileged, is so low that it ought to call into question the viability of many Third World urban transport project appraisal exercises.

Lesson 10 *The implementation costs of many first choice urban transport planning options in the Third World can often render seemingly better technical options ineffective and/or too costly.* The cost of putting a proposal into place, such as road pricing, for example, and the losses associated with the difficulties of doing this, can in certain Third World environments be so large that one may be better off having a system that does not appear to work so well but is in fact easier to introduce and much more acceptable.

FUTURE DIRECTIONS

In addition to the above lessons, a number of other salient points may be deduced from the preceding discussions in this book. Perhaps the most important of these is the conclusion by the author that despite the relatively more flexible approaches to urban transport planning adopted in the USA (see Meyer, 1985) and other industrialised nations, fundamentally, urban transport planning practice has not progressed greatly since the mid-1970s, except perhaps for its greater appreciation of the constraints acting upon it. This is seen as a problem that is expected to become even more pronounced as the environmental lobby is taken more seriously by politicians and the public alike (Dimitriou, 1989).

Ingram (1978) attributes this loss of direction to a series of missed opportunities. He explains:

> I think we are continually making the same mistakes we have made in the past.... There has been a certain amount of fiddling with the structure of the process... but essentially we are making the same mistakes.... I have the sense that in the mid-1950s there was a kind of fork in the road, and one of the things we could have done (which was not done) was to have begun to think more clearly about the planning instrument or the way we characterised the process as a decision-making tool, to essentially enrich the structure of the model.... The other alternative was to look at the shortcomings of modelling. Somehow, however, ever since 1957... it was felt that if we had more traffic analyses and more links in our network analysis, we would have a better model.... Those concerned really wanted to have a mathematical representation of reality.

The combined outcome of the above is that rather than a concern for the planning methodology for urban transport as a whole being the focus of improvements in the field, partial advances in specific techniques of the methodology, many of which went 'overboard' on travel choice, have instead overshadowed developments, as in the case of disaggregate demand analyses. As Ingram (1978) again comments:

> I think disaggregate models prevent people from continuing to think about the underlying problems of the process... the technique has got in the way of thinking more about what to do next.

This outcome has been particularly limiting because these and many other such techniques are too closely derived from the UTP modelling process to provide the new directions so badly needed. They do not, as a result, address many of the important issues and problems discussed earlier in Chapters 3, 4 and 7 but have rather 'side-stepped' them. For many transport planners employing these tools essentially do now what they used to do when they utilised aggregate demand models. This failing is well illustrated with regard to the most recent comprehensive urban transport planning study – for Hong Kong (Hong Kong Government Transport Department and Wilbur Smith Associates, 1989) about which the the following comments have been made (South China Morning Post, 1989):

> The Second Comprehensive Transport Study is inaptly titled. It provides only limited responses to the worsening traffic situation in Hong Kong. What the study discloses in statistical terms, it lacks in ideas and vision, which are essential if the territory is to untangle its traffic snarl-up... it relies too much on old formulae that have been found wanting in the past....

The perpetuation of the lack of new directions in urban transport planning of the kind referred to above, and the resultant danger of this spreading to the Third World, is annually strengthened by the increasing number of professionals (particularly civil engineers and economists) from this part of the globe in receipt of a conventional wisdom type of training. Such persons have been (and are still) trained by institutions, many of which are in the industrialised countries, that are firmly stuck in the technique-ridden ruts of transport planning, and the more straightforward principles of traffic engineering and management.

Innovative thinking in this kind of conventional wisdom perspective has instead been confined to ideas regarding cost revenue generation for urban transport, private/public joint enterprises in transport operations, and to various kinds of privatisation schemes. These are all focused on achieving better operational and administrative efficiency but have very little to do with making transport systems more 'effective' in terms of achieving wider development goals, and arriving at more sensitive planning approaches to the contexts to which they are to be applied. One of the few areas of promise for the Third World has been the development of sketch-planning referred to earlier. However, this too has mainly been confined in scope to an emphasis of investigating how to arrive at a quicker and lower-cost approach to the UTP process, rather than to examine wider issues and new directions.

What the *ad hoc* developments appear to have encouraged is on the one hand, confused thinking regarding future directions in the field, and on the other hand, something which is rather less apparent, namely, a rehabilitation of certain views concerning the utility of the UTP process, particularly regarding specific components of it (see Boyce, 1988).

If past lessons are to be truly learnt regarding the use and misuse of the UTP process and its derivatives, one needs to be capable of drawing the fine but clear line between the need to accept those tools of the process which are sufficiently malleable to be used in other urban transport planning paradigms, and the 'unannounced' and 'indiscriminate rehabilitation' of what in essence is only a marginally revised UTP process.

This latter more pragmatic development could flag the beginning of a new phase in the evolution of the UTP process (see Chapter 2). It is particularly ominous given the signs of a slow but little talked-about rehabilitation of the process. Much of this revaluation arises from the benefits the UTP process and its derivatives offer from its standardisation (and the reduced facilitation costs this encourages) through the wider use of microcomputers. It has been argued, for example, that although the process and its techniques can be criticised for standardising things to a low level, and that subsequently there could have been a better set of techniques on offer, by coming up with a standardised approach, a joint international effort of mutual benefit has been pursued.

Complementing this view is the argument that the standardised direction of developments that has taken place has truncated the distribution of possible analyses in such a way that it has not only cut-off the upper tail of developments (thereby eliminating higher quality or potentially high quality transport analyses) but also the lower tail thus eliminating lower quality transport analyses, with the net benefit of preventing disaster options from being taken on-board.

Further reinforcing this stand is the claim that to abandon the accumulated capital of expertise associated with the UTP package is both disruptive and retrograde – at least until an alternative 'better' approach is found. This is argued on the grounds that the process and its techniques and procedures are well documented, and because many professionals world-wide have had a great deal of experience with such expertise.

What this last viewpoint implies, however, is that 'order' in analysis is a derivative of standardisation, and that conversely, the absence of standardisation leads to 'chaotic' analysis. This is a view that is in direct conflict with the more 'open planning' approaches typical of development planning and policy making experiences that set the context of transport problems in Third World cities, and with which transport planning in these settlements *must* interface. It also goes against the rapidly developing tide of concern for the environment.

The sacrificing of sensitivity in planning for the convenience of standardisation has led Safier (1982) to make a plea to those involved in Third World urban development to recognise the 'intellectual collapse' of many, if not all planning generalisations. In line with the main thrust of this thesis, Safier has long argued for a more balanced approach to planning in Third World contexts by placing much greater priority on the development and policy-making context of such exercises (see Chapter 8).

Interestingly, this is a conclusion that has its parallels in other sectors as well as in the transport field (see Masser, 1987), where it has been concluded that the environment of model building and the application of models have a determining affect on the validity of model outputs. It would therefore appear prudent, where generalisations are employed in urban transport planning, to examine the validity of their use more carefully. Where they do not

Figure 9.1 Shortcomings of conventional urban transport planning: mismatches with Third World contexts

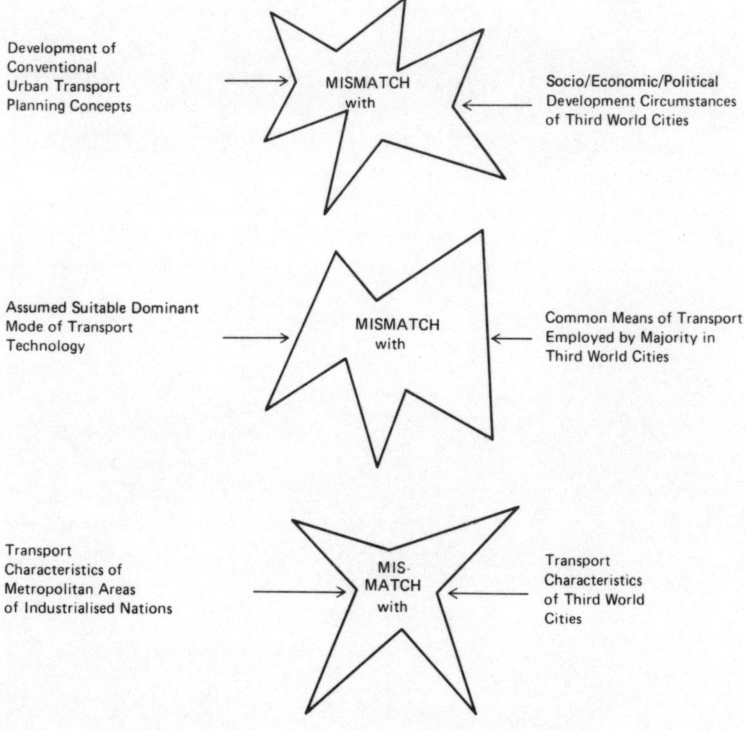

stand up to scrutiny, they should be substituted with principles based on 'home-grown' observations.

The findings of the research reported in this book confirms that the application of the UTP process and its derivatives to the Third World commonly exhibit three serious mismatches which need to be addressed (see Figure 9.1). The first, is a mismatch between the socio-economic and political environments in which the conventional wisdom and its derivatives evolved, and that of the Third World in which it has subsequently been applied. The second mismatch is between the dominant (motorised) modes of transport traditionally encouraged and serviced by the process, and the means of transport employed by the majority of Third World urban inhabitants. Finally, there is the mismatch between characteristics of metropolitan areas of industrialised countries (for which the UTP process was initially designed), and settlements (both large and small) of the Third World.

POSTSCRIPT

The world is now a very different place from that in which the first land use and transportation studies were started in the late 1950s. Western economies are no longer dominated by manufacturing, and new types of services have arisen in response to the inexorable increases in the wealth of the West over the last 30 years. The dependence of the Third World on the West is changing as new types of imperialism are emerging based on the rise of the multinational corporation. The population and resource problems of the Third World become ever more severe as the West is driven headlong on the path to post industrialism. In this milieu, where rapid and often volatile change is the order of the day, it is important to keep what we have learnt about the planning of cities during the last four decades in perspective. The experience recounted in this book is one from which land use and transportation planners must learn and build, for the messages and lessons which flow from these pages are more than they might seem at first sight.

The experiences with systematic transport planning using computer-based analyses and simulation models were but a first attempt at getting to grips with the complexity of urban structure and movement, which was consciously and professionally first recognised in the 1950s. When these studies began, there were massive problems of making such models operational. Computers were slow and small, the organisations into which such science was injected was unaccustomed to operating with such advice, there was unbounded and unwarranted optimism concerning the potential of these quantitative models and processes, and there was a strong technocratic bias to these efforts with little attempt at educating other experts and decision-makers involved in the transport planning process. Moreover, the policy context into which such models were embedded was and remains an extremely volatile one where the chameleon nature of the problems and policies continually undermine the longer-term scientific efforts which such approaches imply.

It is, however, important to learn from these experiences. The immediate conclusion, that computer models and methods are of little use in transport planning either in the developed or developing world, is a false one which has been grasped by the Luddites as ammunition in their quest to fight against the emergence of a computer world. As this book portrays, those involved in developing such models were brave enough to reflect on their experiences and to move on from these. The message of the 1950s that 'traffic is a function of land use' was quickly grasped, while in the 1960s and 1970s, the development of aggregate approaches to travel demand was gradually replaced with more behaviourally-based approaches whose roots lay in microeconomics and psychology. These discrete choice models as they came to be called, were also problematic in that the richness of travel choice and behaviour they sought to capture, together with their obvious policy relevance, was foiled by their very complexity, their poor performance and the formidable data demands which were necessary for their operation.

Moreover, once the initial wave of highway building was over in the West, and as the emphasis on the automobile was tempered by the need for mass transit, by environmental concerns involving pollution, and by the market through various crises related to oil and other non-renewable energy resources, transport planning took a back seat in the activities of government and industry alike. Yet the problems of movement which first led to the development of such planning are emerging once again, or perhaps our perception of them has just been heightened. Whatever. In the West, our highway infrastructure is crumbling, the emergence of new cities on the edges of the old and the ever present phenomenon of gridlock in the suburbs, are all leading to a revival of transport planning. This, however, is a style of transport planning which is considerably more realistic than that which began three decades or more ago. It is more policy relevant, it is based on deeper insights into travel behaviour, and it is sensitive to the way in which the public and private sectors interact to determine the type of transport system that develops. Nevertheless, the process is still heavily based on computer techniques and new types of information system which will clearly affect transport planning in Third World cities during the next decades.

While transport planning lost its focus and was assigned to a back seat in urban planning during the last twenty years, we have quite suddenly entered a world almost completely dominated by computers. Computers are everywhere. In the next decade we will find them embodied into the very hardware of transportation with respect to their use as information systems as well as control devices. Most transport planning is now developed in a computer environment where digital data is the norm, where computer-aided design dominates highway planning, and where computer information systems are central to the operation of the transport system itself. Yet land-use transport models are still problematic in their performance and requirements, although the cost of their application has been considerably reduced. In fact, the sorts of computer environment now becoming the norm for planning enable much greater experimentation with such models and analyses to take place, thus making their use less a symbol or focus for a new age and more a routine activity with less glamour than before.

However, perhaps the single biggest problem which continues to plague land use and transport planning involves the weak theoretical understanding we still have of the ways in which our cities function. This of course is emphasised when it comes to our intervention and control of the development process through planning. In fact, Third World cities are even more complex and lacking superficial order than those in the West; and this more than anything else has defeated those applications of transport planning where there have been direct and perhaps naïve attempts to transfer technology between these two worlds. What is even more problematic is that cities have changed in their complexity during the last forty years; urban processes no longer work in the same way they did in the first industrial age, and planning itself has changed the nature of the urban crisis. These problems have all the characteristics of what Horst Rittel and Mel Webber in 1973 defined as 'wicked problems', problems which actually can and often do get worse rather than better when planners attempt to alleviate or resolve them. Such is the nature of the transport problems presented in this book. It is not simply the nature of the transport planning process which accounts for these difficulties but the failure to develop robust theory in their understanding. And there is now a small but growing and discernible grain of uncertainty that such problems can ever be alleviated, although this lies beyond our rationality.

It sounds almost trite to say that Third World cities are very differently organised and structured from those in the West, although one of the main problems raised in this book is the fact that methods which hardly worked in one context were quickly transferred to an even less appropriate one, often with disastrous results. Moreover, the patterns of dependence between the developed and developing worlds with respect to monetary and technical aid have simply reinforced these differences. In fact the wholesale importation of Western style transport planning into the Third World is but one manifestation of this deeper global crisis.

There is, however, a more fundamental problem which pervades all planning in both the developed and developing world, and that involves the degree to which models, techniques, theories and processes can be generalised and used in more than one context. At a broad level, our understanding of cities and their planning can be obviously generalised, but when it comes to a particular application there can be many characteristics which limit the applicability of standard methods, thus implying that such methods need to be fine-tuned to the circumstances at hand. This is often difficult to achieve usually because resources are limited in terms of skills, time and data; the organisational environment is rarely attuned to the methods being suggested and the dependence on donors, on aid and on consultants tends to limit the degree to which methods can be adapted. All of these problems have been raised in this book, and they are in a sense, independent of the types of methods used. The 'Basic Needs' approach proposed here, however, implies the need for sensitive, adaptive planning, and until both donor and recipient agree that this is necessary the problems of transport planning raised here will remain unresolved.

What then for the future? We are entering an era which in many respects is quite different from that which dominated the mid-century when the types of planning evolved here were in high fashion. But the problems raised by those methods are still there and until the structural dependence of the developing on the developed world begins to change, and until the developing world really grasps the nettle of alternative and attainable visions for their future, these problems will not disappear. They may even intensify.

To this end, the lessons emanating from this book are important. It is not simply a question that transport planning must abandon its old models, old approaches and seek new. Of course this is necessary, but it is the need to study the problem of cities *in situ* that is the main issue. The fact that transport modelling emphasises the automobile in contrast to mass transit and walk trips is not just a methodological problem. Systems models can easily be extended to embrace such behaviour and activities but if the planner relies on standard packages and the time to adapt them to the problem in question is limited, if there is no continuity to the planning process and if skills have to be imported to develop such models, the chances of developing relevant planning applications are low. If there is one message that permeates these pages, it is that planning is a generic activity which must be built up in terms of the problem in question and implemented accordingly. Only then will such planning be effective.

Michael J. Batty,
Professor of City and Regional Planning,
University of Wales College at Cardiff and
Professor of Geography and
Director of the National Center for
Geographic Information and Analysis,
State University of New York, Buffalo.

NOTES

2 THE UTP PROCESS AND ITS DERIVATIVES

1 This chapter is largely based on the author's Chapter 5 of *Transport Planning for Third World Cities* (Dimitriou, 1990).
2 By the late 1980s, a significant proportion of the World Bank's own in-house professional staff involved in project preparation and appraisal of urban transport projects were recruited from consultancy firms, many of them (such as Wilbur Smith Associates) most intimately involved in the early developments and subsequent modification and dissemination of the process and its derivatives.
3 Goals are desired ends towards which efforts and resources are focused. Policies may be seen as guidelines in the form of combinations of 'operational objectives' which are designed to determine how to achieve pre-set goals. Strategies, on the other hand, concern the arrangement of policies and goals in a sequence of time and place and in terms of pre-agreed priorities to achieve certain ends.
4 The widespread international transfer of the UTP process is a phenomenon not referred to in the article by Gakenheimer and Wheaton.
5 The belief that conceptual disarray still prevails (particularly in Third World transport planning practice) is an extension by the author of Gakenheimer and Wheaton's evolutionary stages.2

3 CRITIQUE OF THE PROCESS: FUNCTIONS, ASSUMPTIONS AND CONCEPTS

1 The Highway Revenue Act of 1956, in support of the US Federal Highway Act of the same year, created a Highway Trust Fund from increased federal taxes on: petrol and other motor fuels, excise taxes on tyres, and established new taxes on retreaded tyres as well as a weight tax on heavy trucks and buses. Funds from these sources were dedicated solely to highway purposes – a decision which broke with congressional precedent not to earmark taxes for specific authorised purposes (Weiner, 1987).

4 CRITIQUE OF THE UTP PROCESS: ISSUES AND PERFORMANCE

1 Wilbur Smith's Associates three volumes of books for the Automobile Manufacturer's Association (1961, 1965 and 1966) catalogued the results of transport plans of the time. It was an influential statistical effort and an extremely valuable background contribution which the promoters used to try to prove the urgency of building the interstate highway system in the USA.

2 By policy, one refers to a formal intention declared by the government providing the basis for continued government action.

5 TRANSPORT AND THIRD WORLD CITY DEVELOPMENT

1 This chapter has been published as Chapter 1 in *Transport Planning for Third World Cities* edited by the author, assisted by G.A. Banjo, published by Routledge, London (1990).

2 Given the dramatic political events of 1990, whereby the previously centrally planned economies of Eastern Europe and the USSR are turning toward more market-orientated economies, this categorisation becomes increasingly one of historic rather than current relevance.

6 TRANSPORT PROBLEMS OF THIRD WORLD CITIES

1 This chapter has been previously published as Chapter 2 in *Transport Planning for Third World Cities* edited by the author and assisted by G.A. Banjo, published by Routledge, London (1990).

2 It should be noted that some Third World cities, such as Sao Paulo and Mexico City, possess motorisation rates in excess of those of many cities in the industrialised world.

3 It is unclear, however, whether this figure is unusually high as a result of the construction of the city's metro system during these years.

4 The source of this statistic does not make clear whether the percentage quoted refers to all traffic accidents or those of urban areas alone.

5 The informal transport sector may be defined as that part of the transport sector provided by bodies and private companies which are neither government nor quasi-government. The provision of such transport services is often illegal in that the vehicles used are unlicensed and/or operate along unauthorised routes.

6 Problems may be defined as obstacles to, and a departure from, the desired end(s).

7 For further discussion of this particular aspect, the reader is encouraged to refer to the early writings of Altshuler (1965) on 'Opportunism vs. Professionalism in Planning' and Benveniste (1972) on 'The Prince and the Pundit'.

8 Technology-transfer as defined by Streeten (1974) is 'the transfer of skills, knowledge and procedures for making, using and doing useful things' – for the purpose of this discussion, 'things' relate to efforts to tackle and resolve urban transport problems of Third World cities.

9 Concern for such aspects led the Japanese government to commission a study of technology-transfer considerations in the Third World transport field (see International Development Centre of Japan, 1987).

10 Goals may be defined (after Barlow, 1978) as 'idealised end-states of the total environment (in this case, of the urban transport sector) toward which planners strive'.

7 A CRITICAL REVIEW OF THE APPLICATION OF THE UTP PROCESS AND ITS DERIVATIVES TO THIRD WORLD CITIES

1 The US DOT package developed by Bob Dial in 1977 was initially designed to house the UTP process that was developed in the USA and has subsequently been passed on directly to Third World countries but also indirectly, through the Transport Road Research Laboratory (TRRL) of the UK Government. Via this latter route, the package especially reached innumerable British colonial and ex-colonial territories via its aid programme. The cost of the use of the US DOT UTP package in 1978 was minimal (approximately US $60); the high cost aspect was (and still is) learning how to use it.

2 A similar issue to this was investigated for five years by students of the MIT – Harvard Joint Center for Urban Studies for the Cindad Guayana New City Study of Venezuela under the supervision of Professor Lloyd Rodwin of MIT in the early 1970s.

8 ELEMENTS AND FRAMEWORK OF A DEVELOPMENTAL APPROACH TO TRANSPORT PLANNING FOR THIRD WORLD CITIES

1 This part of the book draws from a number of sources, namely: the preceding discussions contained in Chapters 3 to 7; a paper entitled 'A Developmental Approach to Urban Transport Planning' first presented by the author with Michael Safier in 1982 and subsequently expanded upon in the final chapter of a book recently edited by the author (Dimitriou, 1990a); as well as a UNDP/UNCHS funded study directed and conducted by the author (TDC S.A., 1988).

2 IUIDP, as outlined here, is an integrated urban development approach to infrastructure planning as initiated by the Indonesian government with the intention of introducing more systematic investment programming and cost-effective implementation procedures in seven sub-sectors of urban infrastructure development, including road transport (see Dimitriou, 1991).

3 This section of the chapter is based upon the joint paper entitled 'A

Developmental Approach to Urban Transport Planning' written by the author with M. Safier (1982).

4 This part of the chapter is based on aspects of a study conducted for Training and Development Consultants S.A., Lausanne, on contract to UNDP/UNCHS and the Ministry of Public Works of the Government of Indonesia between 1987/8 for which the author was the Project Director. Professor Budhy Soegijoko of the Institute of Technology Bandung acted as consultant and Sharif Horthy of TDC was Project Manager.

5 This estimate is based on 1984 figures.

6 Transport speed-bands is a term coined in a study conducted in Indonesia by TDC S.A. (1988) which denotes a segregated continuous network of transport infrastructure to be shared as a matter of policy by certain transport modes operating within a common travel speed range. Up to five speed-bands were identified in the Javanese cities studied. These were: speed-band 1 (up to about 15 km/hr) for walking and pushcarts; speed-band 2 (between 10 and 20 km/hr) for bicycles and cycle rickshaws; speed-band 3 (between 25 and 40 km/hr) for low-powered motorcycles, bemos and baja; and speed-band 4 (50–100 km/hr) for minibuses, buses, motorcars and high-powered motorcycles.

7 A road utilisation function is a measure of the road space utilised by a particular transport mode. It is seen as an important added contribution to the assessment of the vehicle's true economic cost, analogous to a 'passenger car unit' (pcu) measure which in industrialised countries is defined as a vehicle's contribution to saturated traffic flow compared to that of a standard motorcar. Due to the fairly standard road and traffic conditions in industrialised nations, pcu values are conveniently regarded as intrinsic to a transport mode and generally independent of extraneous factors. This makes the pcu concept not very useful in Third World countries, except at the higher levels of the road hierarchy (TDC S.A., 1988).

REFERENCES

2 THE UTP PROCESS AND ITS DERIVATIVES

Atkins, S. T. (1986) 'Transportation planning models – what the papers say', *Traffic Engineering and Control*, 27 (9), 460–468.

ARGE Intertraffic-Lenz Consult (1975) *The Jakarta Metropolitan Area Transportation Study*, Arge Intertraffic-Lenz Consult, Jakarta.

Banister, D. (1984) 'The TSU approach – the first ten years of the transport studies unit', *Transport Reviews*, 4 (3), 299–302.

Banister, D., Bould, M. and Warren, G. (1984) 'Towards needs based transport planning', *Traffic Engineering and Control*, 25 (7/8), 372–375.

Banjo, G. A. (1982) 'Towards an appropriate time valuation practice in the Third World', *Proceedings of PTRC Annual Meeting*, University of Warwick, PTRC Education and Research Services Ltd., London.

Banjo, G. A. (1984) 'Towards a new framework for transport planning in the Third World', *ARRB Proceedings*, 12, Part I.

Banjo, G. A. and Dimitriou, H. T. (1983) 'Urban transport problems of Third World cities: the third generation', *Habitat International*, 7 (3/4).

Barat, J. (1990) 'Institutional frameworks for planning transport in Third World cities', in *Transport Planning for Third World Cities* edited by H. T. Dimitriou, assisted by G. A. Banjo, Routledge, London.

Barrett, R. (1983) 'Institution Building for Traffic Management', *World Bank Technical Paper*, No. 8, World Bank, Washington DC.

Ben-Akiva, M. and Lerman, S. R. (1985) *Discrete Choice Analysis: Theory and Applications to Travel Demand*, MIT Press, Cambridge, Massachusetts.

Black, J. (1981) *Urban Transport Planning: Theory and Practice*, John Hopkins University Press, Baltimore.

Blunden, W. R. and Black, J. A. (1984) *The Land-Use/Transport System*, second edition, Pergamon Press, Oxford.

Brokke, G. E. and Carroll, J. D. (1959) 'Program for Assigning Traffic to a Highway Network', *Highway Research Board Bulletin*, No. 224, HRB, Washington DC.

Brotchie, J. F., Dickey, J. W. and Sharp, R. (1980) *TOPAZ – General*

Planning Techniques and its Applications at Regional, Urban and Facility Planning Levels, Springer-Verlag, Berlin.

Bruton, M. J. (1970) *Introduction to Transportation Planning*, Hutchinson Technical Education, London.

Buchanan, C. D. (1963) *Traffic in Towns*, HMSO, London.

Carpenter, S. and Jones, P. M. (eds) (1983) *Recent Advances in Travel Demand Analysis*, Gower Publishing Company, Aldershot.

Carroll, J. D. (1956) General Discussion, *Highway Research Board Bulletin*, No. 130, HRB, Washington DC.

Chicago City (1955–61) *Chicago Area Transportation Study*, Final Reports: Vol. I, II and III, Chicago.

Choi, Y. (1986) 'Land use transport optimization (LUTO) model on strategic planning in Hong Kong', *Asian Geographer*, 5 (2), 155–176.

Creighton, R. L. (1970) *Urban Transportation Planning*, University of Illinois Press, Urbana.

Darbera, R. (1978) 'Methodological and institutional issues in urban transportation planning for less developed countries', *Proceedings of PTRC Annual Meeting*, University of Warwick, PTRC, Education and Research Services Ltd., London.

Detroit City (1953–55) *Detroit Area Metropolitan Traffic Study*, Final Reports: Vol. I and II, Detroit.

Dickey, J. W. (1975) *Metropolitan Transportation Planning*, McGraw-Hill, New York.

Dimitriou, H. T. (1977) 'A call for the effective integration of urban and transport planning in developing countries', *Proceedings of PTRC Annual Meeting*, University of Warwick, PTRC Education and Research Services Ltd., London.

—— (1982) 'Transport and the Urban Poor in the Third World', Paper presented to Habitat International Council (NGO Committee on Human Settlements) at Town and Country Planning Association, London.

—— (1990) 'The urban transport planning process: its evolution and application to Third World cities', in *Transport Planning for Third World Cities*, edited by H. T. Dimitriou, assisted by G. A. Banjo, Routledge, London.

Echenique, M. (1975) 'Urban development models: fifteen years of experience', in *Urban Development Models* R. Baxter (ed.), The Construction Press, Cambridge.

Foot, D. (1981) *Operational Urban Models: An Introduction*, Methuen, London.

Freeman Fox and Wilbur Smith Associates (1964 – 1966) *London Traffic Survey*, Vol. I and II, London.

Freeman Fox and Wilbur Smith Associates (1970 – 1974) *Bogota Transport and Urban Development Study: Phase 1*, London and New Haven, Connecticut.

Gakenheimer, R. A. (1978) Transcript of Interview with Author, Massachusetts Institute of Technology, Cambridge, Massachusetts, 17th and 21st March.

Gakenheimer, R. A. and Wheaton, W. C. (1976) 'Priorities in urban transportation research', *Transportation*, 5 (1), Elsevier Scientific Publishing Company, Amsterdam, 73–91

Hamburg, J. R. and Creighton, R. L. (1959) 'Predicting Chicago's land use pattern', *Journal of the American Institute of Planners*, Vol. 25, No. 2, pp. 67.72.

Heanue, K. and Ettinger, J. (1978) Transcript of Interview with Author, Washington DC.

Hill, D. M., Brand, D. and Hansen, W. B. (1966) 'Prototype Development of Statistical Land-Use Prediction Model for Greater Boston Region, *Highway Research Record*, No. 114, Washington DC.

Hillegass, T. J. (1973) 'A Brief History of the Evolution of Urban Transportation Planning Techniques: 1940–1970', *Federal Highway Administration*, Washington DC.

Hong Kong Government Transport Department and Wilbur Smith Associates, (1989) *Hong Kong Second Comprehensive Transport Study*, Final Report, Government of Hong Kong.

Hutchinson, B. and Batty, M. (eds) (1986) *Advances in Urban Systems Modelling*, North Holland Elsevier, Amsterdam.

Jamieson Mackay and Partners, (1975) *Istanbul Urban Transport and Land Use Study*, Greater Istanbul Master Plan Bureau, Istanbul.

Jansen, G. R. M., Nijkamp, P. and Ruijgrok, C. J. (eds) (1985) *Transportation and Mobility in an Era of Transition*, North Holland Press, Amsterdam.

Jones, P. M. (1977) 'Assessing Policy Impacts Using the Household Activity-Travel Simulator', *Transport Studies Unit, Working Paper*, No. 18, Oxford University, Oxford.

—— (1983) 'The practical application of activity-based approaches in transport planning: an assessment', in S. Carpenter and P. Jones (eds) *Recent Advances in Travel Demand Analysis*, Gower Publishing Company, Aldershot.

—— (1987) Response to Questionnaire on Behavioural Analysis, Network on Transport, Communications and Mobility Project, European Science Foundation, Strasbourg.

Khan, M. A. and Willumsen, L. G. (1986) 'Modelling car ownership and use in developing countries', *Traffic Engineering and Control*, 27, (11), 554–560.

Kocks, KG/RHEIN-RUHR Eng. GMBH, (1975) *Bangkok Transportation Study*, Final Report, Dusseldorf and Bangkok.

Lane, R., Powell, T. J. and Prestwood Smith, P. (1971) *Analytical Transport Planning*, Duckworth, London.

Linn, J. F. (1983) *Cities in the Developing World*, World Bank Research Publication, Oxford University Press, Oxford.

Lowry, I. S. (1964) 'A Model of Metropolis', *RAND Corporation Report*, No. RM–4035 – RC, Santa Monica, California.

Madras Metropolitan Development Authority (MMDA), (1974) *Madras Area Transportation Study*, Vol. I, II, and III, Transportation Unit, Directorate of Town and Country Planning, MMDA, Government of Tamil Nadu, Madras.

Manheim, M. (1978) Transcript of Interview with author, Massachusetts Institute of Technology, Cambridge, Massachusetts, March.

Martin, B. and Wohl M. (1961) *Traffic Systems Analysis for Engineers and Planners*, McGraw-Hill, New York.

McNeill, D. (1977) 'Urban Transport in Developing Countries', *Development Planning Unit Working Paper*, No.1, University College, London.

Meyer, M. D. and Miller, E. J. (1984) *Urban Transportation Planning: A Decision-Orientated Approach*, McGraw-Hill Book Company, New York.

Mitchell, R. and Rapkin, C. (1954) *Urban Traffic: A Function of Land Use*, Colombia University Press, New York.

Mohan, R. (1979) 'Urban Economic and Planning Models: Assessing the Potential for Cities in Developing Countries', *World Bank Staff Occasional Paper*, No. 25, John Hopkins University Press, Baltimore.

Morlock, E. K. (1978) *Introduction to Transportation Engineering and Planning*, McGraw-Hill Book Company, New York.

Newman, P. and Kenworthy J. (1989) *Cities and Automobile Dependency*, Gower Publishing Company, Aldershot.

Nijkamp, P. and Reichman, S. (eds) (1987) *Transportation Planning in a Changing World*, Gower Publishing Company, Aldershot.

Overseas Technical Co-operation Agency (OTCA), (1970) *Urban Transportation System for Tehran*, OTCA, Government of Japan, April, Tokyo.

Paddilla, S. (1978) Transcript of Interview with Author, University of Puerto Rico, San Jose, April.

Putman, S. H. (1983) *Integrated Urban Models*, Pion Ltd, London.

Rimmer, P. J. (1986) 'Look east: the relevance of Japanese urban transport planning and technology to Southeast Asian cities', *Transportation Planning and Technology*, 11 (1), 47–67.

Supernak, J. and Stevens, W. R. (1987) 'Urban transportation modelling: the discussion continues', *Transportation*, 14 (1), 73–82.

Talvitie, A. (Undated) 'A Look at the Conceptual Foundations of the Transportation Planning process', Unpublished Paper, Helsinki.

Thomson, J. M. (1984) 'Toward Better Transport Planning in Developing Countries', *World Bank Staff Working Paper*, No. 600, IBRD, Washington DC.

US Department of Transport (DOT), (1973) 'The Urban Transport Planning Process', *UMTA and Federal Highway Administration*, Washington DC.

Viola, P. (1976) 'Large scale land-use transport studies: how relevant to Asian cities', *Proceedings of PTRC Annual Meeting*, University of Warwick, PTRC Education and Research Services Ltd, London.

Voorhees, A. N. and Morris, R. (1959) 'Estimating and Forecasting Travel for Baltimore by Use of a Mathematical Model', *Highway Research Board Bulletin*, No. 224, HRB, Washington DC.

Webster, P. H., Bly, P. H. and Paulley, N. J. (eds) (1988) *Urban Land Use and Transport Interaction*, Policies and Report of the International

Study Group on Land Use/Transport Interaction, Avebury Press, London.

Weiner, E. (1976) 'Evolution of Urban Transportation Planning', *Urban Analysis Programme, US Department of Transportation*, April, Washington DC.

—— (1986) 'Urban Transportation Planning in the United States: A Historical Overview', *US Department of Transportation Report*, No DOT-1-86-09, DOT, Washington DC.

—— (1989) *'Urban Transportation in the US'*, Praeger, New York.

Wilbur Smith Associates (1963) *Athens Basin Transportation Survey and Study*, New Haven, Connecticut.

—— (1967) *Traffic and Transportation Plan: 1966–86, for Calcutta Metropolitan Planning Organisation*, Sree Saraswaty Press Ltd., Calcutta.

—— (1974a) *Urban Transport Policy and Planning Study for Metropolitan Kuala Lumpur*, Wilbur Smith Associates, New Haven, Connecticut.

—— (1974b) *Lagos Metropolitan Area Transportation Planning Study*: Final Report, for Federal Ministry of Public Works, Military Government of Nigeria, Lagos.

Wilbur Smith Associates in Association with Parsons, Brinckerhoff-Tudor-Bechtel, (1974–7) *Singapore Mass Transit Study*, Government Printers, Singapore.

Wilson, A. G., Bayliss, D., Blackburn, A. J. and Hutchinson, B. G (1969) 'New Directions in Strategic Transportation Planning', *Centre for Environmental Studies Working Paper*, No.36, CES, May, London.

Wynn, F. H. (1959) 'Studies of Trip Generation in the Nation's Capital: 1956–58', *Highway Research Board Bulletin* No. 230, HRB, Washington DC.

Zahavi, Y. (1979) 'The UMOT Project', Report Prepared for US Department of Transportation, Washington DC. and Ministry of Transport of the Federal Republic of Germany, Bonn, *US Department of Transport Report*, No. RSPA-DPB-20-79-3, Bonn and Washington DC.

Zahavi, Y. Beckman, M. J. and Golob, T. F. (1981) 'UMOT/Urban Interactions', *US Department of Transportation Report*, No. DOT/RSPA/DPB-10/7, DOT, Washington DC.

3 CRITIQUE OF THE PROCESS: FUNCTIONS, ASSUMPTIONS AND CONCEPTS

Bell, G., Blackledge, D. A. and Bowen, P. (1983) *The Economics and Planning of Transport*, Heinemann, London.

Bruton M. J. (1970) *Introduction to Transportation Planning*, Hutchinson Technical Education, London.

Chicago City (1959–62) *Chicago Area Transportation Study*, Final Reports: Vol. I (1959), Vol. II (1960) and Vol. III (1962), IL: Harrison Lith, Chicago.

Creighton, R. (1970) *Urban Transportation Planning*, University of Illinois, Urbana.

Detroit City (1955–56) *Detroit Area Metropolitan Traffic Study*, Final Reports: Vol. I and II, MI: Speaker-Hines and Thomas, State Printers, Detroit.

Dimitriou, H. T. (1990) 'The urban transport planning process: its evolution and application to Third World cities' in *Transport Planning for Third World Cities*, edited by H. T. Dimitriou, assisted by G. A. Banjo, Routledge, London.

Gakenheimer, R. (1976) *Transportation Planning as a Response to Controversy: The Boston Case*, MIT Press, Cambridge, Massachusetts.

—— (1989) Correspondence with the author.

Gakenheimer, R. and Meyer, M. D. (1990) 'Urban transport corridor planning' in *Transport Planning for Third World Cities*, edited by H. T. Dimitriou, assisted by G. A. Banjo, Routledge, London.

Gakenheimer, R. and Wheaton, W. C. (1976) Priorities in urban transportation research, *Transportation*, Elsevier Scientific Publishing Company, Amsterdam, Vol. 5, pp. 73–91.

Manheim, M. L. (1990) 'Developments in urban transport planning: their relevance to Third World practice' in *Transport Planning for Third World Cities*, edited by H. T. Dimitriou, assisted by G. A. Banjo, Routledge, London.

Mitchell, R. and Rapkin, C. (1954) *Urban Traffic: A Function of Land Use*, Colombia University Press, New York.

Plant, J. F. (1988) 'Beyond the beltway: urban transportation policy in the 1980s', *Journal of Urban Affairs*, 10 (1), 29–40.

Quarmby, D. (1967) 'Choice of travel mode for journey to work', *Journal of Transport Economics Policy*, 1 (3).

Washington D. C. (1955) *Washington Area Transportation Study*, National Capital Planning Commission, Washington DC.

Webber, M. (1969) *On Strategies for Transport Planning*, OECD, Paris.

Webster, P. H., Bly, P. H and Paulley, N. J. (eds) (1988) *Urban Land Use and Transport Interaction*, Policies and Report of the International Study Group on Land Use/Transport Interaction, Avebury Press, London.

Weiner, E. (1987) *Urban Transportation Planning in the United States*, Praeger, New York.

Williams, H. C. W. L. (1987) 'Some reflections on transportation models' in *Transportation Planning in a Changing World*, by Nijkamp and Reichman, Gower Publishing Company, Aldershot.

Ziv, J. C. (1977) 'La Genèse des Modèles de Trafic aux Etats-Unis', Unpublished PhD Thesis, Cornell University, Ithaca, New York State.

4 CRITIQUE OF THE UTP PROCESS: ISSUES AND PERFORMANCE

Beed, C. S. C. (1981) *Melbourne Development and Planning*, Clewara Press, Melbourne.

Brewer, G. D. (1973) *Politicians, Bureaucrats, and the Consultant*, Basic Books, New York.

Bruton, M. J. (1970) *Introduction to Transportation Planning*, Hutchinson Technical Education, London.

Chicago City (1955–61) Chicago Transportation Study, Final Reports: Vols I, II and III, Chicago.

Dimitriou, H. T. (1989) 'A Developmental Approach to Urban Transport Planning', Unpublished PhD Thesis, University of Wales College at Cardiff, Cardiff.

Gakenheimer, R. (1976) *Transportation Planning as a Response to Controversy: The Boston Case*, MIT Press, Cambridge, Massachusetts.

—— (1989) Correspondence with author.

—— (1990) Correspondence with author.

Gakenheimer, R. and Meyer M. D. (1990) 'Urban transport corridor planning' in *Transport Planning for Third World Cities*, edited by H. T. Dimitriou assisted by G. A. Banjo, Routledge, London.

Hamer, M. (1987) *Wheels within Wheels: A Study of the Road Lobby*, Routledge, London.

Heanue, K. E. (1989) Correspondence with the author.

Hong Kong Government Transport Department and Wilbur Smith Associates (1989) *Hong Kong Second Comprehensive Transport Study*, Final Report, Government of Hong Kong.

Manheim, M. L. (1990) 'Developments in urban transport planning: their relevance to Third World practice' in *Transport Planning for Third World Cities*, edited by H. T. Dimitriou, assisted by G. A. Banjo, Routledge, London.

Mitchell, R. B. and Rapkin, C. (1954) *Urban Traffic: A Function of Land Use*, Columbia University Press, New York.

Newman, P. and Kenworthy, J. (1989) *Cities and Automobile Dependence*, Gower Publishing Company, Aldershot.

Neutze, M. (1977) *Urban Development in Australia: A Descriptive Analysis*, George Allen and Unwin, Sydney.

Plant, J. F. (1988) 'Beyond the beltway: urban transportation policy in the 1980s', *Journal of Urban Affairs*, 10 (1), 29–40.

Snell, M. P. (1974) American Ground Transport: 'A Proposal for Restructuring the Automobile, Truck, Bus and Rail Industries', US Government Policy Office, Washington D. C.

Webster, P. H., Bly P. H. and Paulley, N. J. (1988) *Urban Land Use and Transport Interaction*, Policies and Report of the International Study Group on Land-use/Transport Interaction, Avebury Press, London.

Wilbur Smith Associates (1961) *Future Highways and Urban Growth*, New Haven, Connecticut.

—— (1965) *Parking in the City*, New Haven, Connecticut.

—— (1966) *Transportation and Parking for Tomorrow's Cities*, New Haven, Connecticut.

Ziv, J. C. (1977) 'La Genèse des Modèles de Trafic aux Etats-Unis', Unpublished PhD Thesis, Cornell University, Ithaca, New York State.

Zupan, J. F. and Pushkarev, B. S. (1977) *Public Transportation and Land Use Policy*, Indiana University Press, Bloomington.

5 TRANSPORT AND THIRD WORLD CITY DEVELOPMENT

Bauer, P. T. (1980) *Dissent on Development*, Weidenfeld and Nicholson, London.

Crook, C. (1989) 'The Third World: trial and error' in A Survey of the Third World, *The Economist*, The Economist Newspaper Ltd., London, 23rd September, pp. 5–8.

Dimitriou, H. T. and Safier, M. (1982) 'A developmental approach to urban transport planning', *Proceedings of Universities Transport Study Group Seminar*, University College, London.

Dimitriou, H. T. (1990) 'Transport and Third World city development' in *Transport Planning for Third World Cities*, edited by H. T. Dimitriou assisted by G. A. Banjo, Routledge, London.

Gakenheimer, R. (1986) 'Transportation as a component of national urban strategy', *Habitat International*, 10 (12), 1/2, 133–139.

Gakenheimer, R. and Meyer, M. D. (1990) 'Urban transport corridor planning' in *Transport Planning for Third World Cities*, edited by H. T. Dimitriou assisted by G. A. Banjo, Routledge, London.

Galbraith, J. K. (1974) 'On the modern city – or history as the future', *Royal Institute of British Architects Journal*, London, October.

Harris, N. (1984) 'Some trends in the evolution of big cities', *Habitat International*, 8 (1), 7–28.

—— (1986) *The End of the Third World: Newly Industrializing Countries and the Decline of an Ideology*, Penguin Books, Harmondsworth, Middlesex.

Independent Commission on International Development Issues, under the Chairmanship of Willy Brandt (1981) *North-South: A Program for Survival*, Pan Books, London.

Linn, J. F. (1983) *Cities in Developing Countries*, World Bank Research Publication, Oxford University Press, Oxford.

Mabogunje, A. L. (1980) *The Development Process*, Hutchinson University Library, London.

Meier, R. (1962) *A Communications Theory of Urban Growth*, MIT Press, Cambridge, Massachusetts.

Mitchell, R. B. and Rapkin, C. (1954) *Urban Traffic: A Function of Land Use*, Columbia University Press, New York.

Myrdal, G. (1971) *Asian Drama*, Pantheon Press, New York.

Needham, B. (1977) *How Cities Work*, Pergamon Press, Oxford.

Newman, P. and Kenworthy, J. (1989) *Cities and Automobile Dependence*, Gower Publishing Company, Aldershot.

Proudlove, A. and Turner, A. (1990) 'Street management' in *Transport Planning for Third World Cities* edited by H. T. Dimitriou, assisted by G. A. Banjo, Routledge, London.

Rao, M. S. V and Sharma A. K. (1990) 'The role of non-motorised urban travel' in *Transport Planning for Third World Cities* edited by H. T. Dimitriou assisted by G. A. Banjo, Routledge, London.

Richardson, H. (1977) 'City Size and National Spatial Strategies in

Developing Countries', *World Bank Staff Working Paper*, No. 252, World Bank, Washington DC.

Rimmer, P. J. (1986) *Rikisha to Rapid Transit: Urban Public Transport Systems and Policy in Southeast Asia*, Pergamon Press, Oxford.

Roberts, B. (1978) *Cities of Peasants*, Edward Arnold, London.

Rostow, W. W. (1961) *The Stages of Economic Growth*, Cambridge University Press, Cambridge.

Safier, M. (1981) 'Urban Development and Cities in a Global Context', Unpublished Lecture given at DPU Special Programme on 'National Planning and Urban Development', University College, London.

Seers, D. (1969) 'The meaning of development', *International Development Review*, 11 (4), 2–6.

—— (1977) 'The new meaning of development', *International Development Review*, 19 (3), 3.

Soegijoko, B. T. (1986) 'The Becaks of Java', *Habitat International*, 10 (1/2), 155–164.

Stretton, H. (1978) *Urban Planning In Rich and Poor Countries*, Oxford University Press, Oxford.

Thomson, J. M. (1977) *Great Cities and Their Traffic*, Victor Gollancz, London.

Todaro, M. P. (1981) *Economic Development in the Third World*, Longman, New York.

UN Secretariat (1977) 'Measurement of basic minimum needs', *Asian Development Review*, 5 and 6.

Webber, M. M. (1969) *On Strategies for Transport Planning*, OECD, Paris.

White, P. R. (1990) 'Inadequacies of urban public transport systems' in *Transport Planning for Third World Cities*, edited by H. T. Dimitriou, assisted by G. A. Banjo, Routledge, London.

World Bank (1972) 'Industry', *World Bank Sector Working Paper*, Washington DC.

—— (1975) *Urban Transport: Sector Policy Paper*, Washington DC.

—— (1984) *World Development Report*, Oxford University Press, Oxford.

—— (1986) *Urban Transport: A World Bank Policy Paper*, Washington DC.

—— (1988) *World Development Report*, Oxford University Press, Oxford.

—— (1990) *World Development Report*, Oxford University Press, Oxford.

Worsley, P. (1980) 'How many worlds', in *Why the Third World?*, edited by Wolf-Phillips, Third World Foundation, Monograph, No. 7, London.

6 TRANSPORT PROBLEMS OF THIRD WORLD CITIES

Altshuler, A. (1965) *The City Planning process: A Political Analysis*, Cornell University Press, Ithaca.

Armstrong-Wright, A. (1986) 'Urban Transit Systems: Guidelines for Examining Options', *World Bank Technical Paper*, No. 52, World Bank, Washington DC.

Asia Magazine (1990) 'Stuck in Asia', *Asia Magazine*, Editorial, 28 (E–25), Hong Kong, September.

Bangladesh Bureau of Statistics (1989), 'Statistical Year Book', Ministry of Planning, Dacca.

Banjo, G. A. and Dimitriou, H. T. (1983) 'Urban transport problems of Third World cities: the third generation', *Habitat International*, 7 (3/4).

Barlow, P. (1978) 'Developing Goals and Objectives', *Transport Planning Research Reports*, No. TPRR 1–10, National Institute for Transport and Road Research, Pretoria.

Barrett, R. (1983) 'Institution Building for Traffic Management' *World Bank Technical Paper No.8*, World Bank, Washington DC.

Benveniste, G. (1972) *The Politics of Expertise*, Croom Helm, London.

Bouladon, G. (1967a) 'The transport gaps', *Science Journal*, 3, 41–46.

—— (1967b) 'Transport', *Science Journal*, 3, 93–99.

Carlsson G. and Hedman, K-O, 'A Systematic Approach to Road Safety in Developing Countries', Policy Planning and Research Staff, Infrastructure and Urban Development Department, Report No. 1NU63, World Bank, Washington DC, January.

Dickey, J. W., and Miller, L. H. (1984) *Road Project Appraisal for Developing Countries*, John Wiley and Sons, Chichester.

Dimitriou, H. T. (1977) 'A call for the effective integration of urban and transport planning for developing countries', *Proceedings of PTRC Summer Annual Meeting*, University of Warwick, PTRC Education and Research Services Ltd, London.

—— (1982) 'Transport and the Urban Poor in the Third World', Paper presented to Habitat International Council (NGO Committee on Human Settlements) at Town and Country Planning Association, London.

—— (1988) 'Urban transport and manpower development and training needs of four Asian cities', *Habitat International*, 12 (3), 65–90.

—— (1990) 'The urban transport planning process' in *Transport Planning for Third World Cities*, edited by H. T. Dimitriou assisted by G. A. Banjo, Routledge, London.

Economist (1989) 'Traffic jams: the city and the commuter and the car', Editorial, *The Economist*, February, pp. 23–26.

Hillman, M. (1975) 'Social goals for transport policy', *Proceedings of Transport for Society Conference*, Institution of Civil Engineers, London.

Ichihara, K. (1983) 'Survey on road safety conditions in major Southeast Asian cities', 3, *Proceedings of SEATAC Workshop*, SEATAC, Bangkok.

International Development Centre of Japan, (1987) *Technology Transfer for Better Transport Systems in Developing Countries*, IDC, Tokyo.

Jacobs, G. D. and Sayer, I. A. (1977) 'A Study of Road Accidents in Selected Urban Areas in Developing Countries', *Transport and Road Research Laboratory Report*, No. LR 775, TRRL, Crowthorne.

Kumar, R. K. and Rao, M. S. V. (1975) 'An appraisal of transportation planning and travel forecasting techniques', *Indian Highways Journal*, 3 (9), Delhi.

Linn, J. F. (1983) *Cities in the Developing World*, World Bank Research Publications, Oxford University Press, Oxford.

Madras Metropolitan Development Authority (MMDA) (1977) 'Madras; A Few Facts', MMDA, Madras.

McNeill, D. (1977) 'Urban Transport in Developing Countries', *Development Planning Unit Working Paper*, No. 1, University College, London.

Newman, P. and Kenworthy, J. (1989) 'Cities and Automobile Dependence: An International Sourcebook', Gower Technical, Aldershot.

Potter, S. (1976) 'Transport and New Towns: Transport Assumptions Underlying the Design of New Towns 1946–1976', New Towns Study Unit, *The Open University*, Milton Keynes.

Proudlove, A. and Turner, A. (1990) 'Street management' in *Transport Planning for Third World Cities* edited by H. T. Dimitriou, assisted by G. A. Banjo, Routledge, London.

Rao M. S. V. and Sharma, A. K. (1990) 'The role of non-motorised urban travel' in *Transport Planning for Third World Cities*, edited by H., T. Dimitriou, assisted by G. A. Banjo, Routledge, London.

Roberts, B. (1978) *Cities of Peasants*, Edward Arnold, London.

Ross, A. and Mwirana, M. (1990) 'Road Safety – Review of World Bank Experience: Need for Action', *General Operational Review Paper*, World Bank, Washington DC, March.

Ross Silcock Partnership (1990) 'Towards Safer Roads in Developing Countries', *Transport and Road Research Laboratory*, Crowthorne.

Spencer, A. H. (1988) 'Urban transport' in *South East Asian Transport: Issues in Development* edited by Leinbach, T. R. and Chia L. S., Oxford University Press, Kuala Lumpur.

Streeten, P. (1974) 'Some problems in the use and transfer of an intellectual technology in the social sciences and development, *Proceedings of Conference in Bellagio*, Italy, World Bank, Washington DC.

TDC S. A. – Training and Development Consultants (1988) *IUIDP Policy Planning and Design Guidelines for Urban Road Transport*, Final Report to Department of Public Works, Government of Indonesia and UNDP/UNCHS, Jakarta.

Urban Edge (1990a) 'Gridlock weary: some turn to peddle power', *Urban Edge*, 14 (2), World Bank, Washinton DC, March.

—— (1990b) 'Road safety a lethal problem in Third World, *Urban Edge*, 14 (5), World Bank, Washington DC, June.

Viola, P. (1976) 'Large scale land-use transport studies: how relevant to Asian cities?', *Proceedings of PTRC Annual Meeting*, University of Warwick, PTRC Education and Research Services Ltd., London.

World Bank, (1975) 'Urban transport', *World Bank Sector Policy Paper*, Washington DC.

—— (1986) *Urban Transport*, A World Bank Policy Study, Washington DC.

—— (1990) *World Development Report*, Oxford University Press, Oxford.

Zahavi, Y. (1976) 'Travel Characteristics of Developing Countries', *World Bank Staff Working Paper*, no. 20, Washington DC.

—— (1980) 'Urban Travel Patterns', *Economic Development Institute Report*, World Bank, Washington DC.

Ziv, J. C. (1977) 'La Genèse des Modèles de Trafic aux Etats-Unis', Unpublished PhD Thesis, Cornell University, Ithaca.

7 A CRITICAL REVIEW OF THE APPLICATION OF THE UTP PROCESS AND ITS DERIVATIVES TO THIRD WORLD CITIES

Gakenheimer, R. (1990), Correspondence with the author.

Heanue, K. E. (1989), Correspondence with the author.

Newman, P. and Kenworthy, J. (1989), *Cities and Automobile Dependence*, Gower Publishing Company, Aldershot.

South Magazine (1989) 'Going for the fast lane', Editorial, London, July pp.12–16.

Thomson, J. M. (1983), 'Towards better urban transport planning', *World Bank Staff Working Papers* no. 600, Washington DC.

Zahavi, V. (1979), 'The UMOT Project', Report Prepared for US Department of Transportation, Washington DC and Ministry of Transport of Federal Republic of Germany, Bonn, *US Department of Transportation Report*, no. RSPA-DPB–20–19–3, Bonn and Washington DC.

World Bank (1990), *World Development Report*, Table 28, Oxford University Press, Oxford.

8 ELEMENTS AND FRAMEWORK OF A DEVELOPMENTAL APPROACH TO TRANSPORT PLANNING FOR THIRD WORLD CITIES

Barat, J. (1990) 'Institutional frameworks for planning transport' in *Transport Planning for Third World Cities*, edited by H. T. Dimitriou, assisted by G. A. Banjo, Routledge, London.

Bouladon, G. (1967a) 'The transport gaps', *Science Journal Reprint*, April.

—— (1967b) 'Transport', *Science Journal Reprint*, October.

Breman, J. (1976) 'A dualistic labour system: Parts I, II and III', *Economic and Political Quarterly*, XI/49, pp. 1870–1876 (Part I); pp. 1905–1908 (Part II) and pp. 1939–1944 (Part III).

Brotchie, J., Newton, P., Hall, P. and Nijkamp, P. (1985) *The Future of Urban Form*, Croom Helm, Beckenham.

Cuthbert, R. (1983) 'Assessment of PCU values', part of 'The Jakarta traffic management study', *Traffic Engineering and Control*, 24 (8), 366–369.

Dimitriou, H. T. (1988) Urban transport and manpower development and training needs of four Asian cities', *Habitat International*, 12 (3), 65–90.

—— (1989) 'The Development Approach to Urban Transport Planning', Unpublished PhD Thesis, University of Wales at Cardiff, Cardiff.

—— (1990) 'Towards a developmental approach to urban transport planning' in *Transport Planning for Third World Cities* edited by H. T. Dimitriou, assisted by G. A. Banjo, Routledge, London.

—— (1991) 'An integrated approach to urban infrastructure development: an examination of the Indonesian experience', *Cities Journal*, August.

Dimitriou, H. T. and Safier, M. (1982) 'A developmental approach to urban transport planning', *Proceedings of Universities Transport Study Group Seminar*, University College, London.

Gakenheimer, R. and Meyer, M. D. (1990) 'Urban transport corridor planning' in *Transport Planning for Third World Cities*, edited by H. T. Dimitriou, assisted by G. A. Banjo, Routledge, London.

Harris, B. (1987) 'A Software Package for Micro-computer Based Planning for Small Cities in Developing Countries', Unpublished Paper, University of Pennsylvania, Philadelphia.

Kammeir, H. D. (1986) 'Microcomputer based assessment of the accessibility of central services', *Asian Geographer*, 5 (2), 177–191.

Moser, C. O. N. (1978) 'Informal sector or petty commodity production', *World Development*, 6 (9/10), 1041–1064.

Ocampo, R. B., (ed) (1982) 'Low-Cost Transport in Indonesia', *International Development Research Centre*, Ottowa.

Patsalidis, A., Rathbone, D. B. and Wilmot C. G. (1978) 'Sketch-Planning Tools', *Transport Planning Research Reports*, TPRR 7, National Institute for Transport and Road Research, CSIR, Pretoria, South Africa.

Proudlove, A. and Turner, A. (1990) 'Street management' in *Transport Planning for Third World Cities*, edited by H. T. Dimitriou, assisted by G. A. Banjo, Routledge, London.

Roth, G. (1987) *The Provision of Public Services in Developing Countries*, Published for the World Bank, Oxford University Press, New York.

Royce, N. D. (1978) 'Scenarios and Long Term Planning', *Transport Planning Research Reports*, TPRR 6, National Institute for Transport and Road Research, CSIR, Pretoria, South Africa.

Sandbrook, R. (1982) *The Politics of Basic Needs*, Heinemann Press, London.

Sasaki, Y. (1970) 'Concept of a Transport Hierarchy', Athens Centre of Ekistics, Athens.

TDC S. A. Training and Development Consultants (1988) 'IUIDP Policy, Planning and Design Guidelines for Urban Road Transport', Final Report to Department of Public Works, Government of Indonesia and UNDP/UNCHS, Jakarta and Nairobi.

Thomson, A. M. (1984) 'Urban poverty and basic needs' in *Basic Needs and the Urban Poor* edited by P. J. Richards and A. M. Thomson, Croom Helm, London.

UN Secretariat, (1977), 'Measurement of Basic Minimum Needs', *Asian Development Review*, Asian Development Bank, Manila.

Weeks J. (1975) 'Policies for expanding employment in the informal urban sector of developing countries, *International Labour Review*, III (1), 1–13.

Willumsen, L. G. (1990) 'Urban Traffic Modelling with Limited Data' in *Transport Planning for Third World Cities*, edited by H. T. Dimitriou assisted by G. A. Banjo, Routledge, London.

World Bank (1990) *World Development Report 1990: Poverty*,

International Bank for Reconstruction, Washington DC and Oxford University Press, New York.

CONCLUSIONS

Boyce, E. D. (1988) 'The renaissance of large scale models', *Papers of the Regional Science Association*, University of Illinois, Urbana-Champaign, 65, 1–10.

Dimitriou, H. T. (1990) 'The urban transport planning process: its evolution and application to Third World cities' in *Transport Planning for Third World Cities*, edited by H. T. Dimitriou, assisted by G. A. Banjo, Routledge, London.

Dimitriou, H. T. (1989) 'A Developmental Approach to Urban Transport Planning', Unpublished PhD Thesis, University of Wales at Cardiff, Cardiff.

Hong Kong Government Transport Department and Wilbur Smith Associates (1989) *Hong Kong Second Comprehensive Transport Study*, Final Report, Government of Hong Kong, Hong Kong.

Ingram, G. (1978) Transcript of Interview with Author, World Bank, Washington DC, April.

Masser, I. (1987) 'Policy research for transport planning: a synthesis' in *Transportation Planning in a Changing World*, by Nijkamp, R. and Reichman, C., Croom Helm, London.

Meyer, M. D. (1985) 'Urban transportation planning in the United States: current trends and future directions', in *Transportation and Mobility in an Era of Transition* by Jansen, G. R. M., Nijkamp, P. and Rujgrok, C. J. (eds), Elsevier Science Publishers, North-Holland.

Safier, M. (1982) Unpublished comments to Universities Transport Studies Seminar Group, University College, London.

South China Morning Post (1989) 'Transport must take a broader view', Editorial, Hong Kong, 25th April.

APPENDIX 1

Persons Interviewed on US developments (interviews held between 17 March and 31 April 1978)

Person interviewed	Affiliation	Place of interview
Prof. Russel Ackoff	Sometime of University of Pennsylvania	Philadelphia
Prof. Alan Altshuler*	Massachusetts Institute of Technology	Cambridge Massachusetts
Prof. Edward Banfield*	Harvard University	Cambridge Massachusetts
Prof. David Braybrooke	Dalhousie University	London
Clem Bezold	Institute for Alternative Futures	Washington DC
Douglas Carroll*†	Sometime of Tri-State Regional Planning Commission	New York
Richard Chesser	Florida State Department of Highways	Miami
Thomas Dean*	Sometime of Planning Research Corporation	Washington DC
Tom Edgerton	Highways Research Board	Washington DC
Joel Ettinger*	Urban Mass Transportation Authority	Washington DC
Prof. Garry Fauth	Harvard University	Cambridge Massachusetts

PERSONS INTERVIEWED ON US DEVELOPMENTS

Person interviewed	Affiliation	Place of interview
Prof. Ralph Gakenheimer*	Massachusetts Institute of Technology	Cambridge Massachusetts
Prof. Jose Gomez-Ibanez*	Harvard University	Cambridge Massachusetts
Cambell Graeub	Highways Research Board	Washington DC
John Hamburg	John Hamburg and Associates	Washington DC
Prof. Britton Harris*	University of Pennsylvania	Philadelphia
Kevin Heanue*	Federal Highways Authority	Washington DC
Terence Hill*	Chicago Transit Authority	Chicago
Tom Hillegass*	Urban Mass Transportation Authority	Washington DC
George Jamial	City of Chicago Transport Authority	Chicago
Prof. John Kain*	Harvard University	Cambridge Massachusetts
Prof. Alan Kornhauser*	Princeton University	Princeton
George Krambles	Chicago Transit Authority	Chicago
Herbert Levinson*	Sometime of Wilbur Smith Associates	New Haven
George MacDonald	Wilbur Smith Associates	Miami
Prof. Marvin Manheim*	Sometime of Massachusetts Institute of Technology now of Northwestern University	Cambridge Massachusetts
Prof. Robert Mitchell*	Sometime of University of Pennsylvania	Philadelphia
Tim Mulder	Chicago Area Transportation Study	Chicago

Person interviewed	Affiliation	Place of interview
Milton Picarsky*	Chicago Regional Transportation Authority	Chicago
Dr Boris Pushkarev*	New York Regional Planning Association	New York
Prof. Chester Rapkin*	Princeton University	Princeton
Leonard Rubenstein	Philip Hirschop and Associates	Washington DC
Morton Schneider	John Hamburg and Associates	Washington DC
Prof. Paul Shuldiner*	University of Massachusetts	Boston/Amhurst
Prof. Peter Stopher*	Northwestern University	Chicago
Alvin Toffler	Journalist/Writer	New York
Prof. Vukan Vuchic*	University of Pennsylvania	Philadelphia
Prof. Alan Voorhees	Sometime of University of Illinois	Chicago
Edward Whitlock	Sometime of Wilbur Smith Associates	New York
Hiram Walker	Urban Mass Transportation Authority	Washington DC
Alan Walkan	Dade County Transportation Authority	Miami

Note: *Persons quoted in the text.
†Doug Carroll has died since the interview reported upon here.

APPENDIX 2

Questions for interviews on US developments (interviews held between 17 March and 31 April 1978)

Question 1 If you had to summarise the main phases of development of the urban transport planning process since the Chicago (CATS) study, what would you say they were?

Question 2 What were, and now have become, the main functions of the urban transport planning process? Is it, or has it ever been primarily to plan new expressways? Is it, or has it ever been seen to be a method of primarily 'solving' traffic congestion?

Question 3 To what extent is the ability of a government to control urban development (to a greater or lesser degree) a significant factor in determining an urban transport planning approach?

Question 4 To what degree do you think the urban transport planning process as it has now developed successfully achieves the tasks it set out to perform?

Question 5 What would you say are the main foundation assumptions of the urban transport planning process? To what extent do you think they are more a reflection of utopianism than reality and how deterministic do you believe them to be?

Question 6 What would you say constitutes the major difference between a 'travel need' and a 'travel aspiration'?

Question 7 Do you believe there to be any significant element of 'transport consumerism' within the urban transport planning process? In other words, does the approach encourage the indiscriminate abandonment of old transport technology for new?

Question 8 How comprehensive do you believe the urban transport planning process to be? It has been argued that too much attention is paid to transport-user aspects, and that perhaps the comprehensiveness lies in the in-depth analysis of this rather than other aspects – what are your views?

Question 9 To what degree has the quantitative inputs to the urban transport planning process determined the design of the process? If its dependence on quantitative data inputs are great, how appropriate is the process in instances where data is either unavailable or too costly to collect?

Question 10 How important has the concept of achieving 'internal operational efficiency' of an urban transport system been in determining developments in transport planning evaluation studies, as opposed to the 'external benefits' the system provides in servicing urban activities?

Question 11 What constitutes the 'land-use/transport system'? How may it be defined?

Question 12 Was there (and is there) any evidence of large multi-national car manufacturing lobbies having any influence on the developments of transport models, and therefore the urban transport planning process in general?

Question 13 To what extent could transport planners operate without models and to what degree were these models by-and-large used to justify policy decisions (or non-decisions) already taken?

Question 14 How vulnerable do you believe the urban transport planning process is (and has been) in the evolution of its process to the convenience factors of simulation modelling?

Question 15 What are the major parameters that control urban travel and travel demand?

Question 16 Have transport models primarily been developed to answer design questions rather than strategic or policy issues?

APPENDIX 3

Persons interviewed on Third World developments (17 March – 31 April 1978)

Person interviewed	Affiliation	Place of interview
Prof. Brian Berry*	Sometime of Harvard University now of Carnegie Mellon University	Cambridge Massachusetts
Thomas Dean*	Sometime of Planning Research Corporation	Washington DC
Prof. William Doebele*	Harvard University	Cambridge Massachusetts
Prof. Garry Fauth	Harvard University	Cambridge Massachusetts
Prof. Ralph Gakenheimer*	Massachusetts Institute of Technology	Cambridge Massachusetts
Prof. Jose Gomez-Ibanez*	Harvard University	Cambridge Massachusetts
Leslie Gordan	Harvard Institute of International Development	Cambridge Massachusetts
Prof. Sigmund Grava	Sometime of Columbia University now of Parsons Brinckerhoff	New York
Prof. Britton Harris*	University of Pennsylvania	Philadelphia
Prof. John Harris*	Boston University	Boston
Richard Henrickson*	US Agency for International Development	Washington DC

PERSONS INTERVIEWED ON THIRD WORLD DEVELOPMENTS

Person interviewed	Affiliation	Place of interview
Richard Ingram*	World Bank	Washington DC
Prof. John Kain*	Harvard University	Cambridge, Massachusetts
Herbert Levinson*	Sometime of Wilbur Smith Associates	New Haven
Prof. Charles Lindblom	Yale University	New Haven
Prof. Marvin Manheim*	Sometime of Massachusetts Institute of Technology now of Northwestern University	Cambridge Massachusetts
Cord Nelson	Sometime of Ford Foundation	New York
Wilfred Owen*	Brookings Institution	Washington DC
Prof. Hermenegildo Oritz	University of Puerto Rico	San Hose
Prof. Salvador Padilla*	Sometime of University of Puerto Rico	San Hose
Prof. Lloyd Rodwin*	Sometime of Massachusetts Institute of Technology	Cambridge Massachusetts
Prof. Peter Stopher*	Northwestern University	Chicago
Thomas Sudra*	Sometime of Massachusetts Institute of Technology now of United Nations	Cambridge Massachusetts
Tony Tummarallo*	US Agency for International Development	Washington DC
Prof. Alan Voorhees	Sometime of University of Illinois	Chicago
Peter Watson*	World Bank	Washington DC

Note: * Persons quoted in the text.

APPENDIX 4

Questions for interviews on Third World developments (interviews held between 17 March and 31 April 1978)

Question 1 What have been the most important significant adaptations to the UTP process – and how relevant do you believe these to be to Third World cities?

Question 2 Have all the major adjustments and improvements to the UTP process been incorporated in most Third World applications?

Question 3 Some major amendments to the UTP process were made in the West as a result of issues which surfaced from public debate. Because of the typical absence of this kind of debate in the Third World, does this mean that Third World urban transport planning will more likely be less socially orientated or less developed?

Question 4 What would you say are the main foundation assumptions of the UTP process – to what extent do you believe they are more a reflection of utopianism than reality, and how deterministic do you believe them to be?

Question 5 What are the most significant issues of cross-cultural intervention that international development agencies should consider when preparing urban transport planning projects?

Question 6: Under what circumstances should non-nationals be involved in foreign transportation planning projects – what and whose standards should guide such an involvement?

Question 7 To what extent do you believe that foreign planning consultants in developing nations are able to perceive the client's needs as the client sees such needs, and if so, what are the dangers of viewing needs at the level of needs, alone?

Question 8 If international collaboration in planning projects for Third World nations requires sensitive adaptations in the participants' social behaviour, the professional methods employed and basic aims and values patronised – to what extent do you think international agencies and consultants have made these adjustments?

Question 9 Are many Third World cities at an inherent advantage at not having committed their transport system as yet to the motorcar – if so, what advantages do you believe them to have?

Question 10 Was there (and is there) any evidence of large multi-national car manufacturing companies having an influence on the development of transport models and therefore the UTP process in general – if so, what influence do such companies have today in the application of the process to Third World cities?

Question 11 What are the major parameters that control travel and travel demand, and how do these differ in Third World cities from those in the industrialised countries?

Question 12 Have transport models primarily been developed to answer 'design questions' rather than strategic or policy issues, and if so, what are the implications of this, particularly for Third World cities?

Question 13 Do you think one should adopt a comprehensive planning approach in Third World nations or should one attempt to tackle only those problems considered most critical?

Question 14 To what extent is the basic dilemma of transport planning in the West prevalent in Third World nations – namely, whether to invest in transport to reduce travel needs or to build ahead of travel demand?

Question 15 Given that different development approaches

generate alternative spectrums of physical planning approaches – what transport planning priorities should be adopted for Third World cities – i.e. how does urban transport most influence urban growth in Third World nations, and how does it affect the achievement of development goals best?

Question 16 How important is it to appreciate the role of cities in Third World development before deciding what the contribution of urban transport is to cities?

Question 17 To what extent are planners who work in the Third World equally aware of the problems of resource utilization as they are of resource availability in such scarce-resource environments?

Question 18 To what degree can one make universal generalisations in planning both for Third World cities and elsewhere?

Question 19 Do you believe that the resistance to new technological innovations in the transport field in Third World nations is less than in the West – i.e. is there less vested institutionalised interest in maintaining/protecting the current transport technology, and if so, does this then lead to 'freer' planning?

Question 20 Relevant problem-solving exercises have to be seen within the context of a detailed response to a particular economic, political, cultural and resource availability context. To what extent is the UTP process able to meet these requirements?

Question 21 Do you believe that urban planning and urban transport planning in Third World countries are pursued with compatible goals in mind?

Question 22 To what degree is the necessity to differentiate between land uses to assess various traffic generating powers possible to adhere to in Third World cities, given the multi-purpose nature of many land-uses and the dynamic nature of such fragmented land-uses?

Question 23 Does the inability to predict with any degree of confidence future land-uses and socio-economic trends affect the validity of the UTP process in Third World cities?

Question 24 Do you think that sustained systematic efforts to clarify the major planning goals meet with resistance in Third World nations – do you believe, for example, that this exercise threatens to expose different values and aims of the various government agencies?

APPENDIX 5

Weiner's chronology of significant events in the history of US urban transport planning[1]

1916 • Federal Aid Road Act: created Bureau of Public Roads, beginning of federal aid highway program

1921 • Federal Highway Act: required state highway departments, established federal-aid highway system, contract authority, state matching

Early highway planning

1934 • Federal Aid Highway Act: 1.5 per cent HP&R Program (permissive), statewide highway planning surveys begun

1937 • Toll Roads and Free Roads report

1941 • Inter-regional Highways report

Beginnings of urban transportation planning

1944 • First Home Interview Manual published

• Federal Aid Highway Act: established federal aid Secondary and Urban Extensions programs, directed designation of 40,000 mile national system of interstate highways, but provided no funding

1945 • Chicago Transit Authority (CTA) created

1947 • Housing Act: created Housing and Home Finance Agency (HHFA)

• MTA created in Boston

1948 • San Juan, Puerto Rico transportation study – trip generation by land-use type

1950 • TRB Compendium of O-D practices published

1953 • Federal Aid Highway Act: first funding for interstate system

1953 • Detroit Metropolitan Area Traffic Study (DMATS) started – used tabulating machines

1954 • Housing Act: established 701 Comprehensive Urban Planning Program

1955 • A. M. Voorhees' Gravity Model
- Chicago Area Transportation Study (CATS) started – prototype for future urban transportation studies
- Washington Metropolitan Area Traffic Study (WMATS) started

1956 • Federal Aid Highway Act: created funding for National System of Interstate and Defense Highways
- Highway Revenue Act: established Highway Trust Fund, 90 per cent federal share
- San Francisco Rapid Transit Commission recommends 123 mile system Highway Traffic Estimation published – highlights Fratar technique

1957 • Traffic assignment algorithms
- Baltimore Transportation Study started

1958 • Pittsburgh Area Transportation Study (PATS) started
- Hartford Area Traffic Study started
- National Committee on Urban Transportation, Better Transportation for Your City published
- Sagamore Conference on Highways and Urban Development – region-wide comprehensive planning

1959 • Penn-Jersey (Philadelphia) Transportation Study started

1961 • Housing Act: created program of transit loans and demonstration grants, allowed 701 funds for urban transportation studies

Urban transportation planning comes of age

1962 • Joint Report on Urban Mass Transportation
- President Kennedy's Transportation Message
- Federal Aid Highway Act: mandated 3C urban transportation planning process, 1.5 per cent required for HP&R purposes, 0.5 per cent optional
- Hershey Conference on Freeways in the Urban Setting
- Bay Area rapid transit system bond issue passed

1963 • IM 50–2–63 Guidelines for 3C planning process – defined 3C process including 10 elements

1964 • Urban Mass Transportation Act: created transit capital grants (66.67 per cent federal share), R&D program
• *Improved inter-governmental co-ordination*

1965 • Housing and Urban Development Act: created HUD, 701 grants for comprehensive planning to COGs and Regional Planning Councils
• Williamsburg Conference on Highways and Urban Development – social and community values

1966 • Department of Transportation Act: created DOT
• Amendments to the Urban Mass Transportation Act: created transit technical studies program, management training grants, New Systems study
• Demonstration Cities and Metropolitan Development Act: created 204 Review area wide process for federal aid projects, Model Cities program

1967 • PPM 50–9: consolidated previous guidance on urban transportation planning
• Dartmouth Conference on Urban Development Models

1968 • Federal Aid Highways Act: created TOPICS, prohibited takings of parks, wetlands or wildlife refuge, required public hearings
• Reorganization Plan No.2: established Urban Mass Transportation Administration (UMT) in DOT
• Inter-governmental Co-operation Act: required co-ordination of federal programs with local governments
• IM 50–4–68: Operations Plans for 'Continuing' Urban Transportation Planning – five elements: surveillance, reappraisal, service, procedural development and annual report
• Tomorrow's Transportation: New Systems for the Urban Future

Environment and two-hearing process

1969 • National Environmental Policy Act (NEPA): created EIS process, established CEQ, required systematic, interdisciplinary approach to planning and decision making
• A–95 Project Notification and Review process: required area-wide planning agencies to comment on federally-aided projects

- PPM 20–8, Two Hearing Process: required full consideration of social, economic, and environmental impacts
- Environmental Quality Improvement Act: established Office of Environmental Quality

Beginnings of multi-modal urban transportation planning

1970
- Urban Mass Transportation Assistance Act: established long-term commitment of transit funds, $ 10 billion over 12 years, Elderly and Handicapped requirements
- Clean Air Act Amendments: created EPA, emission standards specified, required national ambient air quality standards be established, SIPs and TCPs, focus on traffic management
- Federal Aid Highway Act: Federal Aid Urban system (FAUS), 70 per cent federal share for non-interstate projects, local selection of routes, allowed highway funds for bus projects, required guidelines on economic, social and environmental impacts, required guidelines for highway project consistency with SIPs
- Mt. Pocono Conference on Urban Transportation Planning
- Boston Transportation Planning Review

1971
- IM 50–3–71: established annual certification of 3C process

1972
- PPM 9–4: Process Guidelines for Highway Projects
- Williamsburg Conference on Urban Travel Forecasting
- UMTA's External Operating Manual: described planning requirements for transit projects

1973
- Federal Aid Highway Act: allowed FAUS and interstate funds to be transferred to transit projects
- Rehabilitation Act: Section 504 access for elderly and handicapped persons
- CEQ guidelines on preparation of EISs

1974
- National Mass Transportation Assistance Act: authorized federal transit operating assistance, federal share 80 per cent for capital and 50 per cent for operating projects, same planning regs as highways, 0.5 fare for E+H, rural program

Transition to short-term planning

1973
- OPEC Oil Embargo

1974 • Emergency Highway Energy Conservation Act: 55 mph speed limit

1975 • Energy Policy and Conservation Act: established CAFE standards

• Joint FHWA/UMTA planning regulations: required MPOs, Prospectus, UPWP, TIP & Annual Element (AE), TSM measures

• Office of Technology Assessment's Report on Automated Guideway Transit – SLT, GRT, PRT

1976 • Policy on Major Urban Mass Transportation Investments: established criteria of multi-modal, region-wide planning, incremental implementation, TSM measures, cost-effectiveness

• Federal Aid Highway Act: allowed interstate transfers to other highways and busways, established 3R program

• Section 504 Regulations: special efforts, suggested 5 per cent of funds

1977 • Clean Air Act Amendments: extended deadlines, required 'conformance'and 'sanctions'

• Department of Energy Organization Act: created DOE

• National Urban Development and New Communities Development Act: required National Urban Policy Report rather than report on growth

Urban economic development

1978 • National Urban Policy Report: revitalization of central cities and older suburbs

• Policy Toward Rail Transit: required high density corridors, local supporting policies

• National Energy Act: energy conservation goal, promote carpools and vanpools

• Surface Transportation Assistance Act: interstate completion deadline of 1990: projects under contract by Sept. 1985, I-substitutions by Sept. 1983, created bridge R&R program, transit Section 5 program expanded to four tiers, rural program, same planning requirement for highways and transit, 'Buy America' requirement

• Council on Environmental Quality's Regulations: 'scoping' and 'tiering'

- Transportation and Air Quality guidelines: integrated air quality planning into the 3C planning process
- Aspen Conference on Future Urban Transportation: automobile will continue to be dominant mode

1979 • Urban Initiatives program guidelines: joint development, leveraging federal investments, stimulate economic development
- Final Section 504 Regulations on Accessibility for the Handicapped: full access in 3 years, 50 per cent of buses

1980 • Joint FHWA/UMTA Environmental regulations: single set of environmental procedures of highway and transit projects, single EIS/AA document

Decentralization of decision making

1981 • Air Quality Conformance and Priority Procedures
- President Reagan's Memorandum on Regulations: postponed regulations for 60 days
- Executive Order 12291: procedures for evaluating regulations, benefits must exceed costs
- Interim Section 504 regulations: certify special efforts were being made

1982 • Airlie House Conference on Urban Transportation Planning in the 1980s: need for greater flexibility and reduced requirements
- Executive Order 12372 Inter-governmental Review of Federal Programs: replaced A–95, states establish own review process, federal government must 'accommodate' or 'explain,' 'single point of contact'
- Woods Hole Conference on Future Directions of Urban Public Transportation: split between conventional transit and paratransit advocates
- Easton Conference on Travel Analysis methods for the 1980s: gap between research and practice
- Surface Transportation Assistance Act of 1982: 5 per cent increase in gas tax; revenue from 4 cents to highways for interstate completion and expanded highway and bridge rehabilitation; revenue from other 1 cent into Mass Transit Account of Highway Trust Fund for Discretionary Grants only for capital needs (75 per cent federal share), new

Section 9 Formula Grant program for capital and operating projects (cap on operating assistance)
- Paratransit Policy: encouraged paratransit as supplement or substitute for conventional transit
- Revised Urban Transportation Planning Regulations: removed all items not actually required, increased state and local flexibility

1983
- Advent of Microcomputers
- Section 504 Regulations (NPRM): DOT-wide, detailed criteria

Private sector participation

1984
- Urban Mass Transportation Major Capital Investment Policy (Notice): specified cost-effectiveness measures
- Policy on User-side Subsidies: eligible for federal funds
- Policy on Private Enterprise Participation in the Urban Mass Transportation Program

1986
- Charter Bus Regulations (NPRM): would prohibit charter bus services by public transit operators unless no one willing and able

LIST OF ABBREVIATIONS USED IN APPENDIX 5

AASHO American Association of State Highway Officials
AGT Automated Guideway Transit
ANPRM Advanced Notice of Proposed Rulemaking
BOB Bureau of the Budget
BPR Bureau of Public Roads
3C Continuing, Comprehensive, and Co-operative
CAFE Corporate Average Fuel Economy
CATS Chicago Area Transportation Study
CEQ Council on Environmental Quality
COG Council of Governments
DMATS Detroit Metropolitan Area Traffic Study
DPM Downtown People Mover
DOE Department of Energy
DOT Department of Transport
EIS Environmental Impact Statement
EPA Environmental Protection Agency
FAUS Federal Aid Urban System

FHWA	Federal Highway Administration
FONSI	Finding of No Significant Impact
FY	Fiscal Year
GRT	Group Rapid Transit
HEW	Department of Health, Education, and Welfare
HHFA	Housing and Home Finance Agency
HHS	Department of Health and Human Services
HP&R	Highway Planning and Research
HRB	Highway Research Board
ICE	Interstate Cost Estimate
HUD	Department of Housing and Urban Development
IM	Instructional Memorandum
IPG	Inter-modal Planning Group
LRV	Light Rail Vehicle
MPO	Metropolitan Planning Organization
NEPA	National Environmental Policy Act of 1969

NOTES

1 Appendix 5 is extracted from *Urban Transportation in the United States: A Historical Overview*, prepared by Edward Weiner, US Department of Transportation, Office of the Secretary, Washington DC, February 1986, Appendix B, pp. 141–6.

2 The list of abbreviations are from Appendix B in the same source, pp. 147–148.

APPENDIX 6

Tables

TABLE A6.1 BASIC INDICATORS

	Population (millions)	Area (thousands of square kilometres)	GNP per capita		Average annual rate of inflation[a]		Life expectancy at birth (years)	Adult illiteracy (per cent)	
	mid-1988		Dollars 1988	Average annual growth rate (per cent) 1965-88	1965-80	1980-88	1988	Female 1985	Total 1985
Low-income economies	2,884.0*t*	36,977*t*	320*w*	3.1*w*	8.8*w*	8.9*w*	60*w*	58*w*	44*w*
China and India	1,904.0*t*	12,849*t*	340*w*	4.0*w*	2.8*w*	5.8*w*	63*w*	56*w*	42*w*
Other low-income	980.0*t*	24,149*t*	280*w*	1.5*w*	18.2*w*	13.8*w*	54*w*	62*w*	51*w*
1 Mozambique	14.9	802	100	–	–	33.6	48	78	62
2 Ethiopia	47.4	1,222	120	–0.1	3.4	2.1	47	–	38
3 Chad	5.4	1,284	160	–2.0	6.2	3.2	46	89	75
4 Tanzania	24.7	945	160	–0.5	9.9	25.7	53	–	–
5 Bangladesh	108.9	144	170	0.4	14.9	11.1	51	78	67
6 Malawi	8.0	118	170	1.1	7.2	12.6	47	69	59
7 Somalia	5.9	638	170	0.5	10.3	38.4	47	94	88
8 Zaire	33.4	2,345	170	–2.1	24.5	56.1	52	55	39

	Population (millions) mid-1988	Area (thousands of square kilometers)	GNP per capita		Average annual rate of inflation[a]		Life expectancy at birth (years) 1988	Adult illiteracy (per cent)	
			Dollars 1988	Average annual growth rate (per cent) 1965-88	1965-80	1980-88		Female 1985	Total 1985
9 Bhutan	1.4	47	180	–	–	8.9	48	–	–
10 Lao PDR	3.9	237	180	–	–	–	49	24	16
11 Nepal	18.0	141	180	–	7.8	8.7	51	88	74
12 Madagascar	10.9	587	190	–1.8	7.7	17.3	50	38	33
13 Burkina Faso	8.5	274	210	1.2	6.5	3.2	47	94	87
14 Mali	8.0	1,240	230	1.6	9.3	3.7	47	89	83
15 Burundi	5.1	28	240	3.0	6.4	4.0	49	74	66
16 Uganda	16.2	236	280	–3.1	21.2	100.7	48	55	43
17 Nigeria	110.1	924	290	0.9	13.7	11.6	51	69	58
18 Zambia	7.6	753	290	–2.1	6.4	33.5	53	33	24
19 Niger	7.3	1,267	300	–2.3	7.5	3.6	45	91	86
20 Rwanda	6.7	26	320	1.5	12.5	4.1	49	67	53
21 China	1,088.4	9,561	330	5.4	0.1	4.9	70	45	31
22 India	815.6	3,288	340	1.8	7.5	7.4	58	71	57
23 Pakistan	106.3	796	350	2.5	10.3	6.5	55	81	70
24 Kenya	22.4	580	370	1.9	7.3	9.6	59	51	41
25 Togo	3.4	57	370	0.0	6.9	6.1	53	72	59
26 Central African Rep.	2.9	623	380	–0.5	8.5	6.7	50	71	60
27 Haiti	6.3	28	380	0.4	7.3	7.9	55	65	62
28 Benin	4.4	113	390	0.1	7.5	8.0	51	84	74
29 Ghana	14.0	239	400	–1.6	22.8	46.1	54	57	47
30 Lesotho	1.7	30	420	5.2	8.0	12.2	56	16	26
31 Sri Lanka	16.6	66	420	3.0	9.4	11.0	71	17	13
32 Guinea	5.4	246	430	–	–	–	43	83	72

	Population (millions) mid-1988	Area (thousands of square kilometers)	GNP per capita: Dollars 1988	GNP per capita: Average annual growth rate (per cent) 1965-88	Average annual rate of inflation[a]: 1965-80	Average annual rate of inflation[a]: 1980-88	Life expectancy at birth (years) 1988	Adult illiteracy (per cent): Female 1985	Adult illiteracy (per cent): Total 1985
33 Yemen, PDR	2.4	333	430	–	–	4.5	51	75	59
34 Indonesia	174.8	1,905	440	4.3	34.2	8.5	61	35	26
35 Mauritania	1.9	1,026	480	–0.4	7.7	9.4	46	–	–
36 Sudan	23.8	2,506	480	0.0	11.5	33.5	50	–	–
37 *Afghanistan*	–	652	–	–	4.9	–	–	–	–
38 *Myanmar*	40.0	677	–	–	–	–	60	–	–
39 *Kampuchea, Dem.*	–	181	–	–	–	–	–	–	–
40 *Liberia*	2.4	111	–	–	6.3	–	50	77	65
41 *Sierra Leone*	3.9	72	–	–	7.8	–	42	79	71
42 *Viet Nam*	64.2	330	–	–	–	–	66	–	–
Middle-income economies	1,068.0*t*	37,352*t*	1,930*w*	2.3*w*	20.4*w*	66.7*w*	66*w*	31*w*	26*w*
Lower-middle-income	741.7*t*	24,451*t*	1,380*w*	2.6*w*	21.7*w*	80.8*w*	65*w*	32*w*	27*w*
43 Bolivia	6.9	1,099	570	–0.6	15.7	482.8	53	35	26
44 Philippines	59.9	300	630	1.6	11.7	15.6	64	15	14
45 Yemen Arab Rep.	8.5	195	640	–	–	11.6	47	97	86
46 Senegal	7.0	197	650	–0.8	6.5	8.1	48	81	72
47 Zimbabwe	9.3	391	650	1.0	5.8	12.1	63	33	26
48 Egypt, Arab Rep.	50.2	1,001	660	3.6	7.3	10.6	63	70	56
49 Dominican Rep.	6.9	49	720	2.7	6.8	16.8	66	23	23
50 Côte d'Ivoire	11.2	322	770	0.9	9.5	3.8	53	69	57
51 Papua New Guinea	3.7	463	810	0.5	8.1	4.7	54	65	55
52 Morocco	24.0	447	830	2.3	6.0	7.7	61	78	67
53 Honduras	4.8	112	860	0.6	5.6	4.7	64	42	41
54 Guatemala	8.7	109	900	1.0	7.1	13.3	62	53	45

	Population (millions) mid-1988	Area (thousands of square kilometers)	GNP per capita: Dollars 1988	GNP per capita: Average annual growth rate (per cent) 1965-88	Average annual rate of inflation[a] (per cent) 1965-80	Average annual rate of inflation[a] (per cent) 1980-88	Life expectancy at birth (years) 1988	Adult illiteracy (per cent) Female 1985	Adult illiteracy (per cent) Total 1985
55 Congo, People's Rep.	2.1	342	910	3.5	6.7	0.8	53	45	37
56 El Salvador	5.0	21	940	–0.5	7.0	16.8	63	31	28
57 Thailand	54.5	513	1,000	4.0	6.3	3.1	65	12	9
58 Botswana	1.2	582	1,010	8.6	8.1	10.0	67	31	29
59 Cameroon	11.2	475	1,010	3.7	8.9	7.0	56	55	44
60 Jamaica	2.4	11	1,070	–1.5	12.8	18.7	73	–	–
61 Ecuador	10.1	284	1,120	3.1	10.9	31.2	66	20	18
62 Colombia	31.7	1,139	1,180	2.4	17.4	24.1	68	13	12
63 Paraguay	4.0	407	1,180	3.1	9.4	22.1	67	15	12
64 Tunisia	7.8	164	1,230	3.4	6.7	7.7	66	59	46
65 Turkey	53.8	779	1,280	2.6	20.7	39.3	64	38	26
66 Peru	20.7	1,285	1,300	0.1	20.5	119.1	62	22	15
67 Jordan	3.9	89	1,500	–	–	2.2	66	37	25
68 Chile	12.8	757	1,510	0.1	129.9	20.8	72		6
69 Syrian Arab Rep.	11.6	185	1,680	2.9	8.3	12.9	65	57	40
70 Costa Rica	2.7	51	1,690	1.4	11.3	26.9	75	7	6
71 Mexico	83.7	1,958	1,760	2.3	13.0	73.8	69	12	10
72 Mauritius	1.1	2	1,800	2.9	11.8	7.8	67	23	17
73 Poland	37.9	313	1,860	–	–	30.5	72	–	–
74 Malaysia	16.9	330	1,940	4.0	4.9	1.3	70	34	27
75 Panama	2.3	77	2,120	2.2	5.4	3.3	72	12	12
76 Brazil	144.4	8,512	2,160	3.6	31.5	188.7	65	24	22
77 *Angola*	9.4	1,247	–	–	–	–	45	–	59
78 *Lebanon*	–	10	–	–	9.3	–	–	–	–

	Population (millions) mid-1988	Area (thousands of square kilometers)	GNP per capita: Dollars 1988	GNP per capita: Average annual growth rate (per cent) 1965-88	Average annual rate of inflation[a] 1965-80	Average annual rate of inflation[a] 1980-88	Life expectancy at birth (years) 1988	Adult illiteracy (per cent) Female 1985	Adult illiteracy (per cent) Total 1985
79 *Nicaragua*	3.6	130	–	–2.5	8.9	86.6	64	–	–
Upper-middle-income	326.3*t*	12,901*t*	3,240*w*	2.3*w*	18.9*w*	45.0*w*	68*w*	31*w*	24*w*
80 South Africa	34.0	1,221	2,290	0.8	10.1	13.9	61	–	–
81 Algeria	23.8	2,382	2,360	2.7	10.5	4.4	64	63	50
82 Hungary	10.6	93	2,460	5.1	2.6	6.4	70	c	c
83 Uruguay	3.1	177	2,470	1.3	57.8	57.0	72	4	5
84 Argentina	31.5	2,767	2,520	0.0	78.2	290.5	71	5	5
85 Yugoslavia	23.6	256	2,520	3.4	15.3	66.9	72	14	9
86 Gabon	1.1	268	2,970	0.9	12.7	0.9	53	47	38
87 Venezuela	18.8	912	3,250	–0.9	10.4	13.0	70	15	13
88 Trinidad and Tobago	1.2	5	3,350	0.9	14.0	5.3	71	5	4
89 Korea, Rep. of	42.0	99	3,600	6.8	18.7	5.0	70	–	–
90 Portugal	10.3	92	3,650	3.1	11.7	20.1	74	20	16
91 Greece	10.0	132	4,800	2.9	10.5	18.9	77	12	8
92 Oman	1.4	212	5,000	6.4	19.9	–6.5	64	–	–
93 Libya	4.2	1,760	5,420	–2.7	15.4	0.1	61	50	33
94 *Iran, Islamic Rep.*	48.6	1,648	–	–	15.6	–	63	61	49
95 *Iraq*	17.6	438	–	–	–	–	64	13	11
96 *Romania*	23.0	238	–	–	–	–	70	c	c
Low- and middle-income	3,952.0*t*	74,349*t*	750*w*	2.7*w*	16.5*w*	46.8*w*	62*w*	51*w*	40*w*
Sub-Saharan Africa	463.9*t*	22,240*t*	330*w*	0.2*w*	12.5*w*	15.5*w*	51*w*	65*w*	52*w*
East Asia	1,538.0*t*	14,017*t*	540*w*	5.2*w*	8.7*w*	5.6*w*	66*w*	41*w*	29*w*
South Asia	1,106.8*t*	5,158*t*	320*w*	1.8*w*	8.3*w*	7.5*w*	57*w*	72*w*	59*w*

	Population (millions) mid-1988	Area (thousands of square kilometers)	GNP per capita: Dollars 1988	GNP per capita: Average annual growth rate (per cent) 1965-88	Average annual rate of inflation[a] 1965-80	Average annual rate of inflation[a] 1980-88	Life expectancy at birth (years) 1988	Adult illiteracy (per cent) Female 1985	Adult illiteracy (per cent) Total 1985
Europe, M.East, & N.Africa	395.6*t*	11,420*t*	2,000*w*	2.4*w*	13.2*w*	25.8*w*	64*w*	53*w*	41*w*
Latin America & Caribbean	413.6*t*	20,293*t*	1,840*w*	1.9*w*	29.4*w*	117.4*w*	67*w*	19*w*	17*w*
Severely indebted	495.5*t*	20,057*t*	1,730*w*	2.0*w*	28.3*w*	107.9*w*	66*w*	23*w*	20*w*
High income economies	784.2*t*	33,739*t*	17,080*w*	2.3*w*	7.9*w*	4.9*w*	76*w*	–	–
OECD members	751.1*t*	31,057*t*	17,470*w*	2.3*w*	7.7*w*	4.7*w*	76*w*	–	–
†Other	33.1*t*	2,682*t*	8,380*w*	3.1*w*	15.9*w*	10.8*w*	71*w*	–	–
97 †Saudi Arabia	14.0	2,150	6,200	3.8	17.2	–4.2	64	–	–
98 Spain	39.0	505	7,740	2.3	12.3	10.1	77	8	6
99 Ireland	3.5	70	7,750	2.0	12.0	8.0	74	–	–
100 †Israel	4.4	21	8,650	2.7	25.2	136.6	76	7	5
101 †Singapore	2.6	1	9,070	7.2	4.9	1.2	74	21	14
102 †Hong Kong	5.7	1	9,220[b]	6.3	8.1	6.7	77	19	12
103 New Zealand	3.3	269	10,000	0.8	10.2	11.4	75	c	c
104 Australia	16.5	7,687	12,340	1.7	9.3	7.8	76	c	c
105 United Kingdom	57.1	245	12,810	1.8	11.1	5.7	75	c	c
106 Italy	57.4	301	13,330	3.0	11.4	11.0	77	4	c
107 †Kuwait	2.0	18	13,400	–4.3	16.4	–3.9	73	37	30
108 Belgium	9.9	31	14,490	2.5	6.7	4.8	75	c	c
109 Netherlands	14.8	37	14,520	1.9	7.5	2.0	77	c	c
110 Austria	7.6	84	15,470	2.9	6.0	4.0	75	c	c
111 †United Arab Emirates	1.5	84	15,770	–	–	0.1	71	–	–
112 France	55.9	552	16,090	2.5	8.4	7.1	76	c	c
113 Canada	26.0	9,976	16,960	2.7	7.1	4.6	77	c	c
114 Denmark	5.1	43	18,450	1.8	9.3	6.3	75	c	c

	Population (millions) mid-1988	Area (thousands of square kilometers)	GNP per capita: Dollars 1988	GNP per capita: Average annual growth rate (per cent) 1965-88	Average annual rate of inflation[a] 1965-80	Average annual rate of inflation[a] 1980-88	Life expectancy at birth (years) 1988	Adult illiteracy (per cent) Female 1985	Adult illiteracy (per cent) Total 1985
115 Germany, Fed. Rep.	61.3	249	18,480	2.5	5.2	2.8	75	c	c
116 Finland	5.0	338	18,590	3.2	10.5	7.1	75	c	c
117 Sweden	8.4	450	19,300	1.8	8.0	7.5	77	c	c
118 United States	246.3	9,373	19,840	1.6	6.5	4.0	76	c	c
119 Norway	4.2	324	19,990	3.5	7.7	5.6	77	c	c
120 Japan	122.6	378	21,020	4.3	7.7	1.3	78	c	c
121 Switzerland	6.6	41	27,500	1.5	5.3	3.8	77	c	c
Total reporting economies	4,736.2*t*	108,088*t*	3,470*w*	1.5*w*	9.8*w*	14.1*w*	64*w*	50*w*	39*w*
Oil exporters	593.3*t*	17,292*t*	1,500*w*	2.0*w*	15.1*w*	21.4*w*	61*w*	43*w*	35*w*
Nonreporting nonmembers	364.5*t*	25,399*t*	–	–	–	–	70*w*	–	–

Source: Table 1, World Bank, 1990

Note 1: For data comparability and coverage, see the technical notes. Figures in italics are for years other than those specified.
Note 2: For economies with populations of less than 1 million, see Box A.1. For nonreporting economies, see Box A.2. † Economies classified by United Nations or otherwise regarded by their authorities as developing. a. See the technical notes. b. GNP data refer to GDP. c. According to Unesco, illiteracy is less than 5 per cent.

TABLE A6.2 POPULATION GROWTH AND PROJECTIONS

	Average annual growth of population[a] (per cent)			Population (millions)			Hypothetical size of stationary population (millions)	Age structure of population (per cent)			
								0–14 years		15–64 years	
	1965–80	1980–8	1988–2000	1988	2000[a]	2025[a]		1988	2025	1988	2025
Low-income economies	2.3w	2.0w	1.9w	2,884t	3,620t	5,200t		35.7w	27.1w	59.8	65.1w
China and India	2.2w	1.6w	1.5w	1,904t	2,283t	2,917		31.8w	22.1w	63.2	67.4w
Other low-income	2.6w	2.8w	2.6w	980t	1,337t	2,284t		43.4w	33.4w	53.4	62.2w
1 Mozambique	2.5	2.7	3.1	15	21	41	93	43.9	38.6	53.0	58.2
2 Ethiopia	2.7	2.9	3.3	47	70	156	471	47.2	43.7	49.5	53.8
3 Chad	2.0	2.4	2.7	5	7	14	30	41.6	37.7	54.9	58.3
4 Tanzania	3.3	3.5	3.4	25	37	74	158	48.8	37.9	49.0	59.2
5 Bangladesh	2.7	2.8	2.4	109	145	219	346	44.7	28.2	52.1	67.4
6 Malawi	2.9	3.4	3.5	8	12	26	79	46.4	43.4	51.0	54.0
7 Somalia	2.7	3.0	3.1	6	9	17	41	45.8	40.2	51.4	56.7
8 Zaire	2.8	3.1	3.0	33	47	87	173	46.2	35.4	51.4	61.0
9 Bhutan	1.6	2.1	2.4	1	2	3	5	40.0	33.0	56.7	62.7
10 Lao PDR	1.9	2.6	2.9	4	6	10	19	43.7	35.0	53.5	60.9
11 Nepal	2.4	2.6	2.5	18	24	37	61	42.7	29.8	54.9	65.2
12 Madagascar	2.5	2.8	2.6	11	15	24	42	46.2	31.5	50.7	64.7
13 Burkina Faso	2.1	2.6	2.9	9	12	23	52	45.1	39.0	51.9	58.3
14 Mali	2.1	2.4	3.0	8	11	24	63	46.6	41.8	50.5	55.7
15 Burundi	1.9	2.8	3.1	5	7	15	33	45.3	39.6	51.5	57.8
16 Uganda	2.9	3.2	3.5	16	24	51	128	48.4	41.5	49.2	56.2
17 Nigeria	2.5	3.3	3.1	110	159	302	617	48.0	36.4	49.4	60.4

	Average annual growth of population[a] (per cent)			Population (millions)			Hypothetical size of stationary population (millions)	Age structure of population (percent)			
								0–14years		15–64years	
	1965–80	1980–8	1988–2000	1988	2000[a]	2025[a]		1988	2025	1988	2025
18 Zambia	3.0	3.7	3.5	8	11	24	56	49.0	39.7	48.6	57.6
19 Niger	2.6	3.5	3.3	7	11	24	82	46.7	44.8	50.5	52.8
20 Rwanda	3.3	3.3	3.8	7	10	23	70	47.7	44.0	49.7	53.6
21 China	2.2	1.3	1.3	1,088	1,275	1,566	1,835	27.7	20.5	66.7	66.6
22 India	2.3	2.2	1.8	816	1,007	1,350	1,862	37.2	24.0	58.4	68.4
23 Pakistan	3.1	3.2	3.1	106	154	285	556	45.0	34.9	52.4	61.5
24 Kenya	3.6	3.8	3.4	22	34	62	113	50.9	31.9	46.1	64.7
25 Togo	3.0	3.5	3.3	3	5	9	19	47.7	36.5	49.3	60.4
26 Central African Rep.	1.9	2.7	2.6	3	4	7	13	42.6	34.7	54.9	61.7
27 Haiti	2.0	1.8	1.9	6	8	11	17	39.3	27.1	56.8	67.3
28 Benin	2.7	3.2	2.9	4	6	11	21	47.2	34.4	50.0	62.2
29 Ghana	2.2	3.4	3.0	14	20	36	66	46.6	34.0	50.2	62.4
30 Lesotho	2.3	2.7	2.6	2	2	4	6	43.1	30.5	53.3	64.7
31 Sri Lanka	1.8	1.5	1.1	17	19	24	28	32.8	21.0	61.8	65.9
32 Guinea	1.5	2.4	2.6	5	7	14	34	42.1	40.5	54.3	56.2
33 Yemen, PDR	2.1	3.0	3.0	2	3	6	11	45.2	35.1	52.0	61.8
34 Indonesia	2.4	2.1	1.7	175	213	282	370	37.3	23.3	58.9	68.2
35 Mauritania	2.3	2.6	2.7	2	3	5	13	43.9	41.2	52.6	56.1
36 Sudan	2.8	3.1	2.7	24	33	57	107	44.8	34.7	52.1	61.6
37 *Afghanistan*	2.4	–	–	–	–	–	–	–	–	–	–
38 *Myanmar*	2.3	2.1	2.0	40	50	69	94	37.9	23.9	58.0	68.8
39 *Kampuchea, Dem.*	0.3	–	–	–	–	–	–	–	–	–	–
40 *Liberia*	3.0	3.2	2.8	2	3	6	11	45.1	33.9	51.5	62.3

	Average annual growth of population[a] *(per cent)*			*Population (millions)*			*Hypothetical size of stationary population (millions)*	*Age structure of population (percent)*			
								0–14years		*15–64years*	
	1965–80	*1980–8*	*1988–2000*	*1988*	*2000*[a]	*2025*[a]		*1988*	*2025*	*1988*	*2025*
41 *Sierra Leone*	2.0	2.4	2.6	4	5	10	25	43.0	40.2	54.0	56.4
42 *Viet Nam*	–	2.4	2.0	64	8.3	117	160	40.0	24.0	55.7	68.8
Middle-income economies	2.4*w*	2.2*w*	1.9*w*	1,068*t*	1,342*t*	1,923*t*		36.6*w*	26.0*w*	58.6*w*	65.3*w*
Lower-middle-income	2.5*w*	2.3*w*	2.0*w*	742*t*	940*t*	1,354*t*		38.0*w*	26.0*w*	57.7*w*	65.9*w*
43 Bolivia	2.5	2.7	2.7	7	10	16	27	43.9	31.5	52.9	64.2
44 Philippines	2.9	2.5	1.9	60	75	103	139	40.3	23.9	56.2	68.4
45 Yemen Arab Rep.	2.3	3.4	3.6	8	13	29	86	48.4	43.7	48.5	54.3
46 Senegal	2.9	3.0	3.2	7	10	21	48	46.8	40.2	50.5	57.4
47 Zimbabwe	3.1	3.7	2.7	9	13	20	29	45.8	25.4	50.8	68.7
48 Egypt, Arab Rep.	2.1	2.6	2.3	50	66	97	140	40.4	24.9	55.4	67.1
49 Dominican Rep.	2.7	2.4	1.8	7	9	11	15	38.5	23.2	57.9	68.0
50 Côte d'Ivoire	4.1	4.0	3.8	11	18	38	94	49.0	40.7	49.0	56.5
51 Papua New Guinea	2.4	2.4	2.2	4	5	7	11	41.3	27.4	56.0	67.9
52 Morocco	2.5	2.7	2.4	24	32	47	69	41.2	26.1	54.5	68.0
53 Honduras	3.2	3.6	2.9	5	7	11	18	45.1	28.1	51.1	66.9
54 Guatemala	2.8	2.9	2.8	9	12	21	35	45.8	30.7	51.3	64.8
55 Congo, People's Rep.	2.8	3.5	3.3	2	3	7	17	44.9	40.3	51.0	56.7
56 El Salvador	2.7	1.3	2.1	5	6	10	16	45.1	27.7	51.8	67.4
57 Thailand	2.9	1.9	1.3	54	64	83	103	34.2	21.6	61.4	68.2
58 Botswana	3.5	3.4	2.6	1	2	2	4	47.4	25.3	48.8	68.9
59 Cameroon	2.7	3.2	3.2	11	16	33	75	46.6	38.3	49.7	58.3
60 Jamaica	1.3	1.5	0.5	2	3	3	4	34.8	21.1	58.0	68.2
61 Ecuador	3.1	2.7	2.2	10	13	19	26	40.5	24.0	55.3	68.0

	Average annual growth of population[a] (per cent)			*Population (millions)*			*Hypothetical size of stationary population (millions)*	*Age structure of population (percent)*			
								0–14years		*15–64years*	
	1965–80	*1980–8*	*1988–2000*	*1988*	*2000[a]*	*2025[a]*		*1988*	*2025*	*1988*	*2025*
62 Colombia	2.5	2.1	1.6	32	38	50	63	35.9	22.3	59.8	68.2
63 Paraguay	2.8	3.2	2.7	4	6	9	13	40.6	26.9	55.7	66.3
64 Tunisia	2.1	2.5	2.2	8	10	14	19	38.7	23.7	57.3	68.3
65 Turkey	2.5	2.3	2.0	54	68	91	120	35.4	23.2	60.3	67.7
66 Peru	2.8	2.2	2.1	21	26	37	49	39.1	23.7	57.2	68.3
67 Jordan	2.5	3.7	3.6	4	6	12	22	47.2	34.4	50.0	61.9
68 Chile	1.7	1.7	1.3	13	15	19	23	30.8	21.3	63.1	65.7
69 Syrian Arab Rep.	3.4	3.6	3.6	12	18	36	74	48.3	36.0	49.1	60.3
70 Costa Rica	2.7	2.3	2.0	3	3	5	6	36.4	22.1	59.7	66.2
71 Mexico	3.1	2.2	1.9	84	105	142	184	38.6	22.8	57.7	68.2
72 Mauritius	1.6	1.0	0.8	1	1	1	2	29.5	19.3	66.5	67.5
73 Poland	0.8	0.8	0.5	38	40	45	50	25.2	19.7	64.9	62.0
74 Malaysia	2.5	2.6	2.2	17	22	30	40	37.2	23.4	58.9	67.2
75 Panama	2.6	2.2	1.6	2	3	4	5	35.9	21.9	59.4	67.2
76 Brazil	2.4	2.2	1.8	144	178	236	303	35.7	22.8	59.8	66.9
77 *Angola*	2.8	2.5	3.0	9	14	27	69	45.0	40.6	52.6	56.3
78 *Lebanon*	1.7	–	–	–	–	–	–	–	–	–	–
79 *Nicaragua*	3.1	3.4	3.0	4	5	9	14	46.1	28.4	51.0	66.4
Upper-middle-income	2.0*w*	1.8*w*	1.7*w*	326*t*	402*t*	569*t*		33.4*w*	26.0*w*	60.5*w*	64.0*w*
80 South Africa	2.4	2.3	2.3	34	45	65	96	38.2	25.3	58.1	67.1
81 Algeria	3.1	3.1	2.9	24	33	52	78	44.4	25.7	52.2	68.4
82 Hungary	0.4	–0.1	–0.2	11	10	10	10	19.9	17.4	66.7	61.7
83 Uruguay	0.4	0.6	0.6	3	3	4	4	26.2	20.1	62.7	64.1

	Average annual growth of population[a] (per cent)			Population (millions)			Hypothetical size of stationary population (millions)	Age structure of population (percent)			
								0–14years		15–64years	
	1965–80	1980–8	1988–2000	1988	2000[a]	2025[a]		1988	2025	1988	2025
84 Argentina	1.6	1.4	1.1	32	36	44	53	30.1	21.5	61.0	65.0
85 Yugoslavia	0.9	0.7	0.6	24	25	28	30	23.5	18.7	67.6	62.4
86 Gabon	3.6	3.9	2.7	1	1	3	7	38.2	39.4	56.9	56.4
87 Venezuela	3.5	2.8	2.2	19	24	34	45	38.7	23.3	57.7	67.5
88 Trinidad and Tobago	1.1	1.7	1.4	1	1	2	2	33.1	22.1	61.6	65.6
89 Korea, Rep. of	2.0	1.2	0.9	42	47	54	56	27.3	18.0	67.9	66.0
90 Portugal	0.4	0.7	0.4	10	11	11	11	21.8	16.4	65.6	63.5
91 Greece	0.7	0.5	0.2	10	10	10	10	19.9	16.0	66.3	60.9
92 Oman	3.7	4.7	3.9	1	2	5	11	45.5	38.1	52.0	57.3
93 Libya	4.3	4.3	3.6	4	6	14	35	46.0	39.5	51.2	56.7
94 *Iran, Islamic Rep.*	3.1	3.0	3.1	49	70	129	247	43.7	34.0	53.5	61.3
95 *Iraq*	3.4	3.6	3.4	18	26	49	90	46.7	33.1	50.6	62.5
96 *Romania*	1.1	0.4	0.5	23	25	27	31	23.8	20.0	66.2	63.6
Low- and middle-income	2.3*w*	2.0*w*	1.9*w*	3,952*t*	4,961*t*	7,123*t*		36.0*w*	26.8*w*	59.5*w*	65.2*w*
Sub-Saharan Africa	2.7*w*	3.2*w*	3.1*w*	464*t*	672*t*	1,310*t*		46.9*w*	38.0*w*	50.2*w*	58.8*w*
East Asia	2.3*w*	1.5*w*	1.4*w*	1,538*t*	1,824*t*	2,293		30.3*w*	21.3*w*	64.6*w*	67.0*w*
South Asia	2.4*w*	2.3*w*	2.0*w*	1,107*t*	1,401*t*	1,987*t*		38.7*w*	26.1*w*	57.2*w*	67.2*w*
Europe, M.East, & N.Africa	2.0*w*	2.1*w*	2.1*w*	396*t*	505*t*	769*t*		36.5*w*	28.7*w*	57.9*w*	63.4*w*
Latin America & Caribbean	2.5*w*	2.2*w*	1.8*w*	414*t*	514*t*	699*t*		36.9*w*	23.5*w*	58.6*w*	67.1*w*
Severely indebted	2.4*w*	2.1*w*	1.8*w*	496*t*	614*t*	844*t*		36.5*w*	24.5*w*	58.5*w*	66.2*w*
High income economies	0.9*w*	0.7*w*	0.6*w*	783*t*	840*t*	918*t*		20.5*w*	17.9*w*	66.8*w*	60.6*w*
OECD members	0.8*w*	0.6*w*	0.5*w*	751*t*	796*t*	847*t*		19.9*w*	16.8*w*	67.1*w*	60.6*w*
†Other	3.5*w*	3.5*w*	2.9*w*	2.5*w*	32*t*	43*t*	71*t*	35.1*w*	30.3*w*	59.9*w*	60.2*w*

	Average annual growth of population[a] (per cent)			Population (millions)			Hypothetical size of stationary population (millions)	Age structure of population (percent)			
								0–14years		15–64years	
	1965–80	1980–8	1988–2000	1988	2000[a]	2025[a]		1988	2025	1988	2025
97 †Saudi Arabia	4.7	4.2	–	14	–	–	–	45.2	–	52.4	–
98 Spain	1.0	0.5	0.4	39	41	43	41	21.3	16.2	65.9	63.0
99 Ireland	1.2	0.5	0.3	4	4	4	5	27.7	19.8	61.2	64.9
100 †Israel	2.8	1.7	1.7	4	5	7	9	32.0	21.3	59.9	65.2
101 †Singapore	1.6	1.1	1.0	3	3	3	4	24.0	18.0	70.8	61.5
102 †Hong Kong	2.0	1.5	0.9	6	6	7	6	21.9	16.0	69.2	61.3
103 New Zealand	1.3	0.8	0.7	3	4	4	4	23.6	18.3	67.1	62.8
104 Australia	1.8	1.4	1.4	17	20	23	24	22.6	18.1	66.6	63.0
105 United Kingdom	0.2	0.2	0.3	57	59	61	61	19.0	17.4	65.6	61.2
106 Italy	0.5	0.2	0.1	57	58	56	46	17.5	14.1	68.4	60.5
107 †Kuwait	7.1	4.4	2.8	2	3	4	5	37.6	21.3	59.2	65.8
108 Belgium	0.3	0.0	0.0	10	10	10	9	18.4	16.0	67.2	60.1
109 Netherlands	0.9	0.5	0.5	15	16	16	14	18.0	15.6	68.9	59.7
110 Austria	0.3	0.0	0.1	8	8	8	7	18.0	15.4	67.1	60.4
111 †United Arab Emirates	16.5	4.8	2.3	1	2	3	3	31.0	22.1	67.0	61.2
112 France	0.7	0.4	0.4	56	59	63	63	20.5	17.3	66.0	60.6
113 Canada	1.3	0.9	0.9	26	29	32	32	21.3	16.9	68.4	60.7
114 Denmark	0.5	0.0	0.0	5	5	5	5	17.6	15.7	67.1	60.2
115 Germany, Fed. Rep.	0.3	–0.1	0.0	61	61	58	50	15.2	15.0	69.6	59.0
116 Finland	0.3	0.5	0.2	5	5	5	5	19.4	16.4	67.8	58.9
117 Sweden	0.5	0.2	0.4	8	9	9	9	17.6	17.6	64.7	59.3
118 United States	1.0	1.0	0.8	246	270	307	316	21.6	18.0	66.0	61.2
119 Norway	0.6	0.3	0.4	4	4	5	5	19.6	17.1	64.5	61.0

	Average annual growth of population[a] (per cent)			Population (millions)			Hypothetical size of stationary population (millions)	Age structure of population (percent)			
								0–14years		15–64years	
	1965–80	1980–8	1988–2000	1988	2000[a]	2025[a]		1988	2025	1988	2025
120 Japan	1.2	0.6	0.4	123	129	131	121	19.6	15.7	68.9	58.8
121 Switzerland	0.5	0.3	0.4	7	7	7	6	17.0	16.1	68.2	58.4
Total reporting economies	2.1*w*	1.8*w*	1.7*w*	4,735*t*	5,801*t*	8,041*t*		33.4*w*	25.7*w*	60.7*w*	64.6*w*
Oil exporters	2.7*w*	2.7*w*	2.4*w*	592*t*	790*t*	1,261*t*		41.4*w*	29.6*w*	55.1*w*	64.2*w*
Nonreporting nonmembers	1.0*w*	0.9*w*	0.6*w*	365*t*	392*t*	450*t*		25.5*w*	20.1*w*	64.1*w*	63.4*w*

Source: Table 26, World Bank, 1990.

Note: For data comparability and coverage, see the technical notes. Figures in italics are for years other than those specified.

a. For the assumptions used in the projections, see the technical notes.

TABLE A6.3 URBANISATION

	Urban population: As a percentage of total population		Urban population: Average annual growth rate (per cent)		Percentage of urban population: In largest city		Percentage of urban population: In cities of over 500,000 persons		Number of cities of over 500,000 persons	
	1965	1988	1965-80	1980-88	1960	1980	1960	1980	1960	1980
Low-income economies	17*w*	35*w*	3.5*w*	–	11*w*	13*w*	30*w*	43*w*	59*t*	165*t*
China and India	18*w*	40*w*	3.0*w*	–	6*w*	6*w*	36*w*	43*w*	49*t*	114*t*
Other low-income	14*w*	25*w*	4.9*w*	5.2*w*	24*w*	28*w*	17*w*	43*w*	10*t*	51*t*
1 Mozambique	5	24	10.2	11.0	75	83	0	83	0	1
2 Ethiopia	8	13	4.9	5.2	30	37	0	37	0	1
3 Chad	9	31	7.8	7.4	–	39	0	0	0	0
4 Tanzania	5	30	11.7	11.6	34	50	0	50	0	1
5 Bangladesh	6	13	6.4	5.6	20	30	20	51	1	3
6 Malawi	5	14	7.5	7.9	–	19	0	0	0	0
7 Somalia	20	37	5.5	5.6	–	34	0	0	0	0
8 Zaire	26	39	4.6	4.6	14	28	14	38	1	2
9 Bhutan	3	5	3.9	4.9	–	–	0	0	0	0
10 Lao PDR	8	18	5.3	6.1	69	48	0	0	0	0
11 Nepal	4	9	6.4	7.4	41	27	0	0	0	0
12 Madagascar	12	24	5.5	5.9	44	36	0	36	0	1
13 Burkina Faso	5	9	4.1	5.4	–	41	0	0	0	0
14 Mali	13	19	4.4	3.5	32	24	0	0	0	0
15 Burundi	2	7	6.7	9.5	–	–	0	0	0	0
16 Uganda	7	10	4.7	5.1	38	52	0	52	0	1
17 Nigeria	17	34	5.7	6.3	13	17	22	58	2	9

	Urban population				Percentage of urban population				Number of cities of over 500,000 persons	
	As a percentage of total population		Average annual growth rate (percent)		In largest city		In cities of over 500,000 persons			
	1965	1988	1965-80	1980-88	1960	1980	1960	1980	1960	1980
18 Zambia	23	54	7.2	6.7	–	35	0	35	0	1
19 Niger	7	18	7.2	8.0	–	31	0	0	0	0
20 Rwanda	3	7	7.5	8.2	–	–	0	0	0	0
21 China	18	50	2.3	–	6	6	42	45	38	78
22 India	19	27	3.9	4.0	7	6	26	39	11	36
23 Pakistan	24	31	4.3	4.5	20	21	33	51	2	7
24 Kenya	9	22	8.1	8.2	40	57	0	57	0	1
25 Togo	11	25	6.6	7.0	–	60	0	0	0	0
26 Central African Rep.	27	45	4.3	4.9	40	36	0	0	0	0
27 Haiti	18	29	4.2	4.0	42	56	0	56	0	1
28 Benin	11	40	9.0	7.8	–	63	0	63	0	1
29 Ghana	26	33	3.2	4.2	25	35	0	48	0	2
30 Lesotho	6	19	7.5	7.2	–	–	0	0	0	0
31 Sri Lanka	20	21	2.3	1.3	28	16	0	16	0	1
32 Guinea	12	24	4.9	5.7	37	80	0	80	0	1
33 Yemen, PDR	30	42	3.5	4.7	61	49	0	0	0	0
34 Indonesia	16	27	4.8	4.8	20	23	34	50	3	9
35 Mauritania	10	40	9.5	7.8	–	39	0	0	0	0
36 Sudan	13	21	5.6	4.1	30	31	0	31	0	1
37 *Afghanistan*	9	–	6.0	–	33	–	0	–	0	–
38 *Myanmar*	21	24	3.2	2.3	23	23	23	23	1	2
39 *Kampuchea, Dem.*	11	–	–0.5	–	–	–	–	–	–	–
40 *Liberia*	22	43	6.2	5.8	–	–	0	0	0	0

	Urban population				Percentage of urban population				Number of cities of over 500,000 persons	
	As a percentage of total population		Average annual growth rate (percent)		In largest city		In cities of over 500,000 persons			
	1965	1988	1965-80	1980-88	1960	1980	1960	1980	1960	1980
41 *Sierra Leone*	15	26	4.4	5.0	37	47	0	0	0	0
42 *Viet Nam*	–	–	–	3.9	–	21	–	50	–	4
Middle-income economies	42*w*	58*w*	3.9*w*	3.3*w*	29*w*	31*w*	34*w*	47*w*	51*t*	113*t*
Lower-middle-income	40*w*	56*w*	4.0*w*	3.5*w*	29*w*	32*w*	32*w*	47*w*	31*t*	70*t*
43 Bolivia	40	50	3.1	4.3	47	44	0	44	0	1
44 Philippines	32	41	4.1	3.7	27	30	27	34	1	2
45 Yemen Arab Rep.	5	23	10.2	8.8	–	25	0	0	0	0
46 Senegal	33	38	3.3	4.0	53	65	0	65	0	1
47 Zimbabwe	14	27	6.0	6.2	40	50	0	50	0	1
48 Egypt, Arab Rep.	41	48	2.8	3.5	38	39	53	53	2	3
49 Dominican Rep.	35	59	5.2	4.3	50	54	0	54	0	1
50 Côte d'Ivoire	23	45	7.5	6.6	27	34	0	34	0	1
51 Papua New Guinea	5	15	8.2	4.5	–	25	0	0	0	0
52 Morocco	32	47	4.3	4.4	16	26	16	50	1	4
53 Honduras	26	42	5.5	5.6	31	33	0	0	0	0
54 Guatemala	34	33	2.7	2.9	41	36	41	36	1	1
55 Congo, People's Rep.	34	41	4.5	4.8	77	56	0	0	0	0
56 El Salvador	39	44	3.2	1.9	26	22	0	0	0	0
57 Thailand	13	21	5.1	4.7	65	69	65	69	1	1
58 Botswana	4	22	12.6	8.4	–	–	–	–	–	–
59 Cameroon	16	47	8.1	7.2	26	21	0	21	0	1
60 Jamaica	38	51	2.8	2.6	77	66	0	66	0	1
61 Ecuador	37	55	4.7	4.7	31	29	0	51	0	2

	Urban population				Percentage of urban population				Number of cities of over 500,000 persons	
	As a percentage of total population		Average annual growth rate (percent)		In largest city		In cities of over 500,000 persons			
	1965	1988	1965-80	1980-88	1960	1980	1960	1980	1960	1980
62 Colombia	54	69	3.7	3.0	17	26	28	51	3	4
63 Paraguay	36	46	3.8	4.5	44	44	0	44	0	1
64 Tunisia	40	54	4.0	2.9	40	30	40	30	1	1
65 Turkey	34	47	4.2	3.4	18	24	32	42	3	4
66 Peru	52	69	4.3	3.1	38	39	38	44	1	2
67 Jordan	46	67	4.3	5.1	31	37	0	37	0	1
68 Chile	72	85	2.6	2.3	38	44	38	44	1	1
69 Syrian Arab Rep.	40	51	4.6	4.5	35	33	35	55	1	2
70 Costa Rica	38	45	4.0	1.9	67	64	0	64	0	1
71 Mexico	55	71	4.4	3.1	28	32	36	48	3	7
72 Mauritius	37	42	2.5	0.8	–	–	–	–	–	–
73 Poland	50	61	1.9	1.4	17	15	41	47	5	8
74 Malaysia	26	41	4.5	4.9	19	27	0	27	0	1
75 Panama	44	54	3.5	3.0	61	66	0	66	0	1
76 Brazil	50	75	4.5	3.6	14	15	35	52	6	14
77 *Angola*	13	27	6.4	5.8	44	64	0	64	0	1
78 *Lebanon*	50	–	4.5	–	64	–	64	–	1	–
79 *Nicaragua*	43	59	4.7	4.6	41	47	0	47	0	1
Upper-middle-income	45*w*	62*w*	3.6*w*	2.8*w*	31*w*	30*w*	38*w*	48*w*	20*t*	43*t*
80 South Africa	47	58	3.3	3.4	16	13	44	53	4	7
81 Algeria	38	44	3.7	3.9	27	12	27	12	1	1
82 Hungary	43	60	2.0	1.2	45	37	45	37	1	1
83 Uruguay	81	85	0.7	0.8	56	52	56	52	1	1

	Urban population				Percentage of urban population				Number of cities of over 500,000 persons	
	As a percentage of total population		Average annual growth rate (percent)		In largest city		In cities of over 500,000 persons			
	1965	1988	1965-80	1980-88	1960	1980	1960	1980	1960	1980
84 Argentina	76	86	2.2	1.8	46	45	54	60	3	5
85 Yugoslavia	31	49	3.0	2.5	11	10	11	23	1	3
86 Gabon	21	44	7.3	6.7	–	–	–	–	–	–
87 Venezuela	70	83	4.8	2.6	26	26	26	44	1	4
88 Trinidad and Tobago	30	67	5.6	3.9	–	–	0	0	0	0
89 Korea, Rep. of	32	69	5.8	3.7	35	41	61	77	3	7
90 Portugal	24	32	1.7	1.9	47	44	47	44	1	1
91 Greece	48	62	2.0	1.3	51	57	51	70	1	2
92 Oman	4	10	7.6	8.7	–	–	–	–	–	–
93 Libya	26	68	9.8	6.7	57	64	0	64	0	1
94 *Iran, Islamic Rep.*	37	54	5.1	4.1	26	28	26	47	1	6
95 *Iraq*	51	73	5.3	4.8	35	55	35	70	1	3
96 *Romania*	38	49	3.0	0.3	22	17	22	17	1	1
Low- and middle-income	24*w*	41*w*	3.7*w*	6.9*w*	16*w*	18*w*	31*w*	44*w*	110*t*	278*t*
Sub-Saharan Africa	14*w*	28*w*	5.8*w*	6.2*w*	28*w*	36*w*	6*w*	41*w*	3*t*	28*t*
East Asia	19*w*	46*w*	3.0*w*	–	11*w*	13*w*	41*w*	47*w*	46*t*	102*t*
South Asia	18*w*	26*w*	4.0*w*	4.0*w*	11*w*	11*w*	25*w*	40*w*	15*t*	49*t*
Europe, M.East, & N.Africa	37*w*	50*w*	3.5*w*	3.1*w*	28*w*	28*w*	31*w*	40*w*	22*t*	43*t*
Latin America & Caribbean	53*w*	71*w*	4.0*w*	3.2*w*	27*w*	29*w*	32*w*	49*w*	20*t*	49*t*
Severely indebted	50*w*	66*w*	3.8*w*	3.1*w*	26*w*	28*w*	33*w*	47*w*	24*t*	56*t*
High income economies	71*w*	78*w*	1.4*w*	0.8*w*	19*w*	19*w*	47*w*	55*w*	107*t*	157*t*
OECD members	72*w*	77*w*	1.3*w*	0.7*w*	18*w*	18*w*	47*w*	55*w*	104*t*	152*t*
†Other	68*w*	83*w*	4.6*w*	3.5*w*	58*w*	49*w*	51*w*	54*w*	3*t*	5*t*

		Urban population				Percentage of urban population				Number of cities of over 500,000 persons	
		As a percentage of total population		Average annual growth rate (percent)		In largest city		In cities of over 500,000 persons			
		1965	1988	1965-80	1980-88	1960	1980	1960	1980	1960	1980
97	†Saudi Arabia	39	76	8.5	5.8	15	18	0	33	0	2
98	Spain	61	77	2.2	1.3	13	17	37	44	5	6
99	Ireland	49	58	2.1	1.1	51	48	51	48	1	1
100	†Israel	81	91	3.5	2.1	46	35	46	35	1	1
101	†Singapore	100	100	1.6	1.1	100	100	100	100	1	1
102	†Hong Kong	89	93	2.1	1.7	100	100	100	100	1	1
103	New Zealand	79	84	1.6	0.9	25	30	0	30	0	1
104	Australia	83	86	2.0	1.4	26	24	62	68	4	5
105	United Kingdom	87	92	0.5	0.4	24	20	61	55	15	17
106	Italy	62	68	1.0	0.5	13	17	46	52	7	9
107	†Kuwait	78	95	8.2	5.1	75	30	0	0	0	0
108	Belgium	93	97	0.4	0.2	17	14	28	24	2	2
109	Netherlands	86	88	1.2	0.5	9	9	27	24	3	3
110	Austria	51	57	0.8	0.6	51	39	51	39	1	1
111	†United Arab Emirates	41	78	23.7	4.2	–	–	–	–	–	–
112	France	67	74	1.3	0.5	25	23	34	34	4	6
113	Canada	73	76	1.5	1.0	14	18	31	62	2	9
114	Denmark	77	86	1.1	0.3	40	32	40	32	1	1
115	Germany, Fed. Rep.	79	86	0.7	0.1	20	18	48	45	11	11
116	Finland	44	60	2.5	0.4	28	27	0	27	0	1
117	Sweden	77	84	0.9	0.3	15	15	15	35	1	3
118	United States	72	74	1.2	1.0	13	12	61	77	40	65
119	Norway	48	74	3.0	0.9	50	32	50	32	1	1

	Urban population				Percentage of urban population				Number of cities of over 500,000 persons	
	As a percentage of total population		Average annual growth rate (percent)		In largest city		In cities of over 500,000 persons			
	1965	1988	1965-80	1980-88	1960	1980	1960	1980	1960	1980
120 Japan	67	77	2.1	0.7	18	22	35	42	5	9
121 Switzerland	53	61	1.0	1.3	19	22	19	22	1	1
Total reporting economies	34*w*	47*w*	2.7*w*	4.9*w*	17*w*	18*w*	35*w*	46*w*	217*t*	435*t*
Oil exporters	30*w*	46*w*	4.8*w*	4.3*w*	24*w*	26*w*	31*w*	49*w*	16*t*	50*t*
Nonreporting nonmembers	53*w*	67*w*	2.1*w*	1.6*w*	9*w*	7*w*	20*w*	30*w*	31*t*	58*t*

Source: Table 31, World Bank, 1990.

Note: For data comparability and coverage, see technical notes. Figures in italics are for years other than those specified.

INDEX